To Alan,
congratuletio
confirmation
lots o
fot
x

C000181526

I Want to Live These Days with You

I Want to Live These Days with You

A Year of Daily Devotions

DIETRICH BONHOEFFER

Translated by
O. C. Dean Jr.

Westminster John Knox Press
LOUISVILLE • LONDON

Translated by O. C. Dean Jr. from the German *So will ich diese Tage mit euch leben: Jahreslesebuch* published in 2005 by Gütersloher Verlagshaus GmbH, Gütersloh.

© 2005 by Gütersloher Verlagshaus GmbH, Gütersloh, Germany
English translation © 2007 Westminster John Knox Press

Scripture quotations, unless otherwise indicated, are from the New Revised Standard Version of the Bible, copyright © 1989 by the Division of Christian Education of the National Council of the Churches of Christ in the U.S.A., and are used by permission.

Book design by Drew Stevens
Cover design by designpointinc.com

First edition
Published by Westminster John Knox Press
Louisville, Kentucky

This book is printed on acid-free paper that meets the American National Standards Institute Z39.48 standard. ♾

PRINTED IN THE UNITED STATES OF AMERICA

07 08 09 10 11 12 13 14 15 16 — 10 9 8 7 6 5 4 3 2 1

Library of Congress Cataloging-in-Publication Data

Bonhoeffer, Dietrich, 1906–1945
  [So will ich diese Tage mit euch leben. English]
  I want to live these days with you : a year of daily devotions / Dietrich Bonhoeffer ; translated by O. C. Dean, Jr. — 1st ed.
      p. cm.
Includes bibliographical references and index.
    ISBN 978-0-664-23148-4 (alk. paper)
    1. Devotional calendars. I. Title.

BV4811.B58613 2007
242'.2—dc22

                                                                      2007003693

CONTENTS

TRANSLATOR'S PREFACE

Since Dietrich Bonhoeffer wrote before the days of inclusive gender, his works reflect a male-oriented world in which, for example, the German words for "human being" and "God" are masculine, and male gender was understood as common gender. In this respect, his language has, for the most part, been updated in accordance with the practices of the New Revised Standard Version of the Bible (NRSV); that is, most references to human beings have become gender-inclusive, whereas references to the Deity have remained masculine. The main exceptions to the former are in Bonhoeffer's pieces on the Pharisee (October 12–13) and the prophet (December 16), where the author's use of the masculine pronoun is retained.

While scriptural quotations are mostly from the NRSV, it was necessary at times to substitute the King James Version (KJV), the Revised Standard Version (RSV), or a literal translation of Luther's German version, as quoted by Bonhoeffer, in order to allow the author to make his point. In a few other cases, the translation was adjusted to reflect the wording of the NRSV.

O. C. Dean Jr.

PREFACE

When the collection *Dietrich Bonhoeffer: Worte für jeden Tag* [words for every day] appeared in 1995,[1] I was very often asked: Can one present the work of Dietrich Bonhoeffer this way, in small units? Does this not do violence to the texts? Can thoughts be taken out of their context? What can be achieved this way? The answers have come from many readers who through that small volume have gained access to the biography and work of Dietrich Bonhoeffer or adopted these mosaic stones as "stimuli to reflect upon and test their own convictions and the content of their everyday lives." The *daily reader* offered here also raises the questions listed above.

In this volume, every day in the year has its own text, and these texts are more extensive than in *Worte für jeden Tag*. They are oriented thematically by month and thus are removed from their original context. That is also true in regard to the temporal order of the texts, which were written between 1927 and 1944.

"Knowledge cannot be separated from the existence in which it was gained," noted Dietrich Bonhoeffer in 1935.[2] But the connection between *knowledge* and *existence* from different times, which is newly perceived through the juxtaposition of texts, offers special access to Dietrich Bonhoeffer's ideas.

Perhaps the reader's experience will be like that of Dietrich Bonhoeffer's friend Eberhard Bethge, which he describes in a letter to Bonhoeffer: "Every time the thought crystals have become well solidified, you come and stir them up again, so that they offer themselves in a new constellation and for a long time offer the observing eye new pleasing or exciting aspects."[3]

The times of origin of the texts are given in the appendix and expanded with an index of sources. All texts [in the German edition] consciously follow the original writing style and thus the old orthography.

The titles above the individual days are formulations taken from the original text. The main theme of each month is indicated by a quotation at the beginning of the month.

Bible references—to the extent that they are given by Bonhoeffer or indicated in the footnotes of the *Dietrich Bonhoeffer Werke* (*DBW*) by its editors—are provided in the texts and arranged by biblical book in an index at the back of the book. There are indications of relationships between these Bible references and the text. But the references themselves are also supposed to stimulate additional reading, for "Dietrich Bonhoeffer thought a lot of the word of the Bible and of its slumbering power, which will clear the way—as it was in the beginning, is now and forever shall be—but above all soon. On this we can rely, and on it we should wait without wavering!"[4]

For Dietrich Bonhoeffer the Bible was "the answer to all our questions," with the presupposition "that one is ready to really ask them."[5]

"I want to live these days with you"—a line from the poem "Von guten Mächten" [see December 31: *Surrounded by good powers*], written at the end of 1944 in prison,[6]—was chosen as the title of this daily reader. When this line was written, it had a very personal reference: "No prison walls can keep Dietrich from 'living' in these days of the turn of the year with his fiancée, his parents, his friends, and going with confidence into the new year. I am struck by the simple words with which he describes this certainty."[7]

Today his thoughts are a legacy with which *we may live*, in order to experience daily what it means "to be there for others."[8]

The life and work of Dietrich Bonhoeffer have found interest worldwide in the past decades. Between his birthday, February 4, 1906, and the day of his violent death, April 9, 1945, he lived only thirty-nine years, but in his prayers, sermons, and meditations, his letters and notes, we find thinking that has surprising validity for our time and points us to the *worldly existence of the Christian.*[9]

Holy Week 2005   Manfred Weber

Notes

1. Dietrich Bonhoeffer, *Worte für jeden Tag,* ed. Manfred Weber, 5th ed. (Gütersloh: Gütersloher Verlagshaus, 2004).

2. *Dietrich Bonhoeffer Werke (DBW*—see Sources*)* 4:38.

3. *DBW* 8:599.

4. Heinz Joachim Held, "Meine Begegnung mit Dietrich Bonhoeffer," *Bonhoeffer Rundbrief* 75 (Nov. 2004).

5. *DBW* 14:144–45.

6. *DBW* 8:607–8.

7. Albrecht Schönherr, "Die letzte Strophe: Gedanken zu Bonhoeffers Gedicht *Von guten Mächten,*" *Bonhoeffer Rundbrief* 75 (Nov. 2004).

8. *DBW* 8:558.

9. *DBW* 8:653.

TEXTS FOR THE FESTIVALS
OF THE CHURCH YEAR

Advent, Christmas:	December 1–26
Lent:	March 1–April 15
Easter:	April 16–30
Ascension:	May 25–27
Pentecost:	May 31; June 4–13
Day of repentance:	November 21
Reformation:	October 30–31
All Saints' Day:	November 24–28

JANUARY

A NEW BEGINNING

Every new morning is
a new beginning
of our life.
Every day is
a completed whole.

FROM NOW ON?

"The road to hell is paved with good intentions." This saying, which is found in a broad variety of lands, does not arise from the brash worldly wisdom of an incorrigible. It instead reveals deep Christian insight. At the beginning of a new year, many people have nothing better to do than to make a list of bad deeds and resolve from now on—how many such "from-now-ons" have there already been!—to begin with better intentions, but they are still stuck in the middle of their paganism. They believe that a good intention already means a new beginning; they believe that on their own they can make a new start whenever they want. But that is an evil illusion: only God can make a new beginning with people whenever God pleases, but not people with God. Therefore, people cannot make a new beginning at all; they can only pray for one. Where people are on their own and live by their own devices, there is only the old, the past. Only where God is can there be a new beginning. We cannot command God to grant it: we can only pray to God for it. And we can pray only when we realize that we cannot do anything, that we have reached our limit, that someone else must make that new beginning.

THE NEXT STEP

People who want to live solely by their good intentions have no idea where those intentions actually come from. It's worth a closer look. Our so-called good intentions are nothing but anxious byproducts of a weak heart that fears all kinds of evils and sins and now arms itself with very human weapons in order to go against these powers. But whoever is afraid of sin is already in the middle of it. Fear is the net that evil throws over us, so that we become entangled and soon fall. Those who are afraid have already fallen. If we are on a difficult mountain climb and are suddenly consumed with fear, we will surely stumble. Hence, such anxious good intentions do us no good. We can certainly never make a new beginning with them.

How can we make a fresh start? "No one who puts a hand to the plow and looks back . . ." (Luke 9:62). One who guides a plow does not look back—or into the immense distance—but to the next step that must be taken. Backward glances are not a Christian thing to do. Leave fear, anxiety, and guilt behind. And look to the one who gives you a new beginning.

FOR EVERYTHING THERE IS A SEASON

For those who find and give thanks to God in their earthly fortune, God will give them times in which to remember that all things on earth are only temporary, and that it is good to set one's heart on eternity. . . . All things have their time, and the main thing is to stay in step with God and not always be hurrying a few steps ahead or falling behind. To want everything all at once is to be over-anxious. "For everything there is a season . . . to weep, and . . . to laugh; . . . to embrace, and . . . to refrain from embracing; . . . to tear, and . . . to sew . . ." (Eccl. 3:1a, 4a, 5b, 7a), "and God seeks out what has gone by" (3:15b). Yet this last part must mean that nothing past is lost, that with us God again seeks out the past that belongs to us. So when the longing for something past overtakes us—and this happens at completely unpredictable times—then we can know that this is only one of the many "times" that God makes available to us. And then we should not proceed on our own but seek out the past once again with God.

MORNING BY MORNING
HE WAKENS ME

Every new morning is a new beginning of our life. Every day is a completed whole. The present day should be the boundary of our care and striving (Matt. 6:34; Jas. 4:14). It is long enough for us to find God or lose God, to keep the faith or fall into sin and shame. God created day and night so that we might not wander boundlessly, but already in the morning may see the goal of the evening before us. As the old sun rises new every day, so the eternal mercies of God are new every morning (Lam. 3:22–23). To grasp the old faithfulness of God anew every morning, to be able—in the middle of life—to begin a new life with God daily, that is the gift that God gives with every new morning. . . .

Not fear of the day, not the burden of work that I have to do, but rather, the Lord wakens me. So says the servant of God: "Morning by morning he wakens—wakens my ear to listen as those who are taught" (Isa. 50:4). God wants to open the heart before it opens itself to the world; before the ear hears the innumerable voices of the day, the early hours are the time to hear the voice of the Creator and Redeemer. God made the stillness of the early morning for himself. It ought to belong to God.

Do Not Worry about Tomorrow

Possessions delude the human heart into believing that they provide security and a worry-free existence, but in truth they are the very cause of worry. For the heart that is fixed on possessions, they come with a suffocating burden of worry. Worries lead to treasure, and treasure leads back to worry. We want to secure our lives through possessions; through worry we want to become worry free, but the truth turns out to be the opposite. The shackles that bind us to possessions, that hold us fast to possessions, are themselves worries. The misuse of possessions consists in our using them for security for the next day. Worry is always directed toward tomorrow. In the strictest sense, however, possessions are intended only for today. It is precisely the securing of tomorrow that makes me so insecure today. "Today's trouble is enough for today" (Matt. 6:34b). Only those who place tomorrow in God's hands and receive what they need to live today are truly secure. Receiving daily liberates us from tomorrow. Thought for tomorrow delivers us up to endless worry.

THE HOUR OF SALVATION

The curious uncertainty that surrounds the feast of Epiphany is as old as the feast itself. We know that long before Christmas was celebrated, Epiphany was the highest holiday in the Eastern and Western churches. Its origins are obscure, but it is certain that since ancient times this day has brought to mind four different events: the birth of Christ, the baptism of Christ, the wedding at Cana, and the arrival of the Magi from the East. . . . Be that as it may, since the fourth century the church has left the birth of Christ out of the feast of Epiphany. . . . The removal of the birth of Christ from his baptismal day had great significance. In gnostic and heretical circles in the East, the idea arose that the baptismal day was actually the day of Christ's birth as the Son of God. . . . But therein lay the possibility of a dangerous error, namely, a misunderstanding of God's incarnation. . . . If God had not accepted Jesus as his Son until Jesus' baptism, we would remain unredeemed. But if Jesus is the Son of God who from his conception and birth assumed our own flesh and blood, then and then alone is he true man and true God; only then can he help us; for then the "hour of salvation" for us has really come in his birth; then the birth of Christ is the salvation of all people.

THE FIRST SIGN

The story of Jesus at the wedding in Cana (John 2:1–11) reports "the first of his signs" that reveal his glory, a highly miraculous and, to our way of thinking, almost unnecessary sign of his divine glory, in view of the modest nature of the occasion. What is crucial, however, is that even this sign of Jesus' divine power remains hidden from the wedding guests, the steward, and the bridegroom. It instead serves only the faith of the disciples. Jesus does not want to force his recognition as the Son of God, but he wants to be believed as such: "And his disciples believed in him." The glory of Jesus is hidden in his lowliness and is seen only in faith. Here the content of the feast of Epiphany is again closely joined with the Christmas story, and so we understand that the day of Epiphany was once the same as the appearance of the One who "had no form or majesty" (Isa. 53:2). In this way Epiphany points to the time that follows in the church year: the passion.

THE FLIGHT INTO EGYPT

The baby Jesus has to flee with his parents. Could God not protect him from Herod in Bethlehem? Certainly, but we don't need to ask about what God could do or would do, but what God really wants to do. God wants Jesus to flee to Egypt. In this way God shows that from the very beginning Jesus' way is a way of persecution, but God is also showing that he can protect Jesus and that nothing will happen to him as long as God does not allow it. Jesus now lives in Egypt, where his people once had to live in slavery and adversity. The king is now supposed to be where his people were. He is supposed to experience the history of his people in his own body. In Egypt, Israel suffered adversity; in Egypt, adversity also begins for Jesus; in Egypt, God's people and their king live in misery in a strange land. Out of Egypt, however, God led his people into the promised land, and out of Egypt God calls his son back into the land of Israel. What the prophet once said in regard to the people of Israel is now fulfilled in Jesus: "Out of Egypt I called my son" (Hos. 11:1). The flight into Egypt was not blind chance but divine promise and fulfillment. In Egypt, Jesus became one with the sufferings and joys of his people, of God's people, of us all. In Egypt, he is with us in a strange land; with him we will also move out of a foreign land and into God's land.

GOD'S COMMAND TO RETURN HOME

From day to day, from year to year, Joseph waits in Egypt for the divine command to return home. Joseph does not want to act on his own. He waits for God's instruction. Then at night—again in a dream—God sends Joseph the command: "Get up, take the child and his mother, and go to the land of Israel, for those who were seeking the child's life are dead" (Matt. 2:19–20).

The mighty Herod has died, without reaching his goal, but Jesus lives. And so it goes again and again in the history of the church. First adversity, persecution, and danger of death for the children of God, for the disciples of Jesus Christ, but then the hour comes with the news: "They are dead." Nero is dead, Diocletian is dead, the enemies of Luther and the Reformation are dead, but Jesus is alive, and his own live with him. The time of persecution suddenly comes to an end, and it turns out that Jesus is alive.

The baby Jesus returns to the land of Israel, called by God. Jesus comes to take up his kingdom, to ascend his throne. At first Joseph intends to take Jesus to Judea, where the king of Israel is expected to come from (Matt. 2:22–23). But a special divine warning prevents him and commands him to go to Nazareth. In the ear of the Israelite, Nazareth had a bad ring: "Can anything good come out of Nazareth?" (John 1:46). Nevertheless—or really precisely because of this—Jesus is to grow up in Nazareth, "so that what had been spoken through the prophets might be fulfilled, 'He will be called a Nazorean'" (Matt. 2:23).

A Plain Shoot

He will be called a Nazorean" (Matt. 2:23). This prophecy seems hard to understand, especially since we don't find it in this form anywhere else. But we must learn to pay close attention to the biblical text. It says here not that a single prophet but, rather, the *prophets* contain this prophecy. What the evangelist must have in mind is that again and again the Old Testament promises that the future king will appear in lowliness and plainness. To be sure, there is no mention there of Nazareth, but the Gospel writer finds this connection in the well-known passage of Isaiah in which we read that a branch, a sprout, a plain shoot will spring from the stump of Jesse, and that this weak and lowly branch coming from the root of Jesse will be the Messiah of Israel (Isa. 11:1–9). The Hebrew word for branch, however, is *nezer*; yet this word contains the same root sounds as the place named *Nazareth*. The Gospel finds—hidden that deep—the Old Testament promise that Jesus will be poor, despised, and lowly. Thus, in the path to miserable Nazareth, which Joseph and the whole world find hard to comprehend, God's way with the Savior of all the world is again fulfilled. He is to live in deepest poverty, obscurity, and lowliness. He is to share the life of the plain and the despised, so that he can bear the misery of all people and become their Savior.

GOD DECEIVES NO ONE

In the beginning, even before the start of his ministry, Jesus is tempted by the devil. The powers of evil, of falling away from God, approach him and try to bring him down at the very moment when he is assuming his role as Messiah (Luke 4:3–4). Luke reports that Jesus is famished, and then the devil confronts him: If you are the Son of God, tell this stone to become bread. If you have the power of God, then use it for yourself. Perform a miracle: turn the stone into bread, and you will be filled. Why, after all, do you have such power? If you are the Son of God, prove your power. Look, it's not just you who are hungry; millions of people are hungry. And they have eyes only for someone who can give them something to eat. They are not capable of being enthusiastic for you—for God—if you don't give them bread first. . . . In this voice of apparent intercessory love, Jesus recognizes the voice of the devil. It was an outrageous suggestion, and he rejects the devil: "One does not live by bread alone, but by every word that comes from the mouth of God" (Matt. 4:4). Here that means basically: God deceives no one.

ONLY FAITH CAN SLEEP
WITHOUT A CARE

When the disciples were climbing into the boat (Matt. 8:23–27), they seemed quite secure. They seemed to have no fear. Why were they secure? They looked at the beautiful, calm sea and were quite at peace and without a care. But with the rising wind and waves, they lost their peace and became anxious. Jesus was reportedly asleep. Only faith can sleep without a care, for sleep is a reminder of paradise; faith has its security in God alone. The disciples could not sleep. Their security was gone. They had nothing to hold on to. Theirs had been a false security that was only fear in different dress. Such security does not overcome fear and soon disappears, for fear is overcome only by faith, which leaves behind all false securities, leaves them fallen and broken. Faith does not believe in itself, or in a favorable sea, or in favorable conditions, or in its own power, or in any other human power, but solely, completely in God—whether there are storms or not. It is the only faith that is not superstition, that does not lead us back into fear, but rather frees us from fear.

SIMPLE OBEDIENCE

When Jesus demanded voluntary poverty of the rich young man, the latter knew that there were only two choices: to obey or not to obey (Matt. 19:21). When Levi was called from his tax collecting and Peter from his nets, there was no doubt that Jesus was serious about his call. They were to leave everything and follow him (Mark 2:14; 1:16–17). When Peter is called onto the rolling sea, he has to get up and venture forth (Matt. 14:29). In all of this, only one thing was demanded: to rely on the word of Jesus Christ and accept his word as a more secure foundation than all the securities of the world. The powers that wanted to put themselves between the word of Jesus and obedience were just as great in those days as they are today. It was contrary to reason: conscience, responsibility, piety, even the law itself and the principle of Scripture stepped into the middle to forbid this extreme, this lawless "fanaticism." But the call of Jesus broke through all of that and brought forth obedience. It was God's own word. The demand was simple obedience. . . . The concrete call of Jesus and simple obedience have their irrevocable meaning. With it Jesus calls us in the concrete situation, in which he can be believed. He therefore calls concretely — and wants to be understood in just that way — because he knows that only in concrete obedience do we become free to believe.

A NECESSARY DAILY EXERCISE

Why is it that my thoughts wander so quickly from God's word, and that in my hour of need the needed word is often not there? Do I forget to eat and drink and sleep? Then why do I forget God's word? Because I still can't say what the psalmist says: "I will delight in your statutes" (Ps. 119:16). I don't forget the things in which I take delight. Forgetting or not forgetting is a matter not of the mind but of the whole person, of the heart. I never forget what body and soul depend upon. The more I begin to love the commandments of God in creation and word, the more present they will be for me in every hour. Only love protects against forgetting.

Because God's word has spoken to us in history and thus in the past, the remembrance and repetition of what we have learned is a necessary daily exercise. Every day we must turn again to God's acts of salvation, so that we can again move forward. . . . Faith and obedience live on remembrance and repetition. Remembrance becomes the power of the present because of the living God who once acted for me and who reminds me of that today.

WE MUST ASK ABOUT THE BEGINNING

The fact that the Bible speaks of the beginning (Gen. 1:1) is very frustrating for us and for the world, for we cannot talk about the beginning. Where the beginning begins, our thinking ends; it comes to a full stop. And yet it is the most ardent passion of our thinking; it is our wanting to ask about the beginning that ultimately gives existence to every genuine question. We know that we must constantly ask about the beginning, and yet we can never ask about it. Why not? Because the beginning is the infinite, and because we can think of the infinite only as what is without end and thus without beginning. Because the beginning is freedom, and we always think of freedom only in necessity and thus only as the one among others, but never as simply the one before all others. If we ask why this is so, why we always think from the beginning and in reference to it, and yet never conceive of it—indeed, cannot even question it—then this "why" is again only the expression of a series that could be taken back into infinity and yet not reach the beginning. Thinking can never answer its own final why, because this answer would also give birth to another why.

THE DOUBLE QUESTION
ABOUT THE BEGINNING

There arises a double question: Is this beginning (Gen. 1:1) God's beginning, or is it God's beginning with the world? Yet even the asking of this question proves that we do not know what beginning means. If the beginning can be discussed only by those who are in the middle and are anxious about the beginning and the end, by those who break their own chains, by those who in their sin know about their creation only from God, then we can no longer ask whether this beginning was God's beginning or God's beginning with the world. This is so because precisely for us God as the beginning is none other than the One who in the beginning created the world and created us, and because we can know nothing about this same God other than what we know about the Creator of the world. When Luther answered the question of what God did before the creation of the world by saying that he cut switches for people who ask such useless questions, he was thereby not only knocking down the questioner's question but at the same time was also saying that where God is not recognized as the gracious Creator, he must become known as the angry Judge — but this too is always in reference to the middle between beginning and end. There is no possible question that can go behind this God who created in the beginning.

THE BEGINNING IS NOT A
TEMPORAL DESIGNATION

Moreover, there is no question to be asked about the why of creation, about God's world plan, or about the necessity of creation—these very questions are ultimately obviated and revealed as godless questions by the statement: In the beginning God created heaven and earth. Not: in the beginning God had this or that idea about the purpose of the world, ideas about which we would now have to find out more, but in the beginning God *created*. And no question can go behind the creating God, because no one can go behind the beginning. From this we must conclude that the beginning is not a temporal designation. One can always go behind a temporal beginning, but this beginning is simply unique; it is unique not in a quantitative sense, but in a qualitative sense, that is, as something simply unrepeatable, as something entirely free. . . . In the beginning—that is, out of freedom, out of nothing—God created heaven and earth. This is the comfort with which the Bible addresses those of us who stand in the middle, who stand anxiously before the false nothing, the beginningless beginning and the endless end. It is the gospel, it is Christ, the resurrected One himself, that we are talking about here. That God was at the beginning and that he will be at the end, that he is free above the world, and that he lets us know these things: all of this is mercy, grace, forgiveness, comfort.

GOD SPOKE

In contrast to all creation myths in which the deity sacrifices its nature, in which the world springs forth from its fruitfulness, in which creation is thus understood as a self-unfolding, a self-formation, a giving birth of the deity, in which the creation itself is thus a part of the nature of God, in which the suffering of nature, its giving birth and passing away, is thus the suffering of the deity itself—in contrast to all of that, the God of the Bible remains entirely God, entirely the Creator, entirely the Lord, and his creation remains entirely subservient and obedient, worshiping and praising him as the Lord. The biblical God is never the creation; he is always the Creator. He is not the substance of nature, and there is no continuum that connects and unites him with his work—except for his *word*. "Then God said . . ." (Gen. 1:3). The only continuity between him and his work is the word; that is, in creation itself there is no continuum. If the word is not there, the world loses its foundation. This word of God is not his nature or his essence, but his commandment—it is he himself who thinks and creates in this word, the same one who as Creator wants to meet his creation. God's creativity is not his nature or his essence, but his will, his commandment, in which he gives himself to us as he will.

IN THE WORD OF CREATION
WE KNOW THE CREATOR

The fact that God creates in the word means that creation is the command, the order of God, and that this
command is given freely. God *speaks*, that is, he creates
altogether freely and in his creating also still remains completely free vis-à-vis his work. He is not bound to his
work, but he binds his work to himself. He does not go
into his work as substance, but his relationship to his work
is his command; that is, he is never in the world in any way
other than in the fact that he is utterly beyond the world.
He is in the world as word, because he is the one who is
utterly beyond, and he is the one who is utterly beyond,
because he is in the world *in the word*. Only in the word of
creation do we know the Creator; in the word in the middle we have the beginning. Thus we do not know the Creator "out of" his works, as if the substance, the nature, the
essence of the work were ultimately somehow identical
with the nature of God, as if there were some kind of continuum there—say of cause and effect. No, solely because
God through his word confesses himself to these works
and because we *believe* this word about these works—that
is why we believe in God as the Creator.

THE WORK OF THE FIRST WORD

God said, 'Let there be light'; and there was light"
(Gen. 1:3). Because it was dark in the formless deep,
light had to create form. As the formless night gained form
through the morning light, as the light revealed and created the form, so that primal light had to give order to
chaos to reveal and create form. If that word of the darkness to the deep was the first reference to the passion of
Jesus Christ, so the liberation of the subjugated, formless
deep to its own existence through light is a reference to the
light that shines in the darkness (John 1:7). The light
awakens the darkness to its own existence, to the free
praise of the Creator. Without light we would not exist—
for without light there is nothing to be distinguished from,
because there is no form. But without something to be distinguished from, there is no free worship of God. The subservient deep worships God in subservient, dull, unfree
indistinctiveness; in light, form perceives distinction as its
own existence and gives full credit to the Creator. The
transparency, clarity, and freedom of one's own existence
given by light in distinction to other created forms and to
the Creator are the work of the Creator's first word. In his
created light, creation sees his light (Ps. 36:9).

The Eye of God

A nd God saw that the light was good" (Gen. 1:4a). The fact that God sees his work and is pleased by what he sees, because it is good, means that God loves his work and therefore wants to sustain it. Creating and sustaining: those are two sides of the one activity of God. Indeed, it can only be true that the work of God is good and that he does not reject and annihilate it, but loves and sustains it. In the eye of God, his work comes to rest and receives his approval. The eye of God keeps the world from falling back into the void, from undergoing total annihilation. The eye of God sees the world as good, as created—even when it is a fallen world—and we live for the sake of this eye of God, with which he surrounds his work and does not abandon it. The idea that God's work is good does not, in any case, mean that the world is the best of all conceivable worlds, but rather that it lives completely from God, that it lives from him and for him, and that he is its Lord. It is the goodness that is not distinguished from evil that is meant here, that consists in its being under the dominion of God. It is thus the work itself that is good; creation is the good work of God that he does for himself.

THE DAY

The world lives in the changing of the day. The day has its own existence, its own form, its own power. . . . The day was God's first creation, something miraculous and mighty in the hand of God. For us the day has completely lost its creaturely and wondrous nature. We use it—and abuse it—but we don't accept it as a gift. We don't live it. Today more than ever, technology is waging war against the day. . . . The unformed takes on form in the morning and sinks back into formlessness in the evening; the bright contrast of the light dissolves into uniformity in the dark; lively sounds fade away into the silence of the night; sleep follows attentive wakefulness in the light; and there are times of wakefulness and sleep in nature, in history, in peoples—all of this is what the Bible means when it talks about the creation of the day (Gen. 1:4b–5), about the day without human beings that portends everything, including the destiny of human beings. The rhythm that combines rest and movement, that gives and takes and gives and takes again is therefore an eternal allusion to God's giving and taking—and to God's freedom beyond rest and movement. That is the day.

IN MILLIONS OF YEARS OR IN INDIVIDUAL DAYS

When the Bible speaks of six days of creation, it may well have thought of a day as consisting of a morning and a night, yet it may not have meant the day literally but may have thought of it as the power of the day that makes the physical day what it is, as the natural dialectic of creation. When the Bible speaks of "day" here, the discussion does not concern the physical problem at all. It does not matter to biblical thought whether creation happened in rhythms of millions of years or in individual days; we have no reason to value the latter or to doubt the former. But the question as such does not concern us. There is no doubt that the biblical author, to the extent that his words are human words, was subject to his time, his knowledge, and his limitations—nor is there any doubt that through these words only God himself is speaking to us of his creation. The daily works of God are the rhythms in which creation occurs.

THE BLESSING OF GOD AS PROMISE

The blessing of God on human beings is his promise, his certain pledge. Blessing means distinction of the one who is blessed. A blessing is placed on an individual and remains until it is changed into a curse. Blessing and curse are burdens that God lays upon people. They are passed down, often not understood, not comprehended. They are something quite real, not something magic in the sense of a charm, but real. This blessing—be fruitful, feed yourselves, rule, have dominion over the world (Gen. 1:28)— affirms human beings entirely in the world of the living in which they are placed; it is their entire empirical existence that is blessed here, their creaturely nature, their worldliness, their earthiness. Yet what happens if this very blessing ever changes into curse? But what does this blessing mean, other than that God saw that his work was very good (Gen. 1:31)?

PEACE AND COMPLETION

In the Bible rest actually means more than taking a
break. It means resting after completion. It means the
peace of God in which the world lies. It means transfiguration. It means focusing completely on God's being God,
on worshiping God. Yet it is never the rest of a lethargic
God, but rather the rest of the Creator; it is not a turning
loose of the world, but rather the last glorification of the
world that looks to its Creator. Even in his rest God must
remain the Creator: "My Father has worked until now,
and I work too" (John 5:17b Luther). God remains the
Creator, but now as the one who has completed his work.
We understand God's rest only in the sense that it is, at the
same time, the rest of his creation. His rest is our rest (as
his freedom is our freedom, and his goodness our goodness). Therefore, God consecrates his day of rest also for
Adam and for us, whose hearts are restless until they find
their rest in God's rest. For us this rest is the whole promise that is given to the people of God (Heb. 4:9).

Conscience Is Shame before God

Adam can no longer stand before his Maker (Gen. 3:8–13). . . . For him the fall is not enough; he cannot flee fast enough. This flight, Adam's hiding from God, we call conscience. Before the fall there was no conscience. Not until their separation from their Creator are human beings separated from themselves. And indeed this is the function of conscience: to drive one into flight from God in order, on the one hand, to concede against one's will that God is right and, on the other, to let one feel secure in this flight. . . . Conscience drives people away from God and into safe hiding. Here, away from God, they then play the judge themselves and in this way avoid God's judgment. Human beings now really live by their own good and evil, by their deepest separation from themselves. Conscience is shame before God, in which, at the same time, one's own evil is hidden, one justifies oneself, and—against one's own will—reference to the Other is contained. Conscience is not the voice of God in sinful human beings, but defense against this voice, which, however—precisely as defense against one's knowledge and will—still points to this voice.

FROM THE DUST OF THE EARTH

Human beings, whom God created in his own image, that is, in freedom, are the ones who were taken from the dust of the earth (Gen. 2:7). Not even Darwin and Feuerbach could have said it more strongly than it is said here. Human beings come from the dust of the earth. Their connection with the earth is a part of their nature. . . . It is God's earth from which human beings are taken. From it they gain their *bodies*. Their bodies are part of their essence. One's body is not one's prison, one's shell, one's exterior; rather, one's body is oneself. A human being does not "have" a body and "have" a soul. Rather, one "is" body and soul. In the beginning Adam is really his body. He is one. Just as Christ is completely his body, and the church is the body of Christ. People who rid themselves of their body, rid themselves of their existence before God the Creator. . . . They have their existence as existence on earth; they do not come from above. They are not imprisoned and enslaved in the earthly world by a cruel fate, but are called forth by the word of God the Almighty out of the earth, in which they slept and were dead. In themselves they are the dust of the earth, but are called by God into being human.

THE LOVE OF THE CREATOR
FOR THE CREATURE

"Sleeper, awake! Rise from the dead, and Christ will shine on you" (Eph. 5:14). This is also what Michelangelo meant. Resting on the young earth, Adam is so solidly and intimately connected with the ground on which he lies that in his still dreamy existence, he himself is quite unusual, quite miraculous, and yet still a bit of earth; indeed, it is precisely this complete unity with the blessed soil of the created earth that reveals the full glory of the first human being. And in this resting on the earth, in this deep sleep of creation, the man now experiences life through bodily contact with the finger of God—it is the same hand that made the man that now touches him from a distance and awakens him to life. The hand of God does not hold the man nearer, clasped in its grip, but sets him free, and its creative power becomes the longing love of the Creator for the creature. The hand of God in this picture in the Sistine Chapel reveals more knowledge about the creation than many a profound speculation.

EVIL IN PARADISE

The prohibition against eating from the tree of knowledge (Gen. 3:1–3), which is heard by Adam as grace, becomes the law, which gives rise to anger in people and in God. . . . The serpent, one creature of God's among others, becomes the instrument of evil. . . . It is characteristic and essential in the biblical story that the whole event unfolds in the world created by God and that no "devils in the machine" are set in motion in order to dramatize this incomprehensible event and make it understandable. . . . The Bible does not claim to provide information regarding the origin of evil but to bear witness to its character as guilt and as unending human burden. . . . As a creature of God I have done evil—something entirely against God— and for this very reason there is guilt and inexcusable guilt. Therefore, it will never be possible simply to blame the devil who tempted me; rather, this devil will always be found precisely where I, as a creature of God in God's world, should live but don't want to live. And, to be sure, it will be just as impossible to fault creation as incomplete and make it responsible for my evil.

THE DESTRUCTION OF CREATION
BY THE CREATURE

Because the fall of human beings in God's creation is incomprehensible and ultimately inexcusable, the word *disobedience* does not fully describe the situation. It is an outrage, a stepping of creatures outside their allotted range of possible behavior. It is creatures becoming creators, the destruction of their nature as creatures. It is a falling away, a dropping out of the realm of creatureliness. And this falling away is a *lasting* fall, a *plunging* into the abyss, a letting loose, an ever widening and deepening separation. And in all this it is not simply an *ethical failure* but the destruction of creation by the creature. That is, the extent of this fall encompasses the entire created world, which is now robbed of its creatureliness, because the world, like a meteor that has torn loose from the core, is falling blindly into endless space. The question of the why of evil is not a theological question, for it presupposes the possibility of going back behind the existence forced on us as sinners. We could make something else responsible. The theological question is not directed toward the origin of evil but toward the real overcoming of evil on the cross; it asks about the forgiveness of guilt and the reconciliation of a fallen world.

ADAM, DON'T RUN AWAY

Adam, where are you? . . . With these words of the Creator, the fleeing Adam is called out of his conscience; he has to stand before his Creator. . . . This call goes directly against his conscience. Conscience says: Adam, you are naked; hide yourself from the Creator. You can't stand before him. God says: Adam, stand before me. . . . Adam tries to keep on running. I am sinful; I cannot stand before you—as if one can be excused through sin. Precisely because you are a sinner, stand before me and don't run away. But Adam still cannot stand: "The woman whom you gave to be with me, she gave me fruit from the tree, and I ate" (Gen. 1:12). He confesses his sin, but in making his confession, he tries again to escape. . . . The woman, after all, was your creature; it is your own work that caused me to fall; why did you bring forth an imperfect creation? What can I do about that? So, instead of standing, Adam falls back on the art he learned from the serpent, of correcting God's thoughts, of appealing from the Creator God to another, better God. In other words, he escapes again. Adam did not stand and did not confess; he appealed to his conscience regarding good and evil and on the basis of this knowledge complained to his Creator. He did not recognize the grace of the Creator that proved itself precisely in his call to God.

FEBRUARY

COMMANDMENT AND PRAYER

Before God's commandment
human beings are not, like Hercules,
permanently at the crossroads;
they do not eternally wrestle
with the right decision.

The "oh" of our wishes
and the "oh" of prayer
are two different things.

LAW OF LIFE AND
COMMANDMENT OF GOD

In all ages people have had thoughts about the basic rules governing their lives. And it is a quite remarkable fact that the results of almost all such thoughts largely agree with each other and with the Ten Commandments. Again and again, when the living conditions of human beings fall into disorder through strong external or internal disturbances and disorientations, those who are able to maintain clarity and soundness of thought and judgment recognize that without reverence before God, without respect toward parents, without the protection of life, marriage, property, and honor—whatever form these ideals may take—no life together is possible for humans. In order to recognize these laws of life, one does not need to be a Christian but only to follow one's experience and sound reason. Christians rejoice in all the agreements they share with others on such important things. They are ready to work and struggle together with others in order to realize common goals. . . .

Yet Christians never forget the crucial difference that remains between these laws of life and the Ten Commandments. The former are based on reason; the latter come from God.

Do Not Hide Your Commandments from Me

In our personal conduct of life and in God's historical activity, God is often hidden from us; that does not make us anxious. But when the revealed commandment of God fades from our view, so that we no longer perceive from the word of God what we ought to do, that is a serious threat. . . . The cry that God not hide his commandment from me (Ps. 119:19) comes only from the heart of one who knows God's commandment. There is no doubt that God *has* let us know his commandments, and we have no excuse, as though we did not know God's will. God does not abandon us in irresolvable conflicts; he does not turn our lives into ethical tragedies. No, he lets us know his will; he demands its fulfillment and punishes those who disobey. Things are much simpler here than we like. Not that we do not know God's commandments, but that we do not do them—and then gradually, as a consequence of such disobedience, we no longer know what is right—that is our predicament. What the writer says here is not *that* God hides his commandments from us; rather, God is asked for grace that his commandments may not be hidden. It is within God's freedom and wisdom to withdraw from us the grace of his commandment. Then, however, we are left not with resignation but with a pressing and persistent prayer: Do not hide your commandments from me.

THE COMMANDMENT IN FREELY
AFFIRMED, NORMAL LIFE

Before God's commandment human beings are not, like Hercules, permanently at the crossroads. They do not eternally wrestle with the right decision; they are not always caught in the conflict of duties; they do not repeatedly fail and start over. And God's commandment itself does not appear only in those great, moving, critical moments of life experienced in full consciousness. Rather, those who stand before God's commandment may now really be on their way (not always standing at the crossroads); they may really have the right decision behind them (not always before them); and they may—completely without inner conflict—do the one thing and leave the other (which is perhaps theoretically and ethically just as urgent). They may have already made a start and be on their way, led, accompanied, and protected by the commandment, as if by a good angel. And God's commandment itself can now give unified direction and personal guidance in the form of daily, seemingly small, meaningless words, sentences, and aids to life. The commandment has its purpose not in the avoidance of trespass, not in the torment of ethical conflict and decision, but in freely affirmed, normal life in the church, in marriage and family, in work, and in the state.

Daily Guidance

God's commandment cannot be found and known outside of time and place. Rather, it can be heard only in connection with time and place. Either God's commandment is definite, clear, and concrete in the last detail, or it is not God's commandment. . . .

As what is revealed in Jesus Christ, God's commandment is always a concrete talking *to* someone, never an abstract talking *about* someone or something. It is always address and demand, and this comes in such a comprehensive and at the same time defining way that in regard to it, there is no longer any freedom of interpretation and application, but only the freedom of obedience or disobedience.

God's commandment revealed in Jesus Christ encompasses the whole of life. It not only watches, like ethics, over the inviolate boundaries of life, but it is also the heart and fullness of life. It is not only obligation but also permission; it not only forbids, it also liberates for genuine life: it liberates for unpremeditated action. It not only interrupts the process of life when it goes astray, but also accompanies and guides it, without needing to be raised to consciousness. God's commandment becomes the daily divine guidance of our life.

THE COMMANDMENT AS THE ELEMENT OF LIFE

The commandment of God becomes the element "in" which one lives without always becoming conscious of it. The commandment as the element of life means freedom of movement and action, freedom from anxiety about deciding, about acting. It means certainty, peace, confidence, equanimity, joy. . . . Only if the commandment not only threatens me as a violator of boundaries but also transforms me and wins me over with its content, does it free me from the anxiety and uncertainty of decision. . . .

The commandment of God allows us as human beings to live in God's presence. The commandment of God is *permission*. It is different from all human laws because it *commands freedom*. It proves itself as *God's* commandment because it resolves this contradiction, it makes the impossible possible, and its real object, freedom, is beyond everything that can be commanded. That is how high the commandment of God reaches. Nothing less will do.

God's Commandments Cannot Fail

Being put to shame is the opposite of being blessed (Ps. 119:6). My life is put to shame when what I rely on fails. For I now no longer have something that gives my life sense and order, something to which I can appeal. My life becomes a joke, and I myself become ashamed. I relied on my strength. . . . If in the world my eye does not seek people, honors, and goods, but only God's commandments, then I will not be put to shame. For God's commandments cannot fail, because God himself upholds them and along with them everyone who looks to them. . . . I look to God's commandments when my decisions are based not on other people or on my own ideas and experiences, but when I ask ever anew—even against my pious thoughts and experiences—What is God commanding me to do? Even with my most pious ways and decisions, I may come to shame, but never with God's commandment. . . . But this requires earnest attention and indefatigable asking and learning to hear the right commandment and thus to know the inexhaustible goodness of God in all his commandments.

WHEN GOD SAYS "I"

When God says "I," then there is revelation. God could have let the world follow its course and kept quiet about it. Why should God find it necessary to talk about himself? When God says "I," then this is grace. When God says "I," then he is simply saying everything, the first and the last. When God says "I," then that means: "Prepare to meet your God" (Amos 4:12). "I am the Lord"—not *a* lord but *the* Lord. With this, God claims all lordship for himself alone. All right to command and all obedience belong to him and him alone. By bearing witness to himself as the Lord, God frees us from all human slavery. We serve God alone and no human being. Even when we carry out the orders of earthly masters, we in truth serve God alone. It is a great human error of many Christians to believe that God has subjected us in our earthly life to many other masters besides himself and that our life now stays in constant conflict between his commandment and the orders of these earthly masters. . . . All earthly authority is based on the authority of God alone; in it they have authority and honor. Otherwise it is usurpation and has no claim to obedience. . . . Obedience to God alone is the foundation of our freedom.

GOD WANTS TO BE GOD ALONE

I am the LORD your God . . . [therefore] you shall have no other gods before me" (Exod. 20:2–3). It is out of God's love that he wants to save us from errors and trespasses through such prohibitions and to show us the boundaries within which we can live in his community. "You shall have no other gods before me." This is something that is not at all obvious. Peoples of high culture in all ages have known a panoply of gods, and it was part of the greatness and dignity of one god to make room for the others in the pious hearts of people without jealous strife. The human virtue of generosity and tolerance was also ascribed to the gods, but God tolerates no other god beside him; God wants to be God alone. He wants to do and be everything for his people; therefore he also wants to be the only one worshiped by them. There is room for nothing beside God; the whole creation is under God. God wants to be God alone because he alone is God. It is a question here not of our being able to worship other gods in place of God, but of our thinking that we can put anything at all *beside* God.

The Name "God"

"You shall not make wrongful use of the name of the LORD your God, for the LORD will not acquit anyone who misuses his name" (Exod. 20:7). For us, "God" is not a general concept with which we designate the highest, most holy, most powerful being imaginable; rather, "God" is a name. When pagans say "god," it is something quite different from what it is when we, to whom God himself has spoken, say "God." For us, God is our God, the Lord, the One who lives. "God" is a name, and this name is the most sacred thing we possess, for what we have in it is not something we thought up, but God himself in his whole being, in his revelation. If we can say "God," it is only because God, in his incomprehensible grace, has made himself known to us. When we say "God," it is as if we can hear God himself speaking to us, calling us, comforting us, commanding us; we feel him acting for us, creating, judging, renewing. "We give thanks to you, O God; we give thanks; your name is near" (Ps. 75:1). "The name of the LORD is a strong tower; the righteous run into it and are safe" (Prov. 18:10). The word "god" is nothing. The name "God" is everything.

KEEPING THE SABBATH HOLY

The Decalogue contains no commandment to work, but there is a commandment to rest from work. That is contrary to our usual way of thinking. In the third commandment, work is presupposed as something that is natural, but God knows that the work we do can gain so much power over us we can no longer leave it alone. Our activity can promise us everything and make us forget God. Therefore God commands us to rest from our work. It is not work that supports us, but God alone; we live not from work, but from God alone. "Unless the LORD builds the house, those who build it labor in vain. Unless the LORD guards the city, the guard keeps watch in vain. . . . for he provides for his beloved during sleep" (Ps. 127:1, 2d [alternate reading]), says the Bible, against all who would make work their religion. The Sabbath rest is the visible sign that human beings live by the grace of God and not by works. . . .

The Sabbath rest is the indispensable prerequisite for keeping the Sabbath holy. Human beings who are exhausted and have been degraded to working machines need rest so they can clear their minds, cleanse their feelings, and redirect their wills.

REST FROM OUR WORK

Resting on the Sabbath means keeping it holy, and keeping the Sabbath holy is what happens when the word of God is proclaimed in the worship service and when there is willing and reverent attention to this word. The desecration of the Sabbath begins with the failure of Christian proclamation, which in the first instance is the fault of the church and, in particular, of the preacher. Thus the renewal of Sabbath holiness begins with the renewal of preaching.

Jesus broke through the Jewish laws regarding the Sabbath rest. He did this for the sake of the true hallowing of the Sabbath. The Sabbath is hallowed, not through what people do or do not do, but through the deeds of Jesus Christ for the salvation of humankind. For this reason the early Christians replaced the Sabbath with the resurrection day of Jesus Christ and called this the Lord's Day. Therefore, with justification Luther gave not a literal but a spiritually interpretative translation of the third commandment, rendering the Hebrew word "sabbath" with the German word for holiday [*Feiertag*]. Our Sunday is the day on which we let Jesus Christ act for us and for all of humankind. Of course, that should happen every day, but on Sunday we rest from our work so that it may happen in a special way.

HEAVIER AND LIGHTER SINS

Today there are again evildoers and saints — and indeed in public view. The dull gray of the humid rainy day has turned into the black clouds and bright lightning of the thunderstorm. The contours are more than sharp; reality is revealing itself. The apparitions of Shakespeare are haunting us. The evildoer and the saint, however, have little or nothing to do with ethical programs; they arise from primal chasms. With their appearance they tear open the hellish and divine abyss from which they come and let us take a brief look at never imagined secrets. Being evil is worse than doing an evil deed. It is worse when a liar tells the truth than when a lover of the truth lies; it is worse when a misanthrope practices brotherly love than when a lover of people is overcome by hate. A lie is better than the truth in the mouth of the liar; hate is better than a deed of brotherly love by an enemy of humankind. Hence one sin is not just like any other. They have different weight. There are heavier and lighter sins. Apostasy is infinitely worse than a fall. The brightest virtues of the apostate are black as night against the darkest weaknesses of the faithful.

Quality Is the Greatest Enemy of Every Loss of Individuality

Unless we have the courage to restore a genuine feeling for human boundaries and to personally fight for them, we will succumb to an anarchy of human values. . . . When we no longer know what we owe ourselves and others, when the feeling for human quality and the strength to maintain distance are extinguished, then chaos stands at the door. If, for the sake of material comfort, we allow impudence to come too close, then we ourselves have already given up; we have let the flood of chaos break through at the point in the dam where we were stationed, and everything becomes our fault. In other ages it may have been the business of Christianity to bear witness to human equality; today it is precisely Christianity that will have to speak out passionately for the preservation of human boundaries and human quality. Socially this means the forgoing of status, a break with any kind of "star" cult, opening our eyes and looking up and down, and the joy of private life, along with the courage to engage in public life. Culturally it means the experience of quality, a retreat from frantic activity to leisure and quiet, from distraction to focusing, from sensation to reflection, from the ideal of virtuosity to the virtue of artistic creation, from snobbery to modesty, from gluttony to moderation. Quantities compete for space; qualities complement each other.

IN GOD'S LAW

H appy are those whose way is blameless, who walk in
the law of the LORD" (Ps. 119:1). We are identified
as those who, with the psalmist, are on the way. This
means that the question about whether or not we have
made the right beginning no longer needs to be asked, for
it would drive us into fruitless fear. Our job now is to learn
to understand ourselves as people who have been put on
the right path and can do nothing but travel it. Therefore,
there is good reason not to talk about the beginning anymore, to remove it from discussion, and in this very way,
and from this beginning, to decisively hold human beings
accountable. Those who do not abandon the search for the
new beginning are *under* the law and will be worn down
and killed by it. But those who have come from the
beginning that has already taken place are *in* God's law
and will be upheld and maintained in life by it. We
should now be able to understand why our psalm begins
with a beatitude for those who let what happened
through God happen for them, who no longer live in
rebellion against God's action but walk "in the law,"
borne by God's action and secure in it.

THE KNOWLEDGE OF GOOD AND EVIL

According to conscience, our relationship with God and with other human beings is based on our relationship with our self. The conscience pretends to be the voice of God and the norm of relationships with other people. Thus, out of a right relationship with themselves, human beings are supposed to gain a right relationship with God and others. This reversal of things is the claim of people who, in their knowledge of good and evil, have become like God. . . . Bearing the knowledge of good and evil within themselves, they have become judges over God and their fellow human beings, just as they are judges over themselves. Knowing about good and evil in separation from their origin, people enter into reflection on themselves. Their life is now all about understanding themselves, just as it was originally about knowing God. Self-knowledge becomes the essence and aim of life. That remains true even where people push beyond the boundaries of their own self. Self-knowledge is the never-ending effort of people to overcome, through thought, their separation from themselves, to come—through the incessant distinguishing of the self from itself—to unity with themselves.

GOD'S RIGHT AND HONOR

If the purpose of the Decalogue is to see the human right to life, marriage, property, and honor preserved in the name of God, this does not mean that these legal statutes in and of themselves have an absolute, divine worth, but only that in and above them God alone is to be honored and worshiped. Thus the statutes are not a second divine authority in addition to the God of Jesus Christ, but are rather the point at which the God of Jesus Christ creates obedience to himself. . . .

In the Decalogue it is never a question of self-assertion, but solely of God's right and honor; with Jesus as with the Decalogue, it is a matter of concrete obedience toward God. It is precisely in the *renunciation* of one's own right, property, and honor for God's sake that the true origin of these gifts, God himself, can be more highly honored than by insisting on one's own right, which could easily eclipse God's right. Jesus' demand of the rich young man to let go of one of his rights makes it quite clear that his keeping of the Ten Commandments from his youth had not been obedience toward God but a disregard of the living God in the midst of preserving the so-called divine statutes (Matt. 19:16–22).

PRAYER

The fact that we can pray is not something to be taken for granted. It is true that prayer is a natural need of the human heart, but that does not give us any right before God. . . . We pray to the God in whom we believe through Christ. Therefore our prayer can never be a conjuring up of God; we do not need to present ourselves before him. We can know that God knows what we need before we ask for it. That gives our prayer the greatest confidence and a happy certainty. It is neither the formula nor the number of words but faith that reaches God in his fatherly heart, which has long known us. The proper prayer is not a deed, not an exercise, not a pious attitude, but the petition of a child to the heart of the Father. Therefore, prayer is never demonstrative—not before God, not before ourselves, not before others. If God did not know what I need, then I would have to reflect on *what* I say to God, *how* I say it to him, and *whether* I say it to him. Thus faith excludes from what I pray any reflection and any demonstration. Simply put: prayer is hidden. It is, in every sense, the opposite of what is public. When we pray, we no longer know ourselves, but only God, to whom we call. Because prayer is not sent into the world, but is directed to God alone, it is the most undemonstrative action there is.

GOD IS NOT A MATTER OF MOOD

We say that religion is a matter of mood: we must wait until the mood strikes us. And then we often wait for years—perhaps until the end of our life—until we are once again in the mood to be religious. This idea is based on a great illusion. It is all well and good to let religion be a matter of mood but God is not a matter of mood. He is still present even when we are not in the mood to meet with him. Does this idea not disturb us at all? Those who want to rely on their moods are impoverished. In religion, as in art and science, there are—in addition to times of great excitement—times of sober work and practice. Interaction with God must be practiced; otherwise we will not find the right tone, the right word, the right language, when he surprises us. We must learn God's language, laboriously learn it. And we must work at it, so that we will be able to talk with him. Prayer must also be practiced—in earnest work. It is a serious, fateful error when one confuses religion with mawkish sentimentality. Religion is work and perhaps the most difficult and certainly the holiest work that a person can do. It is pitiful to satisfy oneself with the words, "I'm not religiously inclined," when there is a God who wants to be with us.

WORD AND ANSWER

Christianity lives and dies with prayer, for prayer is the heart of the Christian life. Luther said that as a shoemaker makes shoes and a tailor makes clothes, a Christian must pray. Anyone who does not pray is not a Christian. The reason so few people know this today is simply that they do not understand what it means to pray. Praying is not just bidding, nor is it just giving thanks. Praying means, first of all, being so still that we perceive God's word to us; but then it also means giving an answer to this word, whether in words or in deeds. . . . Praying means coming close to God and wanting to remain close, because he has come close to us. We can pray only because Christ is there; in him our prayer has its foundation, for through him we have God as our Father. . . . Christ, however, is also the strength of our prayer, and only through this strength can we pray without ceasing (1 Thess. 5:16–18). Yet precisely because Christ is our strength, which leads us to the Father, prayer makes us happy and strong. Therefore those who pray can no longer be fearful and no longer be sad. In prayer Christ is near us—God is near us. If you go to God, God will come to you.

GOD'S WORD—HUMAN PRAYER

The Psalter assumes a unique position in all of Holy Scripture. It is God's word, and at the same time it is, with few exceptions, human prayer. How are we to understand that? How can the word of God be, at the same time, prayer to God? Relevant to this question is an observation that everyone makes who begins to pray the Psalms. We try first to repeat them personally as our own prayer, but soon we run into passages that we don't believe we can pray as a personal prayer for ourselves. One thinks, for example, of the psalms of innocence, the psalms of revenge, and in part even the psalms of suffering. Nonetheless, these prayers are words of Holy Scripture that we as believing Christians cannot with cheap excuses dismiss as outdated, as superseded, as "religious preliminary stages." Thus we don't want to control the words of Scripture, but at the same time we know that we can't pray these words. . . . The prayer of Psalms that does not want to pass over our lips—that puts us off, that stops us in our tracks—leads us to suspect that someone other than we ourselves is praying here, that the one who protests his innocence here, who calls in God's judgment, who has come into such unfathomable suffering, is none other than Jesus Christ himself.

The Psalter as the Vicarious Prayer of Christ

The human being Jesus Christ, to whom no need, no sickness, no suffering is unknown, and yet who was the completely innocent and righteous One, prays in the Psalter through the voice of his church. The Psalter is in the realest sense the prayer book of Jesus Christ. He prayed the Psalter, and now it has become his prayer for all times. Can we not now comprehend how the Psalter can be both prayer to God and yet God's own word, because the praying Christ meets us there? Jesus Christ prays the Psalter in his church. His church also prays; indeed, individuals also pray, but they pray precisely because Christ prays in them. They pray here not in their own name but in the name of Jesus Christ. They pray not out of the natural longing of their own hearts. Rather, they pray out of the humanity of Christ, which he took upon himself. They pray on the basis of the prayer of the human being Jesus Christ. For this reason their prayer alone has found the promise of being heard. . . . Christ has become the petitioner here. The Psalter is the vicarious prayer of Christ for his church.

THE GREAT SCHOOL OF PRAYER

The Psalter is the great school of prayer. We learn here, *first*, what it means to pray: to pray on the basis of the word of God, to pray on the basis of promises. Christian prayer stands on the solid ground of the revealed word and has nothing to do with vague, self-seeking wishes. We pray on the ground of the prayer of the true human being Jesus Christ. That is what the Scripture means when it says that the Holy Spirit prays in us and for us, that Christ prays for us, and that we can rightly pray to God only in the name of Jesus Christ.

Second, we learn from the prayer of Psalms what we are supposed to pray. As surely as the scope of the prayer of Psalms extends far beyond the individual's total experience, so surely the individual prays in faith the whole prayer of Christ, the prayer of the One who was true human being and who alone had the full measure of the experiences of this prayer. . . .

Third, the prayer of Psalms teaches us to pray as a community. The body of Christ prays, and as an individual I know that my prayer is only a very small fraction of the whole prayer of the church. I learn to join in the prayer of the body of Christ. That lifts me above my personal concerns and lets me pray selflessly. . . . The deeper we grow into the Psalter and the more often we ourselves have prayed, the simpler and richer our prayer will become.

THE SIGH "OH"

The "oh" of our wishes and the "oh" of prayer are two different things. The former comes out of our need as we understand it; the latter comes out of our need as God has taught us to see it. The former is demanding or despairing; the latter is humble and confident. We cannot bring forth even the right "oh" from our own heart. God, through the Holy Spirit, must teach us to say it. In the right "oh" our inexpressible deep needs are summarized before God; these are the "sighs too deep for words" of the Holy Spirit, who represents us before God (Rom. 8:26). This right sigh, however, does not remain hidden from God (Ps. 38:9).

Our wishes are directed toward an improvement of the world, but our prayer begins with our own selves. How yearningly we long for people to change, for evil in the world to come to an end, and for a new righteousness to come into being. But all of that leads us nowhere. All change and renewal must begin with me myself.

"O that my ways may be steadfast in keeping your statutes!" (Ps. 119:5). That is a prayer that has promise. "The craving of the lazy person is fatal, for lazy hands refuse to labor" (Prov. 21:25).

Here, however, we have our hands full. This prayer leads promptly to action, and it leads to action where it is most needed: with me myself.

THANKING AND LEARNING

Thanks that do not come from an upright heart (Ps. 119:7) are hypocritical and presumptuous. Only where God's revealed word has convinced the heart that it wants to obey that word can it thank God for earthly and heavenly gifts. . . . The thanks of the world are ultimately always meant for itself; through thanks one seeks only higher confirmation and consecration of one's own good fortune. The expressed thanks convey the satisfaction of regarding the received gifts as rightful possession. There is also, however, a forbidden gratitude among the godly: even the Pharisee thanked God and sinned (Luke 18:11), for in his thanks he saw only himself. He did not receive the gift in humility but misused it against his neighbor. Thus, he could not give thanks "with an upright heart"— otherwise he would have forgotten himself in gratitude and would not have presented himself as one who had something to show God. Rather, like the prayer of the psalm, he would have presented himself as one who is just beginning to "learn your righteous ordinances" (Ps. 119:7). . . . I thank God because I am acquainted with his ordinances and want to learn them, but I give thanks as one who is still fully involved in learning, as one who—as measured by God's "righteous ordinances"—is still lacking in everything.

GREAT AND SMALL THINGS IN PRAYER

Only those who are thankful for small things also receive great things. We keep God from giving us the great spiritual gifts that he has for us because we do not give thanks for daily gifts. We think we cannot be satisfied with the small amount of spiritual knowledge, experience, and love given to us and always look greedily for greater gifts (Jer. 45:5). We then complain that we lack the great certainty, the strong faith, and rich experience that God has given to other Christians, and we believe that our grievances are righteous. We pray for the great things and forget to give thanks for the daily small (yet in truth not small!) gifts. But how can God entrust great things to one who will not thankfully receive small things from his hand? When we do not give thanks daily for the Christian community in which we are placed—even where there is no great experience, no perceivable wealth, but where there is much weakness, little faith, and much difficulty—when we are always complaining to God that everything is so measly, so small, so unlike what we expected, then we keep God from making our community grow according to the abundance and riches that await all of us in Jesus Christ.

THANKFULNESS

Thankfulness arises not from the human heart's own capabilities, but only from the word of God. Therefore, thankfulness must be learned and practiced. . . . Thankfulness reaches beyond the gift to the giver. It arises from the love that it receives. . . .

The thankful are humble enough to receive something as a gift. The proud take only what is their due. They refuse to accept a gift. . . .

To thankful people everything comes as a gift, because they know that for them there is nothing that is earned. . . .

In thankfulness I gain a proper relationship to my past; in thankfulness the past becomes fruitful for the present. Without thankfulness my past sinks into the dark, the mysterious into nothing. In order that I not lose my past but regain it completely, regret must join thankfulness. In thankfulness and regret my life comes together as a unit. . . . Ingratitude begins with forgetting; forgetting is followed by indifference, indifference by dissatisfaction, dissatisfaction by doubt, and doubt by curse.

SILENCE

We are silent in the early hours of each day, because God is supposed to have the first word, and we are silent before going to sleep, because to God also belongs the last word. We are silent solely for the sake of the word, not in order to show dishonor to the word but in order to honor and receive it properly. Silence ultimately means nothing but waiting for God's word and coming away blessed by God's word. . . . Silence before the word, however, will have its effect on the whole day. If we have learned to be silent before the word, we will also learn to be economical with silence and speech throughout the day. There is an impermissible self-satisfied, prideful, offensive silence. This teaches us that what is important is never silence in itself. The silence of the Christian is a listening silence, a humble silence that for the sake of humility can also be broken at anytime. It is silence in connection with the word. . . . In being quiet there is a miraculous power of clarification, of purification, of bringing together what is important. This is a purely profane fact. Silence before the word, however, leads to the right hearing and thus also to the right speaking of the word of God at the right time. A lot that is unnecessary remains unsaid.

MEDITATION

In meditation it is not necessary for us to try to think and pray in words. Silent thinking and praying that comes from just listening can often be more beneficial. It is not necessary for us to find new ideas in meditation. Often that only distracts us and satisfies our vanity. It is quite enough for the word, as we read and understand it, to penetrate us and live within us. As the word of the shepherds moved Mary "in her heart" (Luke 2:51), as a person's word often stays in our minds, lives and works in us, occupies us, unsettles or delights us, without our being able to do anything about it, so in meditation God's word wants to enter us and remain with us. It wants to move us and work in us. . . . Above all, it is not necessary in meditation for us to have some kind of unexpected, extraordinary experiences. It can happen, but if it does not, that is not a sign that our meditation is futile. From time to time we will notice a great inner barrenness and indifference, a lack of interest and even incapability in meditation. We must not then get stuck in such experiences. Above all, we must not let them keep us—especially now—from holding to our meditation time with great patience and faithfulness.

God, I Call to You

God, I call to you in the early morning;
help me pray and gather my thoughts;
I cannot do it alone.

In me it is dark, but with you there is light.
I am lonely, but you do not leave me.
I am faint-hearted, but with you there is help.
I am restless, but with you there is peace.
In me there is bitterness, but with you there is patience.
I do not understand your ways,
but you know the right way for me.

Father in heaven,
Praise and thanks be to you for the rest of the night.
Praise and thanks be to you for the new day.
Praise and thanks be to you for all your love and
    faithfulness in my past life.
You have shown me many good things;
let me now also accept hard things from your hand.
You will not place on me more than I can bear.
You make all things serve your children for the best.

MARCH

PARTICIPATION IN THE SUFFERING OF GOD

It is not the religious act
that makes the Christian,
but participation in
the suffering of God
in the life of the world.

THE WAY OF LOVE FOR HUMAN BEINGS

Christ's time of passion begins not with Holy Week but with the first day of his preaching. His renunciation of the empire as a kingdom of this world takes place not at Golgotha but at the very beginning. And our story is supposed to give expression to this idea (Luke 4:5–8). Jesus could have been Lord of this world. As the Messiah the Jews had dreamed of, he could have freed Israel and led it to fame and honor. He is a remarkable man, who is offered dominion over the world even before the beginning of his ministry. And it is even more remarkable that he turns down this offer. . . .

He knows that for this dominion he would have to pay a price that is too high for him. It would come at the cost of his obedience to God's will. . . . He remains the free Son of God and recognizes the devil, who wants to enslave him. "Worship the Lord your God, and serve only him" (Luke 4:8). Jesus knows what that means. It means lowliness, abuse, persecution. It means remaining misunderstood. It means hate, death, the cross. And he chooses this way from the beginning. It is the way of obedience and the way of freedom, for it is the way of God. And therefore it is also the way of love for human beings.

THE SOLID GROUND

Everything that we can rightfully expect and ask from God is to be found in Jesus Christ. All of the things we might imagine that a god must and could do—these have nothing to do with the God of Jesus Christ. Again and again we must immerse ourselves very slowly and very calmly in the life, speech, deeds, suffering, and death of Jesus in order to know what God promises and what he fulfills. It is certain that we can always live in the nearness and presence of God and that for us this life is a totally new life; that for us there is no longer anything impossible, because for God nothing is impossible; that no earthly power can touch us without God's will; and that danger and need only drive us closer to God. It is certain that we can demand nothing and yet can ask for everything. It is certain that hidden in suffering is our joy, hidden in dying is our life. It is certain that in all of this we stand in a fellowship that supports us. To all of this, God has said "Yes" and "Amen" in Jesus (2 Cor. 1:20). This Yes and Amen is the solid ground on which we stand. . . . Only if the earth was honored by receiving the human being Jesus Christ, only if a human being like Jesus lived, then, and only then, does it make sense for us human beings to live. If Jesus had not lived, then in spite of all the other people we know, honor, and love, our life would be meaningless.

There Were No Longer Any Shepherds There

The eye of the Savior falls compassionately on his people, on the people of God (Matt. 9:35–36). It was not enough for Jesus that a few had heard his call and followed him. He could not consider setting himself apart aristocratically with his disciples and, in the way of great founders of religions, conveying to them, in isolation from the crowd of people, the teachings of higher knowledge and perfect conduct of life. Jesus came, worked, and suffered for the sake of all of his people. And the disciples, who wanted to have him for themselves, who wanted to keep him from being bothered by the children that were brought to him and by many poor beggars on the roadside (Mark 10:48), had to learn that Jesus would not let his ministry by restricted by them. His gospel of the kingdom of God and his power as Savior belonged to the poor and sick, where he found them among his people. The appearance of the crowd, which in his disciples perhaps evoked aversion, anger, or contempt, filled Jesus' heart with deep compassion and anguish. No reproach, no accusation! God's dear people lay mistreated on the ground, and the blame for that belonged to those who were supposed to provide them with the ministry of God. It was not the Romans who had done this, but the misuse of the Word of God by those called as servants of the Word. There were no longer any shepherds there!

No Time to Lose

"The harvest is plentiful" (Matt. 9:37–38). It is ready to be brought into the barns. The hour has come for these poor and pitiful to be brought home into the kingdom of God. Jesus sees the promise of God breaking over the masses of people. The scribes and zealots saw here only a worn down, burned up, beaten down field. Jesus sees a mature field of waving grain for the kingdom of God. The harvest is plentiful! Only his compassion sees that! Now there is no time to lose. Harvest work suffers no delay. "But the laborers are few." Is that any wonder, since so few have been given this merciful eye of Jesus? Who could even join in this work except those who have gained a share in Jesus' heart, who have received through him seeing eyes? Jesus seeks help. He cannot do the work alone. Who are the coworkers who will help him? God alone knows them and must give them to his Son. Who can offer themselves on their own to be Jesus' helpers? Even the disciples cannot do it. They must ask the Lord of the harvest to send workers at the right hour, for it is time.

SUFFERING MUST BE SOMETHING COMPLETELY DIFFERENT

For the second time I am experiencing Holy Week here [in prison]. Internally I must resist when I read in letters statements that speak of my "suffering." That strikes me as a profanation. One must not dramatize these things. Whether I "suffer" more than most people generally do today seems to me more than questionable. Naturally, many things are dreadful, but is that not true everywhere? Earlier I often marveled at how silently the Catholics pass over these cases. But is that supposed to show greater strength? Perhaps they know better from their history what real suffering and martyrdom are. I believe, for example, that "suffering" definitely also includes bodily suffering. We like to emphasize spiritual suffering, but precisely this is what Christ is supposed to have taken away, and I find nothing about it in the New Testament or in the early Christian acts of the martyrs. Yet there is probably a big difference between whether the "church suffers" and whether this or that happens to one of its servants. I believe that much needs to be corrected here; indeed, speaking frankly, I am often almost ashamed of how much we have spoken of our own suffering. No, suffering must be something completely different; it must have a completely different dimension from what I have experienced thus far.

SUFFERING AND BEING REJECTED

Jesus Christ must suffer and be rejected. This is the "must" of God's promise in which the Scripture is fulfilled. Jesus was the Christ who could still be celebrated in suffering. That suffering could still be the basis of all of the world's pity and wonder. Suffering as something tragic could still carry within it its own value, its own honor and dignity. But Jesus is the Christ who is rejected in suffering. Being rejected takes away from suffering any dignity and honor. Suffering and being rejected are the summary expression for the cross of Jesus. Death on the cross means suffering and dying as one who is rejected and cast out. Jesus must suffer and be rejected by virtue of divine necessity. Any attempt to interfere with what is necessary is satanic—even and precisely when it comes out of the circle of the disciples, for it does not want to let Christ be Christ. . . . Thus for Jesus it now becomes necessary to relate the "must" of suffering to his disciples in a clear and unambiguous way. As Christ is Christ only as the suffering and rejected one, so the disciple is a disciple only as one who suffers and is rejected, as one crucified with Jesus. Discipleship, understood as being bound to the person of Jesus Christ, places the disciple under the law of Christ, that is, under the cross.

THE GOSPEL IS NOT A CHEAP CONSOLATION OF FAITH

The cross is not misfortune and hard fate. It is instead the suffering that comes to us from being bound to Jesus Christ. The cross is not accidental, but necessary suffering. The cross is not suffering bound up with natural existence, but suffering bound up with being a Christian. The cross is essentially not just suffering but suffering and being rejected—and also, strictly speaking, being rejected for Jesus Christ's sake, not because of some other kind of behavior or confession. A Christianity that no longer took discipleship seriously, that made of the gospel only a cheap consolation of faith and for which, otherwise, natural and Christian existence were indistinguishably mixed, would have to understand the cross as daily misfortune, as the urgency and anxiety of our natural life. . . . To be cast out in suffering, to be despised and abandoned by people, as is the unending lament of the psalmist (Ps. 69:7–8), this essential mark of the suffering of the cross can no longer be comprehended by a Christianity that does not know how to distinguish ordinary and Christian existence. The cross means suffering along with Christ.

WITHOUT ANY ILLUSION

As the New Testament proclaims life to the dying, as life and death collide in the cross of Christ, and as life swallows up death—only when we see this do we believe in the church under the cross. Only when we look at reality with clear eyes, without any illusion about our morality or our culture, can we believe. Otherwise our faith becomes an illusion. The believer can be neither a pessimist nor an optimist; both are an illusion. Believers do not see reality in a certain light. They instead see it as it is, and against everything and beyond everything they see, they believe *in God alone* and in his power. They do not believe in the world or in the capability of the world to develop and improve; they do not believe in their power to improve the world and in their goodwill. They do not believe in people or in the good in people that ultimately must triumph; they also do not believe in the church in its human power. Rather, believers believe solely in God, who creates and does the impossible, who creates life out of death, who has called the dying church to life against and in spite of us and through us. But God does it alone.

THE HIGH IDEALS OF JUSTICE, TRUTH, HUMANITY, AND FREEDOM

Wherever the name of Jesus Christ is named, he is there as protection and obligation. That is true of all people who in their battle for justice, truth, humanity, and freedom have again learned to name the name of Jesus Christ. This name protects them and the high ideals for which they stand, while this protection is at the same time an obligation placed on them and these ideals. . . . This is not the calm, steady development of the power of Christ's name, as perceived through the Middle Ages, nor is it the attempt to justify the name of Jesus Christ before the world through a connection with human names and ideals. . . . It is not a "Christian culture" that must make the name of Jesus Christ acceptable to the world; rather, the crucified Christ has become the refuge, justification, protection, and obligation for those higher ideals that have begun to suffer and for their defenders.

VICARIOUS LIVING

Because Jesus—who is life, our life—lived as the incarnate Son of God vicariously for us, all human life has therefore become, through him, essentially vicarious living. Jesus was not the individual who wanted to achieve a perfection of his own. He instead lived only as the one who took up and bore the selves of all people. All of his life, deeds, and suffering were vicarious living. What human beings were supposed to live, do, and suffer was fulfilled in him. In this real vicarious living, of which his human existence was composed, he is the epitome of responsibility. Because he is life, through him all life is defined as vicarious living. . . . As vicarious living and doing, responsibility is essentially a relationship between human beings. Christ became a human being and thereby bore vicarious responsibility for human beings. There is also a responsibility for things, conditions, and values, but only under the strict maintenance of the original, essential, and purposeful determination of all things, conditions, and values through Christ (John 1:3–4), the incarnate God. Through Christ the world of things and values regains its orientation toward humankind, in accordance with creation.

THE MISUSE OF VICARIOUS LIVING

Only in the complete dedication of one's own life to other people is there vicarious living and responsibility. Only the selfless person lives responsibly, and that means that only the selfless person *lives*. Where the divine yes and no become one in a person, life is lived responsibly. Selflessness in responsibility is so total that this is the right place for the Goethe saying about the doer who is always without conscience. A misuse of the vicarious life threatens from two sides: through making one's own self absolute and through making other people absolute. In the first case, the relationship of responsibility leads to oppression and tyranny. This fails to recognize that only the selfless can act responsibly. In the second case, the well-being of the other person, for whom I am responsible, is made absolute while disregarding all other responsibilities, and there arises an arbitrariness of action that mocks responsibility before God, who in Jesus Christ is the God of all people. In both cases the origin, essence, and aim of the responsible life in Jesus Christ is denied, and responsibility becomes a self-made abstract idol.

God Is a God of Bearing

Suffering must be borne, so that it will pass. Either the world must bear it and go down because of it, or it falls on Christ and is overcome in him. So Christ suffers vicariously for the world. . . . The church of Jesus Christ stands before God vicariously by following after Christ under the cross. God is a God of bearing. The Son of God bore our flesh, and for that reason he bore the cross; he bore all our sins and through his bearing achieved reconciliation. So too are disciples called to be bearers. Being a Christian consists in bearing. As the bearing of Christ preserved communion with the Father, so the bearing of his disciples is communion with Christ. Human beings can also cast off the burden loaded upon them, but this does not free them from the burden at all; rather, they now carry a much heavier, unbearable burden. They bear the self-chosen yoke of themselves. Jesus calls all who are laden with many kinds of suffering and burdens to cast off their yoke and take upon themselves his yoke, which is easy, and his burden, which is light (Matt. 11:30). His yoke and his burden are the cross. To walk under this cross is not misery and despair but refreshment and rest for the soul. It is the greatest joy. Here we are no longer under self-made laws and burdens but are under the yoke of the one who knows us and who walks with us himself, under the yoke. Under his yoke we are certain of this nearness and communion. It is he himself whom disciples find when they take up their cross.

FALSE ANXIETY

"Blessed are those who are persecuted for righteousness' sake, for theirs is the kingdom of heaven" (Matt. 5:10). The Scripture speaks here not of persecution for the sake of the righteousness of God or for the sake of Jesus Christ, but of the blessedness of those who are persecuted for the sake of a just—a true, good, human—cause (1 Pet. 3:14; 2:20). The false anxiety of those Christians who avoid any suffering for the sake of a just, good, true cause because they allegedly could have a good conscience only about suffering for the sake of an expressed confession of Christ—a pettiness that is suspicious of any suffering for the sake of a just cause and shrinks from it—is clearly placed in the wrong by this beatitude. Jesus receives those who suffer for the sake of a just cause, even if it is not exactly the confession of his name. He draws them under his protection, under his responsibility, under his claim. So those who are persecuted for righteousness' sake are led to Christ. And so it happens that one appealed to Christ in his hour of suffering and responsibility and confessed himself as a Christian, because he realized only at that moment that he belonged to Christ.

INACTIVE WAITING AND
APATHETIC WATCHING?

We must accept the fact that most people get smart only through experiences with their own body. This explains, *first*, the astonishing inability of most people to take preventive action of any kind—they believe that they will still be able to avoid the danger, until it is finally too late—and it explains, *second*, their apathy regarding the suffering of others. Sympathy arises in proportion to growing anxiety in the face of the threatening nearness of disaster. . . . Christ, according to Scripture, experienced all the suffering of all people in his body as his own suffering—an inconceivably noble idea! He freely took it upon himself. We are certainly not Christ and are not called to redeem the world through our own deeds and suffering. We are not lords but instruments in the hand of the Lord of history. We can sympathize with the suffering of other people only to a very limited degree. We are not Christ, but if we want to be Christian, this means that we should share in the broad heart of Christ—in responsible action that freely seizes the hour, that puts us in danger and in genuine sympathy that flows not from anxiety but from the liberating and redeeming love of Christ for all who suffer. Inactive waiting and apathetic watching are not Christian attitudes.

WHY HAVE YOU FORGOTTEN ME?

"Why have you forgotten me?" (Ps. 42:9). This question comes to the lips of all Christians when everything stands against them, when all earthly hope has been shattered, when in the course of great world events they feel totally lost, when all of life's goals seem unattainable, and everything appears pointless. Then, however, it depends where they direct this question: not to a dark fate but to the God who is and remains my Rock, the eternal Ground on which my life rests. When I fall into doubt, God remains solid as a rock. When I waver, God remains unshakable. When I become unfaithful, God remains faithful. . . . To endure humiliation and to be mocked for the sake of the faith—that has been a distinction of the godly for centuries. It hurts body and soul that no day passes without the name of God being doubted and blasphemed. Where, then, is your God? I confess God before the world and before all enemies of God when in deepest need I believe in God's goodness, when in guilt I believe in forgiveness, when in death I believe in life, when in defeat I believe in victory, when in desolation I believe in God's gracious presence. Those who have found God in the cross of Jesus Christ know how wonderfully God hides himself in this world and how he is closest precisely when we believe him to be most distant.

THE ONE WHO BECAME HUMAN

Who is this God? This God is the one who became human as we became human. He is completely human. Therefore, nothing human is foreign to him. The human being that I am, Jesus Christ was also. About this human being Jesus Christ we say: this one is God. This does not mean that we already knew beforehand who God is. Nor does it mean that the statement "this human being is God" adds anything to his being human. God and human being are not thought of as belonging together through a concept of nature. The statement "this human being is God" is meant entirely differently. The divinity of this human being is not something additional to the human nature of Jesus Christ. The statement "this human being is God" *is the vertical from above,* the statement that applies to Jesus Christ the human being, which neither adds anything nor takes anything away, but qualifies the whole human being as God. . . . Faith is ignited from Jesus Christ the human being. . . . If Jesus Christ is to be described as God, then we do not speak of his omnipotence and omniscience, but of his cradle and his cross. There is no "divine being" as omnipotence, as omnipresence.

THE LOVE OF GOD IS NOT A VAGUE IDEA

As God became a human being and can be known no longer as an idea, but only as one who has become human, so the love of God also took on worldly form. And only as such—and not as a vague idea—is it the love of God.

Love, which, in distinction from all philosophy, is what the gospel is all about, is not a method of interacting with human beings. Rather, it is being drawn into and entering into an event, namely, into God's communion with the world that took place in Jesus Christ. "Love" does not exist as an abstract characteristic of God but as the real event of people and the world being loved by God. "Love" also does not exist as a human characteristic but as the real belonging together and being together of people with people and the world on the basis of God's love for me and for them. As God's love went into the world and surrendered itself to the misunderstanding and ambiguity of everything worldly, so Christian love also exists in no other way than in the world, in the infinite fullness of concrete worldly actions, subject to every misinterpretation and prejudice. . . . The love of God frees us from human vision, which is clouded by self-love and has gone astray, and frees us for the clear knowledge of the reality of neighbor and world. In this way—and only in this way—it prepares us for the acceptance of genuine responsibility.

A LOVE THAT IS FOR US

I give you a new commandment . . ." (John 13:34), says
Jesus. That means that those who know him must
begin a new life with their neighbors, a life according to
the commandment of Jesus. What is this new commandment? ". . . that you love one another. Just as I have loved
you, you also should love one another." . . .

The love of Jesus Christ for us — what is that? To us, is
it only a word? Or have we experienced it? Only those
who have experienced it can, in turn, love others with this
love. Jesus' love — that is love that comes from eternity
and leads toward eternity. It does not cling to temporal
things but surrounds us, because we are supposed to be
eternal. It lets nothing stop it, for it is God's eternal faithfulness to us. Jesus' love — that is love that shrinks from no
pain, no renunciation, no suffering, if it helps the other
person. It is the love with which he loved us solely for our
own sake, with which on earth he took upon himself
mockery and hatred and died on the cross. Jesus' love is
love that takes upon itself the cross. Jesus' love — that is
love that is for us as we are. As a mother loves her child as
it is — and the greater the need, the greater the love,
because she knows that the child requires her love — such
is the love of Jesus for us. He accepts us as we are.

THE SCANDAL OF PIOUS PEOPLE

The lowly God-man is the scandal of pious people and of people in general. This scandal is his historical ambiguity. The most incomprehensible thing for the pious is this man's claim that he is not only a pious human being but also the Son of God. Whence his authority: "But I say to you" (Matt. 5:22) and "Your sins are forgiven" (Matt. 9:2). If Jesus' nature had been deified, this claim would have been accepted. If he had given signs, as was demanded of him, they would have believed him. But at the point where it really mattered, he held back. And that created the scandal. Yet everything depends on this fact. If he had answered the Christ question addressed to him through a miracle, then the statement would no longer be true that he became a human being like us, for then there would have been an exception at the decisive point. . . . If Christ had documented himself with miracles, we would naturally believe, but then Christ would not be our salvation, for then there would not be faith in the God who became human, but only the recognition of an alleged supernatural fact. But that is not faith. . . . Only when I forgo visible proof, do I believe in God.

THE SUCCESSFUL AND THE UNSUCCESSFUL

To a world in which success is the measure and justification of all things, the figure of the condemned and crucified One remains foreign and, at best, pitiable. Decisions are made not by ideas or convictions but by deeds. Success alone justifies the injustice that occurs. Guilt scars over in success. It is pointless to reproach the successful about their methods. To do so is to remain in the past while the successful stride forward from deed to deed, win the future, and make it impossible to revisit the past. . . .

The figure of the crucified One nullifies all thinking oriented toward success, for such thinking is a denial of judgment. . . . Only in judgment is there reconciliation with God and among people. . . . God's yes to the cross means judgment for the successful. The unsuccessful, however, must recognize that it is not their lack of success as such that allows them to stand before God, but solely their acceptance of the judgment of divine love. The fact, then, that precisely the cross of Christ—that is, his failure in the world—leads to historical success is a mystery of the divine governance of the world, from which we can make no rule, but which is repeated here and there in the suffering of his church.

In the Midst of Enemies

Our hearts always like to stay among friends, among those who are upright and honorable. But Jesus Christ was in the midst of enemies, and that's precisely where he wanted to be. And that's where we should be too. This distinguishes us from all other sects and religions, where the pious want to stay among themselves. Christ, however, wants us to be in the midst of our enemies, as he was. In the midst of his enemies he died the death of God's love and prayed: "Father, forgive them; for they do not know what they are doing" (Luke 23:34). Christ wants to win his victory among enemies. Therefore, do not withdraw; do not separate yourselves, but think good things about everyone. Live peaceably with all, "so far as it depends on you" (Rom. 12:18). . . . Our hearts should always be full of peace. Does that mean that we should also remain silent about the word of God for the dear sake of peace? Never. But is there then a more peaceful word and work than preaching the peace that God made with his world and with his people? "So far as it depends on you"—one thing does not depend on you, namely, to remain silent about the word of God. But it *is* your responsibility to speak that word for peace, to speak for the peace of human beings with God, in the midst of a human world that is torn apart and alienated. Jesus made peace with us while we were enemies (Rom. 5:10). Let us bear witness to this peace before everyone!

THE TIMES OF GOD

A defeat shows vigorous and ethical people that their strength must increase before they can stand the test. Therefore, their defeat is never irrevocable. Christians know that in the hour of temptation all their powers will leave them every time. Therefore, temptation is for them the dark hour that can become *irrevocable.* Therefore, they do not seek the testing of their strength but instead pray: *lead us not into temptation.* . . .

Yet the God who makes it become day and night also gives times of thirst and times of refreshment. God gives the storm, and God gives a peaceful journey. God gives times of concern and anxiety, and God gives times of joy. . . .

What is important to Christians is not what life is in itself, but how God now deals with me. God rejects me, and he accepts me again; he destroys my work, and he builds it up again. "I am the LORD, and there is no other. I form light and create darkness, I make weal and create woe; I the LORD do all these things" (Isa. 45:6–7). Thus, Christians live according to the times of God and not according to their own concept of life. Therefore, they do not say they always live in temptation and always on probation. Rather, they pray in times of preservation that God will not let the time of temptation come upon them.

Lead Us Not into Temptation

Then does the hour of temptation not have to come? Is it therefore permissible to pray in this way? Should we not simply pray instead that in the hour of temptation — which surely must come — we will be given the strength to overcome it? This idea claims to know more about temptation than Christ and to be more pious than the one who experienced the greatest temptation. "Does temptation not have to come?" Why does it have to? Must God deliver his own up to Satan? Does he have to lead them to the abyss of apostasy?

Does God have to allow Satan such power? And who are we that we can talk about the idea that temptation *must* come? Do we sit on the divine council of God? And if temptation must indeed come — by virtue of a *divine* "must" that is incomprehensible to us — then Christ, the most tempted of all, calls us to pray against this divine necessity, not to deliver ourselves to temptation in a stoic, resigned fashion, but rather to flee from that dark necessity in which God submits his will to the devil, to appeal to that apparent divine freedom in which God treads the devil under foot. Lead us *not* into temptation! (Matt. 6:13 KJV).

IN THE WILDERNESS

The Gospels report that Jesus was led by the Spirit into the wilderness to be tempted by the devil (Matt. 4:1). So the temptation does not begin with the Father arming the Son with all powers and weapons, so that he can win the battle. No, the Spirit leads Jesus into the wilderness, into solitude, into forsakenness. God removes from his Son all human and creaturely help. The hour of temptation is supposed to find Jesus weak, alone, and hungry. God leaves human beings alone in temptation. Thus Abraham had to be completely alone on Mount Moriah (Gen. 22). Yes, God himself abandons people in the face of temptation. This is what it means when we read in 2 Chronicles 32:31: God left Hezekiah in order to test him; or when the psalmist calls to God again and again: Do not forsake me (Pss. 38:21; 71:9, 18; 119:8).

"Do not hide your face from me. . . . Do not cast me off, do not forsake me, O God of my salvation!" (Ps. 27:9).

What must remain incomprehensible to all human, ethical, and religious thought is that in temptation God does not reveal himself as the one who is gracious and near, who arms us with all gifts of the Spirit. Rather, God forsakes us and is quite distant from us. We are in the wilderness.

THE SIGN OF CAIN

Cain marks the beginning of history, the history of death. Adam, who is destined for death and consumed by the thirst for *life*, fathers Cain, the *murderer*. What is new in Cain, the son of Adam, is that he, even like God himself, reaches for the life of a human being. The human being who may not eat from the tree of life reaches for the fruit of death, the annihilation of life. Only the Creator can annihilate life. Cain acquires this last right of the Creator and becomes a murderer. . . . The history of death stands under the sign of Cain. Christ on the cross, the murdered Son of God—that is the end of Cain's history and thus the end of history in general. That is the last desperate storming of the gates of paradise. And under the swinging sword, under the cross, the human race dies. But Christ lives. The upright post of the cross becomes the tree of life, and in the middle of the world, life is now established anew on the cursed ground.

CHRISTIANS AND PAGANS

People go to God in their need,
for help they plead, for good fortune they ask, and for
    bread,
for rescue from illness, guilt, and death.
They all do it, all of them, Christians and pagans.

People go to God in his need;
they find him poor, reviled, without shelter and bread;
they see him swallowed by sin, weakness, and death.
Christians stand with God in his suffering.

God goes to all people in their need
and satisfies body and soul with his bread;
God goes to his death on the cross, for Christians and for
    pagans,
and forgives them both.

THE REAL VICARIOUS LIVING
OF JESUS CHRIST

Jesus Christ is the epitome of responsible living. He is not the individual who wants to achieve his own ethical perfection; rather, he lives only as the one who has assumed and bears the selves of all people. His whole life, deeds, and suffering are vicarious living. As the one who became human he really takes the place of all human beings. What people should live, do, and suffer comes to him. In this real vicarious living, which comprises his human existence, he is simply the responsible One and the basis of all human responsibility. Responsible action is vicarious action. . . .

The content of Jesus Christ's responsibility for humankind is love, and its form is freedom. The love in question here is the realized love of God for human beings and the love of human beings for God. Because Jesus Christ is the incarnate love of God for human beings, he is therefore not the announcer of abstract ethical ideologies but the concrete performer of God's love. . . .

For Jesus what is at stake is not the exhibition and realization of new ethical ideals, and not some kind of goodness of his own, but solely God's love for human beings. Therefore, he can enter into their guilt; *he can let himself be burdened with their guilt.*

Jesus Enters into the Guilt
of Human Beings

Jesus does not want to be the only perfect human being at the expense of humankind. He does not want, as the only guiltless one, to ignore a humanity that is being destroyed by its guilt; he does not want some kind of human ideal to triumph over the ruins of a wrecked humanity. Love for real people leads into the fellowship of human guilt. Jesus does not want to exonerate himself from the guilt in which the people he loves are living. A love that left people alone in their guilt would not have real people as its object. So, in vicarious responsibility for people and in his love for real human beings, Jesus becomes the one burdened by guilt—indeed, the one upon whom all human guilt ultimately falls and the one who does not turn it away but bears it humbly and in eternal love. As the one who acts responsibly in the historical existence of humankind, as the human being who has entered reality, Jesus becomes guilty. But because his historical existence, his incarnation, has its sole basis in God's love for human beings, it is the love of God that makes Jesus become guilty. Out of selfless love for human beings, Jesus leaves his state as the one without sin and enters into the guilt of human beings. He takes it upon himself.

TAKING ON GUILT

Because what is at stake for Jesus is not the proclamation and realization of new ethical ideals, and thus also not his own goodness (Matt. 19:17), but solely his love for real human beings, he can enter into the communion of their guilt; he can be loaded down with their guilt. Jesus does not want to be the only perfect human being at the expense of humankind. He does not want, as the only guiltless one, to ignore a humanity that is being destroyed by its guilt; he does not want to have some kind of human ideal triumph over the ruins of a humanity wrecked by its guilt. Jesus does not want to exonerate himself from the guilt under which the people are dying. A love that left people alone in their guilt would not have real people as its object. As the one who acts responsibly in the historical existence of humankind, Jesus becomes guilty. It is his love alone that lets him become guilty. Out of his selfless love, out of his sinless nature, Jesus enters into the guilt of human beings; he takes it upon himself. A sinless nature and guilt bearing are bound together in him indissolubly. As the sinless one Jesus takes guilt upon himself, and under the burden of this guilt, he shows that he is the sinless one. In this sinless-guilty Jesus Christ every vicarious, responsible action now has its origin.

BECOMING GUILTY

Because Jesus took upon himself the guilt of all people, everyone who acts responsibly becomes guilty. Those who want to extract themselves from the responsibility for this guilt, also remove themselves from the ultimate reality of human existence. Moreover, they also remove themselves from the redeeming mystery of the sinless guilt bearing of Jesus Christ and have no share in the divine justification that covers this event. They place their personal innocence above their responsibility for humankind, and they are blind to the unhealed guilt that they load on themselves in this very way. They are also blind to the fact that real innocence is revealed in the very fact that for the sake of other people it enters into the communion of their guilt. Through Jesus Christ, the nature of responsible action includes the idea that the sinless, the selflessly loving become the guilty.

PARTICIPATION IN THE
SUFFERING OF GOD

S o, could you not stay awake with me one hour?"
[Jesus asked in Gethsemane] (Matt. 26:40b). That is
the opposite of everything that the religious person
expects from God. Human beings are called to share the
suffering of God in a godless world. Therefore we must
really live in the godless world and may not make the
attempt somehow to conceal, to transfigure its godlessness
religiously; we must live in a "worldly" way and in just this
way participate in God's suffering. We *are allowed* to live in
a "worldly" fashion, which means we are liberated from
false religious attachments and inhibitions. Being a Christian does not mean being religious in a certain way or, on
the basis of some methodology, to make something out of
ourselves (a sinner, a penitent, or a saint); rather, it means
to be a human being. Christ does not create in us a human
type but a human being. It is not the religious act that
makes the Christian, but participation in the suffering of
God in the life of the world. This is the reversal: not to
think first of our own needs, questions, sins, and anxieties,
but to let ourselves be pulled into the way of Jesus, into
the messianic event that is now fulfilled (Isa. 53:4–5):

> Surely he has borne our infirmities and carried our
> diseases; yet we accounted him stricken, struck
> down by God, and afflicted. But he was wounded
> for our transgressions, crushed for our iniquities;
> upon him was the punishment that made us whole,
> and by his bruises we are healed.

APRIL

GOOD FRIDAY AND EASTER

What is liberating about
Good Friday and Easter
is that our thoughts are pulled
far beyond our personal destiny
to the ultimate meaning of all life,
all suffering, and all happening in general,
and then we grasp a great hope.

WHERE ALL LOSE FAITH IN GOD

Christ goes through the cross, only through the cross, to life, to the resurrection, to victory? That, indeed, is the marvelous—and yet for many people so repulsive— theme of the Bible, that the only visible sign of God in the world is the cross. Christ is not gloriously transported from earth into heaven. He must instead go to the cross. And precisely there, where the cross stands, the resurrection is near. Precisely there, where all lose faith in God, where all despair about the power of God, God is fully there, and Christ is alive and near. Where one stands on a razor's edge of becoming an apostate or remaining true, God and Christ are fully there. Where the power of darkness wants to overcome the light of God, there God triumphs and judges the darkness. So it is now also, when Christ thinks about the day that faces his church (Matt. 24:6–14). His disciples ask him for a sign of his return after his death. This is not a one-time return but an eternal return. The end time in the Bible is the whole time and every day between Christ's death and the judgment of the world. Indeed, this is how serious and how crucial the New Testament considers the death of Christ.

BLESSING AND CROSS—
CROSS AND BLESSING

You believe that the Bible does not talk much about health, fortune, strength, and so on. I have thought about this a lot. For the Old Testament, however, this is, in any case, not true. The theological intermediate concept in the Old Testament between God and human fortune and so forth is, as far as I can see, that of blessing. Certainly in the Old Testament—for example, with the patriarchs—it is not a matter of fortune but rather of the blessing of God, which includes all earthly goods. This blessing is the claiming of earthly life for God, and it contains every promise. It would be in line with the usual spiritual conception of the New Testament to regard the Old Testament blessing as superseded by the New Testament. . . . Are we now supposed to set the Old Testament blessing against the cross? That would be to make a principle out of the cross or out of suffering. . . . Incidentally, in the Old Testament, too, those who were blessed had to suffer a great deal (Abraham, Isaac, Jacob, Joseph), but nowhere does this lead (any more than in the New Testament) to fortune and suffering or blessing and cross being placed in mutually exclusive opposition to each other. The difference between Old Testament and New Testament in this regard may lie only in the fact that in the Old Testament blessing also includes the cross, while in the New Testament the cross also includes blessing.

ABLE TO BEAR THE CROSS

Before Jesus takes his disciples with him into suffering, into humiliation and shame, into contempt, he gathers them around him and reveals himself to them as the Lord of God's glory (Matt. 17:1–9). Before the disciples have to descend with Jesus into the abyss of human guilt, evil, and hate, Jesus leads them up on a high mountain, from which their help is to come (Ps. 121:1). Before Jesus' face is struck and spit upon, before his clothing is torn and spattered with blood, the disciples are to see him in his divine brilliance. His face shines like the face of God, and the clothing he has on is dazzling white. It is an enormous grace that the same disciples who in Gethsemane are to experience Jesus' suffering with him can see him as the transfigured Son of God, as the eternal God. The disciples go to the cross with the knowledge of the resurrection. In this they are *entirely like us*. In this knowledge we are supposed to be able to bear the cross.

Next to the transfigured Jesus stand Moses and Elijah. Law and prophecy give honor to Jesus. They talk with him. . . . They talk together about the cross, about the mysteries of God. Old and New Testament meet in the light of the transfiguration and talk together. Promise is now fulfillment. Everything has come to an end.

UNDER THE CROSS

We have peace with God through our Lord Jesus Christ" (Rom. 5:1). Thus, God's battle against us has now also been brought to an end. . . . Jesus Christ died for us on the cross, slain by the wrath of God. He was sent by God himself for this reason. . . . Miraculous mystery: God has made peace with us through Jesus Christ. Under the cross there is peace. Here there is surrender to God's will; here is the end of our own will; here is rest and quiet in God; and here is the peace of conscience in the forgiveness of all our sins. Here under the cross is "access to this grace in which we stand" (Rom. 5:2), daily access to peace with God. Here is the only way in the world to find peace with God. In Jesus Christ alone, God's wrath is stilled, and we are overcome in the will of God. Therefore, the cross of Jesus Christ is for his church the eternal ground of joy and the hope of the coming glory of God. "We boast in our hope of sharing the glory of God" (Rom. 5:2). Here in the cross God's justice and victory have broken out on earth. Here this will one day become apparent to all the world. The peace that we receive here will become an eternal glorious peace in the kingdom of God.

THE CROSS IN YOUR OWN LIFE

There are many Christians who may well bow before the cross of Jesus Christ but who resist and defend themselves against any tribulation in their own life. They believe they love the cross of Christ, but they hate the cross in their own life. So, in truth, they also hate the cross of Jesus Christ. In truth, they are despisers of the cross who with every possible means seek to escape the cross. Those who know within themselves that they regard suffering and tribulation in their life only as something foreign and evil are also people who can know by this that they have not yet found peace with God at all. Basically, they have sought only peace with the world and perhaps believe that with the cross of Jesus Christ they can at best deal with themselves and with all their own questions; that is, they can find an inner peace of the soul. Thus, they have used the cross but have not loved it. They have sought peace only for their own sake. But when tribulation comes, this peace quickly disappears. It was not peace with God, for they hate the tribulation that God sends. . . . Those who love the cross of Jesus Christ, who have found peace in it, will also begin to love the tribulation in their life, and ultimately they can say with the Scripture: "We also boast in our sufferings" (Rom. 5:3).

How Hope Grows

Suffering produces patience" (Rom. 5:3 Luther). Translated literally, patience means holding the course, not throwing off the burden but bearing it. Today we in the church know all too little about the real blessing of bearing. Bearing, not shaking off; bearing, but also not collapsing; bearing as Christ bore the cross, staying under, and there below, finding Christ. . . . God's peace is with the patient. "Patience produces experience" (Rom. 5:3 Luther). The Christian life consists not in words but in experience. No one is a Christian without experience. The topic here is not experience in life but the experience of God. Yet it is also not all kinds of experience of God that are discussed here but the experience that lies in the preservation of faith and the peace of God, the experience of the cross of Jesus Christ. Only the patient are experienced; the impatient experience nothing. . . . Experience produces hope. For every attack withstood is already the prelude to the final victory; every conquered wave brings us closer to the land we long for. Therefore, hope grows with experience, and in the experience of tribulation a reflection of the eternal glory can already be perceived.

"Hope does not disappoint us" (Rom. 5:5). Where there is still hope, there is no defeat.

THE CROSS OF RECONCILIATION

Jesus Christ, the crucified reconciler—that means, first, that through its rejection of Jesus Christ the whole world has become God-less and that no effort of its own part can take this curse from it. The worldliness of the world has received its signature once and for all through the cross of Christ. The cross of reconciliation is liberation for life before God in the middle of the God-less world; it is liberation for life in genuine worldliness. Liberation is the proclamation of the cross of reconciliation, because it leaves behind it vain attempts to idolize the world, because it has overcome separations, tensions, and conflicts between "Christian" and "worldly" and calls us to simple doing and living in faith in the accomplished reconciliation of the world with God. Only through the proclamation of the crucified Christ is there a life in genuine worldliness—that is, worldly life is not in contradiction to proclamation, nor beside it in some kind of worldliness that operates according to its own laws. Rather, it is precisely "in, with, and under" the proclamation of Christ that genuine life in the world is possible and real.

SEE, THE HOUR IS AT HAND

Jesus had kept one secret from his disciples until the Last Supper (Matt. 26:20–25). It is true that he had not left them in the dark about his path of suffering, but he had still not revealed to them the deepest secret. Only in the hour of their last fellowship in their Holy Communion could he say to them: The Son of Man will be handed over into the hands of sinners — through betrayal. "One of you will betray me."

By themselves, his enemies can gain no power over him. It is up to a friend, a very close friend, to hand him over; it is a disciple who betrays him. The most fearful event does not happen from the outside but from within. Jesus' path to Golgotha has its beginning in a disciple's betrayal. While some sleep that incomprehensible sleep in Gethsemane (Matt. 26:40), one betrays him. In the end "all the disciples deserted him and fled" (Matt. 26:56).

The night in Gethsemane comes to completion. *"See, the hour is at hand"* — that hour that Jesus had predicted, that the disciples had long known about, and before whose arrival they quivered; that hour for which Jesus was so completely prepared and for which the disciples were so completely unprepared; the hour that now could no longer be postponed by any means in the world — "See, the hour is at hand, and *the Son of Man is betrayed into the hands of sinners*" (Matt. 26:45).

BETRAYED

"Betrayed," says Jesus. That means that it was not the world that gained power over him, but rather that Jesus is now delivered, handed over, given up by his very own people. His protection comes to an end. They no longer want to be burdened with him: leave him to the others. That's it: Jesus is thrown away; the protective hands of friends fall. May the hands of sinners now do with him what they will. May those seize him whose unholy hands have never been allowed to touch him. May they play with him, mock him, and beat him. We can no longer do anything about it. This is what betraying Jesus means: no longer intervening for him, but handing him over to the power and mockery of the public, letting the world deal with him according to its whim, and no longer standing with him. Jesus is delivered up to the world by his own. That is his death.

Jesus knows what he faces. Steadfastly and decisively, he summons his disciples: "Get up, let us be going" (Matt. 26:46). Threatening enemies had often had to give way before him. He was free to walk through their midst; their hands fell (Luke 4:28–30). His hour had not yet come. Now the hour is at hand. Now he approaches it with free and firm resolve. And with that, there is no more doubt; with that, it is unambiguously clear that the hour has come in which he will be betrayed. He says: "See, my betrayer is at hand" (Matt. 26:46).

INEXPLICABLE, INCOMPREHENSIBLE

W hile he was still speaking, Judas, one of the twelve, arrived; with him was a large crowd with swords and clubs" (Matt. 26:47). Now there are still only two at the center of the drama. The disciples and the pursuers step back; they are both doing their work badly. Only two do their work as they must do it: Jesus and Judas. Who is Judas? That is the question. It's a very old and brooding question for Christianity. Let us stay initially with what the evangelist himself says about it: *Judas, one of the twelve.* Do we feel anything of the horror with which the evangelist wrote this little phrase? Judas, one of the twelve— what else was there to say? Didn't this really say it all: the very dark secret of Judas and at the same time the deepest horror before his deed? Judas, one of the twelve—this says, nonetheless, that it was impossible that this happened. It was quite impossible, and yet happen it did. No, there is nothing else here that can be explained and understood. It is totally inexplicable, incomprehensible; it remains a complete puzzle—and yet the deed took place. Judas, one of the twelve—that means not only that he was one who was around Jesus day and night. It also means something still more incomprehensible: Jesus himself had called and chosen Judas! That is the real mystery, for Jesus knew from the beginning who would betray him.

PASSIONATE LOVE AND
PASSIONATE HATE

"Friend, do what you are here to do" (Matt. 26:50). Do you hear how Jesus still loves Judas, how he still calls him his friend in this hour? Even now Jesus still does not want to let Judas go. He lets Judas kiss him. He does not push him away. No, Judas must kiss him. His fellowship with Jesus must be complete. Jesus knows very well why Judas has come: "Do what you are here to do." And Judas, do you betray the Son of Man with a kiss? One last expression of a disciple's loyalty, combined with betrayal. One last sign of passionate love, paired with a much more passionate hate. One last indulgence of a submissive gesture, made while conscious of his superior power of victory over Jesus. This kiss of Judas is the action of one who is internally conflicted in the deepest way!

He could not leave Christ, and yet he handed him over. Who is Judas? At this point, let us also think about the name he bore: "Judas"—his name means "thanks." Can we not understand this kiss as an expression of thanks and, at the same time, an eternal rejection offered to Jesus by the internally conflicted people the disciple represents? Who is Judas? Who is this betrayer? In view of this question, should we be able to do anything other than ask with the disciples: Lord, is it I? Is it I?

WE ARE BEGGARS

God comes to human beings and gives them grace. The way from eternity into time is the way of Jesus Christ: this is the paradoxical message that moved powerfully through the old world, which had become skeptical about what came from human beings.

We stand before Good Friday and Easter, the days of the mighty deeds of God in history, the deeds in which the judgment and grace of God became visible to all the world: judgment in those hours in which Jesus Christ the Lord hung on the cross, grace in that hour in which death was swallowed up in victory. Human beings did nothing here; God did it all alone. He traveled the path to human beings in unending love. He has judged what is human and has given grace beyond all merit (Rom. 11:6). When the old Luther died, they found on his writing table a slip of paper on which in his last hours he had written these words: We are beggars in the Spirit. And that's the way it will remain, as long as there are human beings. But he who is King in the Spirit, the Lord of all life and all grace, lets us know that our hope and our life stand or fall with the grace of God. His is the deed; his is the way. His is the grace; his is the Spirit. And his is our service and our life. His is the honor above all creation.

THE UNFATHOMABLE LOVE
OF GOD FOR HUMANKIND

The basis of the love of God for humankind lies not in human beings but solely in God himself. The basis on which we as real human beings can live and can love the real human beings around us lies again solely in the incarnation of God, in the unfathomable love of God for humankind.

Ecce homo—see the *man judged by God!* The figure of misery and of pain. This is what the Reconciler of the world looks like. The guilt of humanity has fallen on him; it pushes him into shame and death under God's judgment. This is what it costs God to be reconciled with the world. Only by God executing judgment on himself can there be peace between him and the world and among human beings. But the mystery of this judgment, this suffering and dying, is God's love for the world, for humankind. What happened to Christ happened to all people in him. Only as people judged by God can human beings live before God. Only the crucified human being is at peace with God. In the figure of the crucified One, human beings recognize and find themselves. Accepted by God, judged and redeemed in the cross: that is the reality of being human.

ALL HOPE DASHED?

Father, into your hands I commend my spirit" (Luke 23:46), Jesus prays aloud. "It is finished," and with that he bows his head and dies (John 19:30). It had all happened the way it had to happen. The love of God had appeared on earth in humiliation, shame, and disgrace. On the cross the wrath of God slew his own Son for the wickedness of the world, for the wickedness of the world had nailed the Son to the cross. On Good Friday let us not think right away about the fact that with Easter things were given a new direction. We want to think about how with the death of Jesus the disciples saw all hope dashed. Scattered from each other, they brooded in hopeless sorrow about what had happened. Only when we can take the death of Jesus just as seriously as they did, will we rightly understand what the resurrection message can bring.

THE EMPTY TOMB, A PUZZLE

For the world the empty tomb is an ambiguous historical fact. For believers it is a historical sign of God that follows necessarily from the miracle of the resurrection and confirms it, a sign from the God who deals with human beings in history. There is no historical proof for the resurrection. . . . The decision of the historian in this matter, which remains so scientifically puzzling, will be dictated by the presuppositions of one's worldview. In that respect, however, it loses interest and importance for believers who are grounded in God's acting in history. Thus, for the world there remains an unsolvable puzzle, which in no way can compel faith in the resurrection of Jesus. For believers, however, this puzzle is a sign of the reality about which they already know, a mark of divine activity in history. Scholarship can neither prove nor disprove the resurrection of Jesus, for it is a miracle of God. But faith, to which the resurrected One witnesses as the living One, recognizes in the very testimony of the Scripture the historicity of the resurrection as an action of God, which in its miraculous nature can present itself to science only as a puzzle.

A New, Cleansing Wind

Easter? Our attention falls more on dying than on death. How we deal with dying is more important to us than how we conquer death. Socrates overcame dying; Christ overcame death.

"The last enemy to be destroyed is death" (1 Cor. 15:26). Dealing with dying doesn't mean dealing with death. The overcoming of dying is within the realm of human possibilities; the overcoming of death means resurrection.

Based not on the art of dying, but on the resurrection of Christ, a new, cleansing wind can blow into the present world. . . . If a few people really believed this and let it affect the way they move in their earthly activity, a lot of things would change. To live on the basis of the resurrection—that is what Easter means.

Most people do not know what their lives are actually based on. They are very much surrounded by mental confusion. There is an unconscious waiting for a resolving and liberating word. Yet the time has probably not yet arrived when it can be heard. But that time will come.

The Easter Message

Easter is not a battle between darkness and light that ultimately must end in the victory of light, because darkness is actually a nothing, because death is indeed already life. Easter is not a battle of winter and spring, of ice and sun. Rather, it is the battle of guilty humanity against divine love—or better: of divine love against guilty humanity, a battle in which God seems to be defeated on Good Friday, but in which God, in his very losing, wins on Easter. . . . Good Friday is not the darkness that necessarily has to yield to light . . . it is the day on which the God who became human, the love that became a person, is killed by the people who want to become gods. . . . And here only one thing can help: the mighty act that the eternal God performs among human beings. Easter is not an immanent—that is, an inner-worldly—event, but a transcendent event that is something above and beyond the world, an intervention of God from eternity, by virtue of which God declares his commitment to his Holy One and awakens him from death. Easter is not about immortality but about resurrection from a death that is a real death with all its frightfulness and horrors, resurrection from a death of the body and the soul, of the whole person, resurrection by the power of God's mighty act. This is the Easter message.

A Dangerous Easter Text

I f Christ has not been raised, your faith is futile and you are still in your sins" (1 Cor. 15:17). This is a dangerous Easter text. For if we examine it closely and let it impress us, it could take away our Easter joy. Thus it does not seem appropriate at Easter to speak of such serious, such dangerous things. And yet, among the Christian festivals, there is not one that does not seem threatening to us, if we take it quite seriously. Our whole existence and our entire spiritual being are attacked, brought into judgment, and placed at the crossroads of decision. What is true of the Easter story is true of the Christmas message as well. Yet only when we let the attack work on us anew at the deepest level, can we overcome it and feel the real joy of Easter, which is anything but sentimentality. If Christ has not been raised, then our faith is futile, and that means further that we still live in guilt in relation to God; that means ultimately that we are the most miserable people on the earth. In other words, if Christ did not rise, then the foundation on which our life rests is taken away and everything collapses. Our life falls into meaninglessness. Paul is telling us that our life depends on Easter.

OLD EASTER QUESTIONS

Everything will depend on our rightly understanding what Paul means by the word *raised*. What does resurrection mean, and what can it mean for us? These are the old Easter questions, and we cannot avoid the struggle to answer them, if we think about them at all. An overwhelming fact of life is the ever renewing springtime that allows humankind in all the world to sense something of the primal battle between darkness and light in which, after a hard struggle, light wins the victory. Every year the tremendous display of nature is renewed and awakens in humanity anticipation of the hope for resurrection: all darkness must finally become bright. . . . Already in the death of nature lie the seeds of life. Death is not at all real death but an epoch of life that further persists incipiently in what appear to be stiff bodies. Life and light must win, and death and darkness are only their apparent forms. Such ideas are the common, ancient property of human beings going back to the most primitive spiritual life, and it is to such ideas that our modernized Easter faith harks back and in the process does not even see that Christianity has some quite different things to say about Easter.

GOD'S WORD OF POWER

God spoke his word of power over death. He annihilated it and raised Jesus Christ. What does that mean? How are we to understand it? This raises a lot of questions for us. What is this bodily resurrection? What is the meaning of the empty tomb? How do we understand the appearances? There is an abundance of questions—of curiosity, of interest in superstitions, of many mysterious things—about which we can gain no pleasure. The questions grow from a hundred to a thousand, and we're still not satisfied. The empty tomb must surely have happened, but only one thing is important: God committed himself to Christ and touched him with his eternal life. Now Christ lives. He lives because God lives and because God's love lives. For us, that is enough. We can brood over the "how," but nothing will change regarding the "that." If God lives—that is, if love now lives in spite of the cross—then we are no longer living in our guilt, for God has indeed forgiven us. He has committed himself to Jesus, and Jesus has committed himself to us. If Jesus lives, then our faith receives new meaning. Then we are the most blessed of human beings. A yes from God to guilty humanity, a new meaning for all our doing—that is Easter.

GOD'S YES TO CHRIST

The resurrection of Jesus Christ is God's yes to Christ and his atoning work. The cross was the end, the death of the Son of God, curse and judgment over all flesh. If the cross were the last word about Jesus, then the world would be without hope and lost in death and damnation. The world would have won the victory over God. But God, who alone achieved our salvation, awakened Christ from the dead. That was the new beginning that followed the end like a miracle from above, not according to a fixed law like spring, but out of the incomparable freedom and power of God, which smashes death. . . . The Son gains back his eternal divine glory; the Father has his Son again. Thus is Jesus confirmed and glorified as the Christ of God, which he was from the beginning. In this way, however, the vicarious atoning work of Jesus Christ is also acknowledged and accepted by God. On the cross Jesus had called out his cry of despair (Mark 15:34) and then commended himself into the hands of his Father, who was to make out of Jesus and his work whatever God wanted. In the resurrection of Christ, it became certain that God had said yes to his Son and his Son's work.

GOD'S YES TO US

The resurrection of Jesus Christ is God's yes to us. Christ died for our sins; he was raised for our justification (Rom. 4:25). Christ's death was the judgment of death on us and our sins. Had Christ remained in death, this judgment of death would still be in force and we would still be in our sins (1 Cor. 15:17). But because Christ was raised from death, the judgment on us has been lifted, and we are resurrected with Christ (1 Cor. 15:20–23). This is so because we are in Jesus Christ by virtue of the adoption of our human nature in the incarnation. What happens to him happens to us, for we are adopted by him. That is not a judgment of experience but a judgment of God that must be acknowledged through faith in God's Word. . . .

The resurrection of Jesus Christ requires faith. It is the unanimous witness of all reports—though they are not unified in what they have otherwise recounted about what happened and was experienced—that the resurrected One did not show himself to the world, but only to his own (Acts 10:40–41). Jesus did not present himself to an impartial authority in order to have the miracle of his resurrection certified to the world and thereby to force its recognition. He wants to be believed, preached, and believed again.

GOD'S YES TO CREATION

The resurrection of Jesus Christ is God's yes to creation. Not destruction, but a new creation of physicality is what happens here. The body of Jesus goes forth from the tomb, and the tomb is empty (Mark 16:15–16). How it is possible, how it is thinkable, that the mortal and perishable body is now there as the body that is immortal, imperishable, transfigured (1 Cor. 15:35ff.), remains a mystery for us. Perhaps nothing is made as clear by the various kinds of reports on the resurrected One's encounter with the disciples as the fact that we can in no way imagine the new physicality of the resurrected One. God produced the first creation, and he has made a new creation equal to the first one. Not an idea of Christ, but the bodily Christ himself lives on. In the resurrection we know that God did not surrender the earth but reconquered it. He gave it a new future, a new promise. The same earth that God created bore the Son of God and his cross. On this earth the resurrected One appeared to his own. To this earth Christ will come on the last day. Those who affirm the resurrection of Christ in faith can no longer withdraw from the world, nor can they become slaves to the world, for in the midst of the old creation, they know God's new creation.

CHRISTIAN HOPE OF RESURRECTION

In distinction to other Near Eastern religions, the faith of the Old Testament is not a religion of redemption. Nonetheless, however, Christianity is now always designated as a religion of redemption. . . . It is said that in Christianity the crucial point is that the hope of the resurrection is proclaimed, and that in this way a genuine religion of redemption has thus come into being. The emphasis now falls on what is beyond the boundary of the grave, and this is precisely where I see the error and the danger. Redemption now means redemption from cares, needs, anxieties, and longings, from sin and death into a better beyond. But is this really supposed to be the essence of the proclamation of Christ in the Gospels and in Paul? I don't think so. The Christian hope of the resurrection is distinguished from the mythological because—in a completely new and yet more precise way compared with the Old Testament—it points humankind in the direction of its life on earth. Unlike believers in the myths of redemption, Christians do not have a last escape from earthly tasks and difficulties into the eternal. Rather, they must completely and fully enjoy earthly life, as Christ did. Only when they do this, will the crucified and resurrected One be with them. Only when they do this, will they be crucified and resurrected with Christ. The present age must not be prematurely abolished. In this, Old Testament and New Testament remain united. Myths of redemption arise from human boundary experiences. But Christ meets human beings in the middle of their lives.

THE NEW CREATION

The dead Jesus Christ of Good Friday and the resurrected Lord of Easter Sunday: this is creation out of nothingness, creation from the beginning. The fact that Christ was dead did not mean the possibility of his resurrection: it meant the impossibility; it was nothingness itself. There is absolutely no transition, no continuum between the dead and the resurrected Christ other than the freedom of God, which created his work from nothingness in the beginning. . . . He, who is the beginning, lives, annihilates the nothingness, and creates the new creation in his resurrection. From his resurrection we know about the creation, for if he were not raised, the Creator would be dead and would not bear witness to himself. From his creation, however, we know once again about the power of his resurrection, because he remains the Lord of the nothingness.

THE RECONCILIATION OF THE
WORLD WITH GOD

Those who look at Jesus Christ in actuality see God and the world in one. From now on, they can no longer see God without seeing the world, nor the world without seeing God. *Ecce homo*—see what a human being! In him the reconciliation of the world with God took place. The world is conquered not through smashing it but through reconciliation. Not ideals, programs, not conscience, duty, responsibility, virtue, but the perfect love of God all alone can meet reality and overcome it. It is not a general idea of love, but the love of God really lived in Jesus Christ, that accomplishes that. This love of God for the world does not withdraw from reality back into noble souls transported away from the world but rather experiences and suffers the reality of the world in the severest way. The world amuses itself with the body of Jesus Christ, but the martyred One forgives the world its sin. This is how reconciliation takes place. *Ecce homo*.

AN UNFATHOMABLE MYSTERY

In an incomprehensible reversal of all righteous and pious thinking, God declares himself guilty to the world and thereby extinguishes the guilt of the world. God himself takes the humiliating path of reconciliation and thereby sets the world free. God wants to be guilty of our guilt and takes upon himself the punishment and suffering that this guilt brought to us. God stands in for godlessness, love stands in for hate, the Holy One for the sinner. Now there is no longer any godlessness, any hate, any sin that God has not taken upon himself, suffered, and atoned for. Now there is no more reality and no more world that is not reconciled with God and in peace. That is what God did in his beloved Son Jesus Christ. *Ecce homo* — see the incarnate God, the unfathomable mystery of the love of God for the world. God loves human beings. God loves the world — not ideal human beings but people as they are, not an ideal world but the real world.

THE DOUBTER

What good does the news of this most glorious miracle do me, if I cannot experience and test it myself? Dead is dead, and wishing makes people gullible. So says doubt in any age, and so thinks Jesus' disciple Thomas (John 20:25). From the few words that have come down to us from him (John 11:16; 14:5), we know him as a disciple who is prepared for any sacrifice, but who openly confesses his questions about Jesus and wants clear answers. After Jesus' death he had separated himself from the other disciples and had also stayed away on Easter day. He did not want to let himself be drawn into unhealthy enthusiasm. When the other disciples give him the news, he says, firmly: "Unless I see the mark of the nails in his hands, and put my finger in the mark of the nails and my hand in his side, I will not believe" (John 20:25). Thomas is right, if he wants either to find his faith himself or not to believe at all; but the way in which he seeks it is wrong. In spite of his refusal to believe, Thomas joins the circle of disciples. This is important, for it shows Thomas's willingness to let himself be convinced; it shows the sincerity of his doubt. Nevertheless, it is the free grace of the resurrected One that now also goes after the individual, overcomes the doubter, and creates in him the Easter faith.

FREEDOM TO REVERSE HIMSELF

Jesus arrives, in spite of closed doors (John 20:26–28). Therefore, there could be no doubt about the miraculous nature of his presence. He gives the greeting of peace, which is addressed to all, but this time, no doubt, especially to the restless heart of Thomas. Jesus has come for the sake of his doubting disciple. We see that in his first words to Thomas. Jesus stills the disciple's doubting desire by granting him what he had refused Mary (John 20:17). For there is a difference as to whether we want to take something for ourselves or whether the Lord gives us something. Mary was rebuffed; Thomas is allowed to hear, see, and touch. It is an incomprehensible condescension of the Lord to his doubting disciple to let himself be put to the test by Thomas. "Do not doubt but believe," Christ implores his disciple (John 20:27). The final decision has not been made, even if it is very close. But by addressing the disciple as one who has not yet decided against him, Jesus gives him the freedom to reverse himself. Whether Thomas dared to stretch out his hand is not reported. It is not important, but it is important that in Thomas the Easter faith breaks through: "My Lord and my God!" That is the entire Easter confession. No one had said it before this doubter.

THE RETURN OF LIGHT

The Old Testament day begins with the evening and ends again with the setting of the sun. That is the time of expectation. The day of the New Testament church begins in the morning with the rising of the sun and ends with the dawning of light on the next morning. This is the time of fulfillment, of the resurrection of the Lord. Christ was born in the night, a light in the darkness; midday became night when Christ suffered and died on the cross, but in the early hours of Easter morning, Christ went forth from the tomb as victor. . . . "May your friends be like the sun as it rises in its might" (Judg. 5:31). The early hours of the morning belong to the community of the risen Christ. At the dawning of light it remembers the morning and how death, devil, and sin were forcibly laid low, and how new life and salvation were given to human beings. What do we today, who no longer fear or revere the night, still know of the great joy of our fathers and mothers in early Christendom at the daily return of the light? May we again want to learn something of the praise due the triune God in the early morning—God the Father and Creator, who has preserved our life in the dark night and awakened us to a new day.

MAY

GOD'S YES TO HUMANKIND

The resurrected Christ
bears the new humanity
within himself,
the last marvelous yes of God
to the new humanity.

THE NEW HUMANITY AND THE NEW WORLD

The miracle of the resurrection of Christ turns upside down the idolization of death that reigns among us. When death is the end, then the fear of death is joined with defiance. When death is the end, then earthly life is everything or nothing. . . . The radical nature of saying yes and saying no to earthly life reveals that only death is worth something. To grab everything or throw everything away: that is the attitude of those who believe fanatically in death. But where it is recognized that the power of death is broken, where the miracle of the resurrection and new life shine into the middle of the world of death, there one demands no eternities from life and takes from life what there is—not everything or nothing but the good and the bad, the important and the unimportant, joy and pain. There one does not hold on desperately to life, nor does one lightly throw it away; there one is satisfied with measured time and does not ascribe eternity to earthly things. There one allows death the limited right that it still has. The new humanity and the new world, however, are expected only from a standpoint beyond death, from the power that has overcome death. The resurrected Christ bears the new humanity within himself, the last marvelous yes of God to the new humanity.

HUMAN BEINGS BEFORE GOD

We believe that in Jesus Christ is the incarnate, crucified, and resurrected God. In the incarnation, God's becoming human, we know the love of God for his creation; in the crucifixion we know the judgment of God on all flesh; in the resurrection we know the will of God for a new world. Now, nothing would be more wrong than to tear these three pieces apart, for in each of them the whole is maintained. As it would be inappropriate to establish a separate theology of the incarnation, a theology of the cross, or a theology of the resurrection by falsely making one of these parts absolute, so also is it wrong to use this procedure in thinking about the Christian life. A Christian ethics built solely on the incarnation would easily lead to compromises; an ethics built solely on the cross or resurrection of Jesus Christ would lead to radicalism and fanaticism. Only in unity does the conflict resolve itself. Jesus Christ the human being means that God enters created reality and that we can and should be human beings before God. . . . Jesus Christ the crucified One means that God pronounces his final judgment on his fallen creation. . . . Jesus Christ the resurrected One means that God, out of love and omnipotence, puts an end to death and calls a new creation into being—and gives it new life.

CHRIST REMAINS THE ONLY SHAPER

Non-Christian people shape the world with their ideas, but Christ shapes people into a form like himself. But as the figure of Christ is misjudged when he becomes essentially the teacher of a good and pious life, so also the shaping of human beings is wrongly understood when one sees it only as instructions for a good and pious life. As the one confessed by the Christian faith, Christ is the incarnate One, the crucified One, and the resurrected One. The shaping the Bible talks about means to be changed into his form. To be shaped in a form like the incarnate One means to be a real human being. Human beings can and should be human. Every idea of superhuman beings, every effort to rise above humanity, every idea of being a hero, every demigod-like being, falls away from humanity here, for it is not true. The real human being is not an object of scorn or of deification, but an object of the love of God.

NEW HUMAN BEINGS

Real human beings can in freedom be the creatures of their Creator. To be shaped in a form like the incarnate One means human beings can be what they in reality are. Sham, hypocrisy, senseless effort, compulsion to be different, better, more ideal than one is—all of that is done away with here. God loves real human beings. God became a real human being. To be shaped in a form like the crucified One means to be a human being judged by God. Human beings carry around with them daily the death sentence of God, the necessity of dying before God because of sin. They attest with their lives that before God nothing can stand, except in judgment and in grace. . . . To be shaped in a form like the resurrected One means to be a new human being before God. New human beings live in the midst of death, are righteous in the midst of sin, and are new in the midst of the old. Their secret remains hidden to the world. They live because Christ lives, and they live only in Christ. "Living is Christ" (Phil. 1:21).

THE SHAPING FORCES

We are weary of Christian programs and also weary of the thoughtless, superficial words of a so-called practical Christianity in place of a so-called dogmatic Christianity. The shaping forces in the world come from a quite different side than from Christianity. And so-called practical Christianity fails in the world at least as much as the so-called dogmatic. "Shaping" must therefore mean something quite different from what we normally understand by it, and indeed the Holy Scripture speaks to us about shaping in a sense that is initially quite foreign. The Scripture is not concerned primarily with shaping the world through planning and programming. Rather, in all shaping, Scripture is concerned only with the one shape that has conquered the world (John 16:33), the shape of Jesus Christ. Shaping comes only from this shape. . . . This happens not through endeavors "to be like Jesus," as we normally put it, but by letting the shape of Jesus Christ work on us in such a way that it forms our shape after its own (Gal. 4:9).

The Penultimate

The thrust of the Christian message is not for us to become like one of those biblical figures, but to be like Christ himself. This comes, however, not through some kind of method, but from faith alone. Otherwise the gospel would lose its price, its value. Costly grace would become cheap. . . .

There is a time of God's allowing, waiting, preparing, and there is a last, an ultimate time that judges and breaks off the penultimate. Luther had to go through the monastery, Paul had to go through the piety of the law, and even the thief had to go through guilt on the cross, in order to hear the last word. A path had to be taken, a quite long path of penultimate things had to be trod. All had to sink to their knees under the burden of these things—and yet the last word was not then a coronation but a complete breaking off of the penultimate. In regard to the last word, Luther and Paul were no different from the thief on the cross. Thus, a path had to be trod—though there is, nonetheless, no single path to this goal—and this path had to be traveled to the end, that is, to the place where God puts an end to it. Thus the penultimate still remains, although it is completely abolished and nullified by the ultimate.

OVERCOMING FEAR

Human beings are dehumanized by fear. . . . But they should not be afraid. We should not be afraid! That is the difference between human beings and the rest of creation, that in all hopelessness, uncertainty, and guilt, they know a hope, and this hope is: Thy will be done. Yes. Thy will be done. . . . We call the name of the One before whom the evil in us cringes, before whom fear and anxiety must themselves be afraid, before whom they shake and take flight; the name of the One who alone conquered fear, captured it and led it away in a victory parade, nailed it to the cross and banished it to nothingness; the name of the One who is the victory cry of the humanity that is redeemed from the fear of death—Jesus Christ, the One who was crucified and lives. He alone is the Lord of fear; it knows him as its Lord and yields to him alone. Therefore, look to him in your fear. Think about him, place him before your eyes, and call him. Pray to him and believe that he is now with you and helps you. The fear will yield and fade, and you will become free through faith in the strong and living Savior Jesus Christ (Matt. 8:23–27).

ARE WE STILL USEFUL?

We have been silent witnesses to evil deeds. We have been washed with many waters and have learned the arts of pretence and ambiguous speech. Through experience we have become mistrusting of people and often have not been truthful and honest with them. Through unbearable conflicts we have become worn out and perhaps even cynical—are we still useful? We will need not geniuses, not cynics, not misanthropes, not refined tacticians, but plain, simple, straightforward people. Will our inner power of resistance against what is forced upon us remain strong enough and our uprightness against ourselves ruthless enough for us to find again the path to simplicity and straightforwardness?

THE CONCEPT OF FREEDOM

The concept of freedom is also a great good in German intellectual history (idealism), but it requires closer definition. Freedom *from* something experiences its fulfillment only in freedom *for* something. Freedom solely for the sake of freedom, however, leads to anarchy. Biblically, freedom means free for service to God and neighbor, freedom for obedience to the commandments of God. This presupposes freedom from every internal and external force that hinders us from this service. Thus, freedom does not mean the dissolution of all authority but rather means living under the authorities and obligations ordained and *limited* by the word of God. The question of individual freedoms—such as freedom of speech, freedom of the press, freedom of assembly, and so on—must first be answered in this overall context. It is a question of how far these freedoms are necessary and suitable in order to promote and assure the freedom of life according to God's commandments. For freedom is not primarily an *individual* right but a *responsibility*. Freedom is not primarily oriented toward the individual but toward the neighbor.

FREEDOM AND OBEDIENCE

Jesus stands before God as the One who is obedient and free. As the obedient One, he does the will of the Father, blindly following the law commanded of him. As the free One, he affirms that will out of his most personal knowledge. With open eyes and joyful heart, he creates that will anew out of himself, as it were. Obedience without freedom is slavery; freedom without obedience is arbitrariness. Obedience binds freedom; freedom ennobles obedience. Obedience binds the creature to the Creator; freedom juxtaposes the creature, in his image of God, with the Creator. Obedience shows human beings that they must *say* what is good and what God requires of them (Mic. 6:8); freedom lets human beings create the good themselves. Obedience knows what is good and does it. Freedom dares to act and leaves the judgment of good and evil up to God. Obedience follows blindly; freedom has open eyes. Obedience acts without asking; freedom asks for meaning. Obedience has bound hands; freedom is creative. In obedience human beings follow the Decalogue of God; in freedom human beings create a new decalogue. In responsibility both obedience and freedom are realized. It carries this tension within itself. Any independent act of the one against the other would be the end of responsibility. Responsible action is bound and yet creative.

Do Not Repay Evil with Evil

Do not raise your hand to strike. Do not open your mouth in anger, but remain still. How can the one who wants to do evil things against you hurt you? It does not hurt you: it hurts the other person. Suffering injustice does not hurt the Christian, but doing injustice does. Indeed, evil can do only one thing to you, namely, make you also become evil. If it does, then it wins. Therefore, do not repay evil with evil. If you do, you will not hurt the other person; you will hurt yourself. You are not in danger when evil happens to you, but the person who does you wrong is in danger and will suffer from it, if you do not offer help. Therefore, for the sake of the other person and your responsibility for that person—do not repay evil with evil. . . .

How does that happen? Not by our giving nourishment to the other person's evil, hate to the other person's hate, but by letting evil strike out into empty space and find nothing that can inflame it. How can we overcome evil? By our forgiving it endlessly. How does that happen? By our seeing enemies as they really are: as people for whom Christ died, as people Christ loves.

THE OPEN QUESTION OF CHRIST

God's yes and God's no to history, as they are known in the incarnation and crucifixion of Jesus Christ, bring into every historical moment an eternal, unrelenting tension. History does not become the transitory bearer of eternal values. It is instead through the life and death of Jesus Christ that history first becomes temporal. It is precisely in its temporality that history is affirmed by God. The quest for a historical heritage is thus not the timeless quest for the eternally valid values of the past. Rather, human beings placed in history are themselves accountable here for the present, as it is accepted by God in Christ. . . . The historical Jesus is the continuity of our history. But because Jesus Christ was the promised messiah of the Israelite-Jewish people, the line of our ancestors goes back beyond the appearance of Jesus Christ and into the people of Israel. Western history is, in accordance with God's will, indissolubly bound to the people of Israel, not only genetically but in genuine, constant encounter. The Jew keeps the Christ question open. . . . An expulsion of the Jews from the West must bring with it the expulsion of Christ, for Jesus Christ was a Jew.

I Am with You

In our time there is a seeking, an anxious groping and searching for divine things. A great loneliness has come over our time, a loneliness that is found only where god-forsakenness reigns. In the midst of our large cities, in the greatest, most frantic activity of untold masses of people, we see the greatest amount of loneliness and homelessness. But the longing grows that the time will nonetheless come again when God dwells among people, when God lets himself be found. People have been overcome by a thirst for touching divine things that is burning hot and longs to be quenched. And at the moment many drugs have become available that promise to radically satisfy this thirst and are sought by a hundred thousand greedy hands. In the middle of this frantic activity and vociferous extolling of new ways and means stands the one word of Jesus Christ: "I am with you . . ." (Matt. 28:20). You don't need to do a lot of seeking and questioning and looking for mysterious manifestations. I *am* with you. That is, Jesus does not just promise his coming. He does not prescribe ways in which we can reach him. Rather, he says quite simply: "I am with you." Whether we see him or not, feel him or not, want him or not—that is all the same in view of the fact that Jesus is there with us, that he is simply everywhere we are, and that we can do absolutely nothing about it.

THE WILL OF GOD

The will of God can lie hidden very deep under many available possibilities. And because it is not a predetermined system of rules, but new and different in different life situations, the will of God must be tested again and again. Heart, mind, observation, and experience must work together in this testing. Precisely because it is no longer a question of one's own knowledge of good and evil, but of the living will of God, precisely because it is not at our own human disposal but solely by the grace of God that we know his will, and precisely because this grace is and wants to be new every morning, this testing of the will of God must be taken very seriously. Neither the voice of the heart nor some kind of inspiration nor some kind of generally valid principle can be confused with the will of God, which is revealed anew only to the one testing it. . . . The knowledge of Jesus Christ—the metamorphosis, the renewal, the love, or however one might express it—is something that is alive and not something given once and for all, something fixed and possessed. For this reason each new day brings the question how—today and here and in this situation—I will remain with God, with Jesus Christ, and be preserved in this new life. This very question, however, is the meaning of the testing of what the will of God is.

THE DOCUMENTATION OF THE DIVINE WILL

The Christian idea is the way of God to human beings, and its visible objectification is the cross. This is the point at which we usually turn away from the Christian cause, shaking our heads in dispute and arguing that the cross was first placed at the center of the Christian message by Paul and that Jesus said nothing about this. And yet the correct interpretation of the cross of Christ is nothing more than the starkest intensification of the idea that Jesus himself is divine. The cross is, as it were, the historically visible form assumed by the idea that Christ is divine. God comes to human beings, who have nothing but an empty space for God, and this hollow space, this void in people, in Christian language is called faith. That is to say: in Jesus of Nazareth, God's revealer, God devotes himself to the sinner. Jesus seeks fellowship with sinners and goes after them in boundless love. He wants to be in that void where human beings have nothing. The meaning of Jesus' life is the documentation of this divine will for sinners, for the unvalued. Where Jesus is, there is the love of God. . . . Jesus really dies in despair over his work, over God, but precisely here is the culmination of his message that God loved human beings so much that with them and for them, as documentation of his own will to love, God takes death upon himself.

TESTING WHAT THE WILL OF GOD IS

Now we must really test what the will of God is, what is right in a given situation, what is pleasing to God, for it must now be concretely lived and done. Understanding—the ability to know—and attentive perception of what is given move into lively action here. In the process, the commandment will encompass and permeate everything. Past experiences will come to expression to strengthen or warn us. In no case can we count on and wait for direct inspirations, without all too easily opening ourselves up to self-deception. In view of the issue now at stake, a strong spirit of sobriety will reign. Possibilities and consequences will be well considered. Thus, the whole apparatus of human powers will be put into motion when it is a question of testing what the will of God is. In all of this, however, we will have room for neither the torment of standing before unsolvable conflicts, nor the arrogance of being able to master any conflict, nor the fanatical expectation and assertion of direct inspirations. There will be faith that God certainly reveals his will to anyone who humbly asks him. And then, after all earnest testing, there will also be the freedom to make a real decision.

CENTER AND PARADOXICAL SYMBOL

Because on the cross Jesus in humiliation proves his and God's love for the world, death is followed by the resurrection, for death cannot contain love. "For love is strong as death" (Song 8:6b). That is the meaning of Good Friday and Easter Sunday: the way of God to humankind leads back to God. Thus the divine idea of Jesus comes together with Paul's interpretation of the cross, and the cross becomes the center and paradoxical symbol of the Christian message. A king who goes to the cross must be the king of a miraculous kingdom. Only those who understand the profound paradox of the idea of the cross can understand the meaning of Jesus' saying: "My kingdom is not from this world" (John 18:36). . . . Christ is not the bringer of a new religion but the bringer of God. So, as the impossible way of human beings to God, the Christian religion stands beside other religions. Christians can never do something good on their own by their being Christian, for that remains human—all too human. They live, however, by the grace of God, which comes to human beings and comes to everyone who is open to it and understands it in the cross of Christ. Thus, the gift of Christ is not the Christian religion but the grace and love of God, which culminate in the cross.

No Preference over Others

To speak of God's love for the world (John 3:16) causes no small amount of difficulty today for those who don't want to be stuck with formulas. Indeed, it is clear enough that God's love for the world does not consist in his putting an end to wars and taking away from us poverty, misery, persecution, and catastrophes of all kinds. But this is the very place where we usually seek God's love, and we don't find it. Nonetheless, as difficult as it is for us, and as deeply as it disturbs us that God's love is so hidden from the world, we can be especially thankful, particularly in such times, that we no longer need to look for God's love where it is not to be found, and that it has become all the clearer where alone we will find it: in Jesus Christ. God's love for us is to be found in Christ alone. If God loved the world, the whole fallen creation, then he gave us no preference over others. He loved my worst enemy no less than he loved me. Jesus Christ died for his and our enemies.

CHRISTIANITY WITHOUT DISCIPLESHIP?

Discipleship means being bound to Christ. Because Christ is, there must be discipleship. An idea of Christ, a doctrinal system, or a general religious knowledge of grace or forgiveness of sins makes discipleship unnecessary, is hostile to it, and, in truth, even excludes it. With an idea one enters into a relationship of knowledge, enthusiasm, perhaps even realization, but never into personally obedient discipleship. A Christianity without the living Jesus Christ necessarily remains a Christianity without discipleship, and a Christianity without discipleship is always a Christianity without Jesus Christ. It is an idea, a myth. A Christianity in which there is only the Father God but not Christ as the living Son absolutely abolishes discipleship. Here there is trust in God but not discipleship. Only because the Son of God became human, because he is *mediator*, is discipleship the proper relationship to him. Discipleship is bound to the mediator, and where one speaks properly of discipleship, one speaks of the mediator Jesus Christ, the Son of God. Only the mediator, the God-man, can call one into discipleship. Discipleship without Jesus Christ is the self-selection of what could be an ideal way, or even a martyr's way, but it is without promise.

PIOUS FORMULA OR DIVINE WORD?

With my lips I declare all the ordinances of your mouth" (Ps. 119:13). It is often easy to carry God's word in the heart, but how hard it is sometimes to let it pass through the lips! We have in mind here not empty lip service, but saying aloud what fills the heart. When faced with great suffering, isn't our mouth often closed, because we are afraid of reciting a pious formula instead of the divine word? Is there not an atmosphere of carelessness and godlessness in which we simply can't find the right word and remain silent? Aren't we often enough silenced by false shyness and timidity? Warning and admonition remain unspoken; comfort and concern are denied. How tortuously and anxiously does the name of Jesus Christ sometimes come out of our mouth! It takes a great deal of spiritual experience and practice, and at the same time childlike confident faith, to be able to tell "all the ordinances" of God with one's lips without getting into a spiritual rut or becoming an apostle of custom or an insistent chatterbox. Our whole heart must belong to the word of God before we can also learn to put our lips entirely into the service of Jesus Christ.

THE HIDDEN WISDOM OF GOD

"But we speak God's wisdom, secret and hidden . . ." (1 Cor. 2:7–10). God's thoughts are not obvious, not common sense. God does not let himself be simply grasped right where we want to grasp him. Rather, the church speaks of the *secret, hidden wisdom of God*. God lives in mystery. His being is a mystery to us, a secret from eternity and to eternity. None of the thoughts that we have about God can ever serve to do away with this mystery or to turn God into something generally comprehensible and not mysterious. Rather, all thinking about God must serve to make visible his *mystery*, which is totally beyond us, to make God's secret, hidden wisdom visible in its secretiveness and obscurity—not to rob it of this, so that perhaps through this mystery, the homeland from which God comes will become visible. Every dogma of the church is only a reference to the mystery of God. But the world is blind to this mystery. It wants a god that it can take into account and exploit, or it wants no god at all. The mystery of God remains hidden from it. The world doesn't want it. It makes gods for itself according to its wishes, but the near, mysterious, hidden God it does not know.

An Unmistakable Sign

The upper classes of this world live by calculation and exploitation. In this way they become great in the world, but they do not comprehend the mystery, for the mystery is understood only by children. The world bears an unmistakable sign that attests to its blindness to the mystery of God: the cross of Jesus Christ. If they had known it, "they would not have crucified the Lord of glory" (1 Cor. 2:8). That, therefore, is the unrecognized mystery of God in this world: Jesus Christ. That this Jesus of Nazareth, the carpenter, was himself the Lord of glory: that was the mystery of God. It was a mystery because God became poor, low, lowly, and weak out of love for humankind, because God became a human being like us, so that we would become divine, and because he came to us so that we would come to him. God as the one who becomes low for our sakes, *God in Jesus of Nazareth— that is the secret, hidden wisdom* . . . that "no eye has seen nor ear heard nor the human heart conceived" (1 Cor. 2:9). . . . That it is the one God, the Father and Creator of the world, who in Jesus Christ loved us unto death, who in the Holy Spirit opens our hearts to him, that we love him, that there are not three gods but that God is one, who embraces, creates, and redeems the world from the beginning to the end—that is *the depth of the Deity*, whom we *worship as mystery* and *comprehend as mystery*.

WHAT THE WORLD LIVES ON

Many are the afflictions of the righteous" (Ps. 34:19), but not those of the unrighteous. The righteous suffer from the things that for others are a matter of course and necessary. The righteous suffer from unrighteousness, from the senselessness and wrongness of world events. . . . The world says: that's just the way it is, always will be, and must be. The righteous say: it should not be that way; it is against God. The righteous will always be recognized by the fact that they suffer in this way. To a certain extent, they bring the sensitivity of God into the world. They therefore suffer as God suffers from the world. "But the LORD rescues them"—God's help is not in every human suffering, but God's help is always in the suffering of the righteous, because they suffer with God. God is always present. . . . The answer of the righteous to the sufferings that the world brings them is called blessing. That was God's answer to the world that slew Christ on the cross: blessing. God did not repay like with like, and neither should the righteous. Do not condemn, do not scold, but bless (1 Pet. 3:9). The world would have no hope if this were not so. The world lives by the blessing of God and of the righteous, and it has a future. . . . Only out of the impossible can the world be renewed, and the impossible is the blessing of God.

A CENTRAL PROCLAMATION OF THE NEW TESTAMENT

The central proclamation of the New Testament is that in Christ God loved the world and reconciled it with himself. It presupposes that the world is in need of reconciliation with God, yet is incapable of it on its own. The acceptance of the world is a miracle of divine mercy. Therefore, the relationship of the church to the world is completely determined by the relationship of God to the world. There is a love of the world that is enmity toward God (Jas. 4:4; 1 John 2:15), because it arises from the nature of the world in itself and not from the love of God toward the world. The world "in itself," as it understands itself and as it guards itself against—and even rejects—the reality of the God's love for it in Jesus Christ is subject to the judgment of God over all enmity of Christ. This world is in a life-and-death struggle with the church. Nevertheless, it is the commission and essence of the church to speak to this very world of its reconciliation with God and to reveal to it the reality of God's love, against which the world rages blindly. In this way, even—and especially—the lost and judged world is constantly drawn into the Christ event.

ASCENSION JOY

Ascension joy—inwardly we must become very quiet to hear the soft sound of this phrase at all. Joy lives in its quietness and incomprehensibility. This joy is in fact incomprehensible, for the comprehensible never makes for joy. It is the incomprehensible—and yet true, real, and living—that brings joy. Therefore, proper joy itself is something incomprehensible, both for others and for the one who feels it.

Joy is simply there—ascension joy is simply there—when the church speaks of Christ's exaltation above the world and of his coming again, when he himself meets his joyfully waiting church in the sacrament. Joy is there, not loud but restrained. The world makes it anxious. Sin makes it anxious—but it is there as the heavenly joy of slaves who wait in the night and keep watch with burning lamps until their dear master comes home (Luke 12:35–40). All the joy of Christ in this world is anticipatory—and who will betray out loud their anticipation of joy? And yet what joy is greater than anticipatory joy? Anticipation, then, in expectation of what? In expectation of the last things. The Lord whom we do not see but nonetheless love: he will come again.

Where Is the Path to Joy?

J oy to the world!" Anyone for whom this sound is foreign, or who hears in it nothing but weak enthusiasm, has not yet really heard the gospel. For the sake of humankind, Jesus Christ became a human being in a stable in Bethlehem: Rejoice, O Christendom! For sinners, Jesus Christ became a companion of tax collectors and prostitutes: Rejoice, O Christendom! For the condemned, Jesus Christ was condemned to the cross on Golgotha: Rejoice, O Christendom! For all of us, Jesus Christ was resurrected to life: Rejoice, O Christendom! Jesus Christ, come from God and going to God—this is not a new world of problems, of questions and answers. That is, this is not a new moral law, not a new burden added to the burdens that people already carry. It actually means, above all, God's joy in the world, God's joy ignited in a humanity that hungers for joy. All over the world today people are asking: Where is the path to joy? The church of Christ answers loudly: Jesus is our joy! (1 Pet. 1:7–9). Joy to the world!

THREE GIFTS

In addition to the indwelling of the Father and the Son (John 14:23) and the sending of the Holy Spirit come the gifts (John 14:27–31) that Jesus gives the disciples when he leaves them. The first is *peace*. So that the disciples know what is meant here, Jesus says in clear repetition that it is his peace that he gives to his own. How easily illusion and false hope could arise here otherwise! It is the peace of One who on earth had no place to lay his head and had to go to the cross. It is peace with God and humankind even where the wrath of God and human beings threatens to annihilate us. Only this peace of Christ will prevail. . . .

The second gift is *joy*. Because Jesus goes to the Father who is greater than he, because he is in glory and transfiguration, he gives those who love him joy. . . .

The promise of Jesus gives to his own the power of *faith*. This is the third gift. Nothing happens but what the Lord has predicted. Everything goes according to his word. . . . In all of this, however, the church knows through the word of Jesus that its Lord goes to his Father and will come again. It believes in his word and waits on his promise. In faith it is certain of the sending of the Holy Spirit.

AFRAID OF THE TRUTH

In human life the truth is something foreign, something unusual, something exceptional. Whenever the truth is spoken somewhere, it is as if something quite unexpected and dramatic breaks into our life. It is not unusual when someone trumpets in our ears that we are now going to hear the whole truth. But talking about the truth is still a long way from the real truth. We can distinguish real truth from trite truth because the former has quite definite intentions and something happens—namely, people are redeemed and set free. It suddenly opens people's eyes to the fact that they have been living in lies, unfree and anxious, and thus it gives them back their freedom. And the quite unambiguous statement of the Bible is that human beings are living completely in slavery and lies, and only the truth that comes from God can make people free (John 8:32). . . .

But it is hard to speak of freedom as the Bible does. The *truth* will make you free: in every age that is anachronistic. . . .

We are all afraid of the truth, and this fear is basically our fear of God.

THE CRUCIFIED TRUTH

God—and no other—is the truth. And we are afraid of him, afraid that he will suddenly shine the light of truth on us and expose us in our mendacity. . . .

We are on the defensive against the assertion not only that there are many lies around us and in us, but also that we ourselves are inveterate liars. And we have to defend ourselves until something totally unexpected happens, namely, until God himself meets us as the truth and does what we cannot do—presents us with the truth in his presence. . . . And now something happens over which we no longer have any power: *the truth.* It confronts us in a strange form, not in radiant, unapproachable glory and shining, heart-compelling clarity, but as the crucified truth, as the crucified Christ. And the truth speaks to us. It asks us: Who crucified me? Who crucified the truth? And the answer comes already in the same moment: Look here! You did this. You hated what God's truth said about you, so you crucified it and set up your own truth. You believed that you knew the truth, you possessed it, and you could make people happy with your truth. And in that way you have made yourself God. You have robbed God of his truth, and from God's perspective it became a lie.

OUR TRUTH—GOD'S TRUTH

The truth will make you free" (John 8:32). Not our deeds, our courage, our strength, our nation, our truth, but God's truth alone makes us free. . . . God's truth alone, however, makes me see the other person. It directs my attention, which is focused on me, beyond myself and shows me other people. And by doing that, it performs for me the deed of love, the deed of God's grace. It does away with our lies and creates the truth. It does away with hate and creates love. God's truth is God's love, and God's love makes us free from ourselves and for others. Being free means nothing other than being in love. And being in love means nothing other than being in God's truth. People who love because they are made free by God's truth are the most revolutionary people on the earth. They are the ones who overturn all values; they are the dynamite of human society; they are the most dangerous people. For they have recognized that people have been profoundly deceived and are ready at any time to let the light of truth fall on them—and this for the very sake of love. . . . God preserve us in love, so that we will not dream up a false idea of freedom.

TRUTH IS TO BE DONE

Who comes to the light? "Those who do what is true" (John 3:21)! What does this mean? Truth is supposed to happen; it is not only to be thought or willed, but to be done. Truth arises through action that is the opposite of pretense and darkness, which give rise to evil. But how is one who lives in darkness supposed to do the truth? . . .

You will not come to the light through what you think, Jesus says, but through what you do, and not through just any doing but through doing the *truth*. The truth itself will bring you to the light through your doing. Thus the emphasis in Jesus' words falls first on the word "truth" and only then on the word "do." In all of this, the idea of any sort of works righteousness is just as foreign as a righteousness of thinking. But what it does say is that for us, if we want to come to the light, if we want Pentecost also to happen for us, there is no time to lose. Rather, the time has come to act, to obey the word of God as well as we can. This keeps us from flying off into endless questions and requires us to act earnestly on the spot and to live under the word. . . . Completely by itself, the truth in our actions will strive for the light that will make it apparent.

JUNE

THE UNITY OF THE CHURCH

The unity of the church will consist
not in organizations,
not in dogmas,
not in liturgies,
not in pious hearts,
but in the word of God,
in the voice of Jesus Christ.

WE BELIEVE IN MUCH TOO MUCH

We believe in all kinds of things. Indeed, we believe in much too much. We believe in power; we believe in ourselves; we believe in other people; we believe in humanity. We believe in our nation; we believe in our religious community; we believe in new ideas. But we don't believe in the One who is above them all—in God. For faith in God would take away our faith in all those other things and powers. Faith in them would become impossible. Those who believe in God believe in nothing else in this world, because they know it will fail and pass away. Nor do they need to believe in anything else, for they have the One from whose hands everything comes and into whose hands everything goes. We know about the victories that people win who really believe in themselves, who believe in some kind of power or idea in this world, so that they devote themselves and their lives to it entirely, and can do superhuman, impossible things. How much greater victories would they win if the object of their faith were not a subjective phantom but the living God himself! The miracles of Jesus, the ministry of Jesus: they were nothing but his faith. . . . Faith means trusting and daring *unconditionally*.

... But Do Not Have Love

First of all, what is said here is something very simple, namely, that a life has meaning and value only to the extent that it has love, and that a life is nothing—nothing at all—and has no meaning or value if there is no love in it (1 Cor. 13:1–3). A life has value according to how much love it has. Everything else is nothing, absolutely nothing, completely irrelevant, completely unimportant. Everything bad and everything good, everything large and everything small is unimportant—we are asked only one question: whether or not we have love. . . .

"If I speak in the tongues of mortals and of angels . . ." This is a possibility with which we had not reckoned: that even our holiest words can become unholy, godless, common, if they do not have heart, if they do not have love. . . .

"And if I have prophetic powers, and understand all mysteries and all knowledge . . ." If I knew why I must travel this path and why others must travel that path, if I could perceive even here and now the dark ways of God—would that not be blessedness? . . .

Perception, knowledge, and truth without love are nothing. They are not truth, for truth is God, and God is love. Therefore, truth without love is a lie.

What Is Grace?

The evil, the sinful, the common are overpowering in us, and we remain under their spell as long as we live. And we would despair of the good, of the holy, of ourselves, and of God, if we had not been given the word: "My grace is sufficient for you, for power is made perfect in weakness" (2 Cor. 12:9). It is clear, therefore, that for us *religion* is not the fulfillment of what the world lacks or the provider of good fortune on earth. No, with religion, misfortune, unrest, and deprivation have become powerful in the world. "My *grace* is sufficient for you." *What is grace?* It is something not seen, something we don't get to feel directly. On the contrary, it is something entirely improbable and incredible, according to which we judge what we experience here. It speaks of an event beyond all worlds and wants to draw us away from our own world to another. A dark abyss opens up, and a voice commands: Jump across. I will catch you and hold you fast. I am stretching out my hand. Now bet your life on it, and rely on me and on nothing else. My grace is sufficient for you. I am love. "I have called you by name, you are mine" (Isa. 43:1).

PENTECOST—A LETTER FROM PRISON

So, we are now also celebrating Pentecost still separated, and yet in a special way it is a community festival. When the bells sounded early today, I had a great longing for a worship service. But then I did like John on Patmos (Rev. 1:9–10) and held a service of worship for myself alone that was so beautiful that the loneliness was not felt at all, because you were all there and even the churches in which I had already celebrated Pentecost. Every few hours since last evening, I have been saying to myself the Paul Gerhardt Pentecost hymn with the beautiful verses: "You are a Spirit of joy . . ." and "Give joyfulness and strength . . ." and also rejoicing in the words: "If you faint in the day of adversity, your strength [is] small" (Prov. 24:10), and "for God did not give us a spirit of cowardice, but rather a spirit of power and of love and of self-discipline" (2 Tim. 1:7). The strange story of the "miracle of the languages" (Acts 2:1–13) has also again kept me very occupied. That the confusion of languages at the tower of Babel—which kept people from understanding each other because they each spoke their own language— should come to an end and be overcome by the language of God, which everyone understands and which is the only language through which people can understand each other, and that the church should be the place where this happens: these are all very great and important ideas.

A VOICE WITHIN US

Heal, lead, comfort (Isa. 57:18) — that is what God does on Pentecost.

God sees our ways; it is grace when he does that. He can also let us go our own ways without looking at them. But God has seen them — and he has seen us wounded, lost, anxious. Now he is there to heal us. . . . Memories no longer torment us. All hurts sink into nothingness, into oblivion, as when we are close to a beloved person. God is nearer to us than the past.

God wants to lead us. Not all human ways are under God's leadership. We can often go a long time in our own ways, and there we are a plaything of chance: will it bring us good fortune or misfortune? Our own ways always lead in a circle back to ourselves. God's ways lead to God. God leads us through good fortune and bad, but always and only to God. This is how we recognize God's ways.

God wants to comfort us. God comforts only when there is enough reason for comfort, when people no longer know a way out, when the meaninglessness of life makes them anxious. The world as it really is always makes us anxious. But those who are comforted see and have more than the world. They have life with God. Nothing is destroyed, lost, meaningless, when God comforts. . . .

How does God heal, lead, and comfort? God does these things only by placing a voice within us that says, prays, calls, cries out: "Abba! Father!" (Gal. 4:6). This is the Holy Spirit. This is Pentecost.

GOOD FORTUNE AND MISFORTUNE

God blesses some of his children with good fortune (Gen. 39:23) and lets everything they do prosper. He is with them and gives them other people's goodwill, success, and recognition in their endeavors. Indeed, he gives them great power over other people and through them accomplishes his work. It is also true that they usually have to endure times of suffering and testing, but whatever evil people try to do to them, God always turns it into good. Some of his other children are blessed by God with suffering and even martyrdom. God links himself with good fortune and misfortune to lead people in his way and to his goal. That way means: "Obey his commandments" (1 John 3:24), and the goal is that we abide in God and that God abide in us. Good fortune and misfortune come to their fulfillment in the blessedness of this goal: that we may be in God and God may be in us. And the way to this goal, keeping the commandments of God, is already the beginning of this blessedness. How do we know—through good fortune or misfortune—that we are moving toward this blessedness? By the fact that an irresistible love of this way and toward this goal has been awakened in us, even if we often slip on this path and are in danger of missing the goal. This love comes from God. It is the Holy Spirit that God has given us.

HOLD ON TO THE WORLD

Today, probably more than ever, the question of whether to be modern or old-fashioned remains at the forefront of all interest — not only in matters of style or health, but in all areas of human interest, in science, literature, and religion. "Serve the opportune time" (Rom. 12:11, alternate reading). The spirits are divided on this saying: some people simply ascribe to whatever is modern; others, the consciously old-fashioned, look blissfully back to the good old days. To the question "Do you want to be a modern person?" the former answer just as decisively and self-confidently "yes" as the latter answer "no." What is the position of those who call themselves Christians? How do they stand on the changing of the times? Do Christians have to think conservatively or progressively? Do they have to be old-fashioned or modern? The basic question of every Christian is apparently the question of eternity. How do I reach for eternity here in the middle of time? At this point there seems to be only one answer: Away with time! Become indifferent to everything that happens here, and live only for eternity. Against this, however, our saying calls to us: "Serve the opportune time." If you want to find eternity, then live and serve in time. This saying must strike us as a monstrous contradiction: if you want the imperishable, then hold on to the perishable. If you want the eternal, then hold on to the temporal. *If you want God, then hold on to the world.*

THE SIGNIFICANT HOUR

The present is God's hour of responsibility for us: every present, today and tomorrow, the present in all its reality and diversity. In the whole history of the world, there is always only one significant hour: the present. Whoever flees from the present flees from the hour of God; whoever flees from time flees from God. Serve the opportune time! The Lord of the ages is God; the turning point of the ages is Christ; and the right spirit of the ages is the Holy Spirit. So, hidden in every moment is this threefold reality: I recognize God as the Lord of my life, I bow before Christ as the turning point of my life from judgment to grace, and in the midst of the spirit of the world I endeavor to make room and power for the Holy Spirit. . . . To *serve* the opportune time does not mean to become its *slave*. It does not mean to approve of whatever is *currently popular.* Serving includes the strength of one's own will and one's own thoughts, and not the weakness of going along and following the crowd. *It does not mean serving fashion,* but serving the opportune time. Fashion is what people do — and that can be no more than despicable. The opportune time is what God does, and serving the opportune time does not mean serving people. It means serving God.

Forgoing the Pious Self

First, we must completely forget how to say, "I will," until God, through the Holy Spirit, teaches us to say it in a new and right way. It is precisely in matters of piety that "I will" can wreak the greatest havoc: "I will be godly, I will be holy, I will keep the commandments." We must first have a basic understanding that even in these things, it is not our will but God's will alone that matters. We must also forgo our pious self, so that God can do his work in us. Otherwise our "I will" most certainly will be followed by bankruptcy. But when through God's grace we have stopped saying, "I will," when through God's new beginning with us in Jesus Christ we have been brought onto his path — in spite of our "I will" and "I won't" — then the Holy Spirit begins to speak in us, and we say something quite new and quite different from our previous "I will." . . . "I will observe your statutes" (Ps. 119:8). I do it without compulsion. Rather, you have made me free, so that I can will what I hated. You have bound my will to your statutes. It is God the Holy Spirit who implements in me what was true for Jesus Christ alone: Your will is my will. But because I myself am not the Holy Spirit or the Lord Jesus Christ, I must quickly add to my "I will" the petition: "Do not utterly forsake me" (Luther).

THE TURNING POINT OF THE AGES

Serve the opportune time." The most profound matter will be revealed to us only when we consider that not only does the world have its time and its hours, but also that our own life has its time and its hour of God, and that behind these times of our lives traces of God become visible, that under our paths are the deepest shafts of eternity, and every step brings back a quiet echo from eternity. It is only a matter of understanding the deep, pure form of these times and representing them in our conduct of life. Then in the middle of our time we will also encounter God's holy present. "My times are in your hand" (Ps. 31:15). Serve your times, God's present in your life. God has sanctified your time. Every time, rightly understood, is immediate to God, and God wants us to be fully what we are. . . . Only those who stand with both feet on the earth, who are and remain totally children of earth, who undertake no hopeless attempts at flight to unreachable heights, who are content with what they have and hold to it thankfully—only they have the full power of the humanity that serves the opportune time and thus eternity. . . . The Lord of the ages is God. The turning point of the ages is Christ. The right spirit of the ages is the Holy Spirit.

THE NEW STANDS
FIRMLY ON THE OLD

The task of the Holy Spirit is twofold: *to teach* and *to remind*. On its way through the world, the church requires instruction and knowledge ever anew. Regarding new foes, new questions, and new needs, the church has its teacher in the Holy Spirit, who "will teach you everything" (John 14:26). The church will not remain without instruction and knowledge in any way that is important for it, and it may be certain of this knowledge because the Holy Spirit, and not human reason, is its teacher. Thus in the course of its history, the church will also receive new knowledge; it will not stop learning and listening to the Holy Spirit. The Holy Spirit is not a dead letter but the living God (2 Cor. 3:6). In every decision, therefore, the church may trust the Holy Spirit and firmly believe that he works in the present time on the church and in the church, and he will not leave us groping in the dark if we will only listen earnestly to his teachings. All the teachings of the Holy Spirit, however, remain bound to the word of Jesus. The new stands firmly on the old. Thus reminding is added to teaching. If there were only reminding in the church, it would fall victim to a dead past. If there were only teaching, without reminding, the church would be delivered up to fanaticism. Thus the Holy Spirit, as the right assistance to the church, practices both. It leads the church forward and at the same time holds it fast to Jesus (Matt. 13:52).

THE CHURCH AND GOD'S
AIM ON EARTH

The church as its own community serves the fulfillment of the divine mandate of proclamation in two ways. *First*, everything in this community is directed toward the active proclamation of Christ to all the world, so that the church itself is only an instrument, only the means to an end. *Second*, in this very initiative of the church for the world, the aim and initial fulfillment of the divine mandate of proclamation has occurred—that is, the church, by itself wanting to become only the instrument and means to an end, has become the aim and center of all of God's actions with the world. The concept of representation designates this double relationship most clearly. The Christian church stands in the place where the whole world should stand; in this way it serves the world vicariously and is there for the sake of the world. Conversely, the world comes to its own fulfillment where the church stands; the church is the "new creation" (2 Cor. 5:17), the aim of God's ways on earth. In this double representation the church stands completely in the communion and discipleship of its Lord, who was the Christ precisely by being there completely for the world and not for himself.

The Church of God in the World

When God in Jesus Christ claims space in the world—even if only in a stable, "because there was no place for them in the inn" (Luke 2:7)—then, at the same time, God summarizes in this small space the whole reality of the world and reveals its ultimate foundation. So also the church of Jesus Christ is the place—that is, the space—in the world in which the lordship of Jesus Christ is witnessed and proclaimed over all the world. . . . The space of the church is not there to make a piece of the world controversial, but precisely to attest to the world that it remains the world, specifically, the world loved and reconciled by God. The church does not desire more space than it needs in order to serve the world with its witness to Jesus Christ and to the world's reconciliation with God through Christ. Also, the church can defend its own space only by fighting not for it but for the salvation of the world. Otherwise the church becomes a "society of religion" that fights for its own cause and thereby ceases to be the church of God in the world. The first instruction to those who belong to the church is not, therefore, to do something for themselves—say, create a religious organization or lead a pious life—but to be witnesses of Jesus Christ to the world.

THE IMAGE OF HUMANITY

Why only a part of humanity knows the form of its redeemer is a mystery for which there is no explanation. The desire of the incarnate One to take form in all people still remains unfulfilled. He who bore the form of a human being can take form in only a small flock: this is his church. Therefore, "formation" means, first of all, Jesus Christ taking form, taking shape, in his church. It is the figure of Jesus Christ himself that takes shape here. In a profound and clear designation of the matter itself, the New Testament calls the church the body of Christ. The body is the form, the shape. Thus the church is not a religious community of worshipers of Christ but is instead the Christ who has taken shape among human beings. The church may be called the body of Christ, however, because humanity and thus all people are really assumed in the body of Jesus Christ. The church now has the form that in truth is valid for all humanity. The image according to which it is shaped is the image of humanity. What happens in it happens in an exemplary and representative way in all human beings. It cannot be said clearly enough, however, that even the church does not have its own independent form beside the form of Jesus Christ. The church is nothing but that piece of humanity in which Christ has really taken on human form.

The Church Is Not about Religion

The church is the humanity that was incarnate, condemned, and raised to new life in Christ. Thus, to begin with, it has essentially nothing at all to do with the so-called religious functions of human beings; it has to do rather with the whole of humankind in its existence in the world and in all its relationships.

What the church is all about is not religion but the form of Christ and Christ taking shape among a group of human beings. If we let ourselves vary even just the least bit from this view, we fall back inevitably into programs for the ethical or religious formation of the world. . . .The starting point of Christian ethics is the body of Christ, the form of Christ in the form of the church and the shaping of the church according to the form of Christ. Only if what happens in the church is truly valid for all of humanity does the concept of formation gain—indirectly—its importance for all human beings. Again, however, it is not as if the church is now presented as the model for the world, but the formation of the world can be discussed only in such a way that humanity is drawn into the church in its true form, which belongs to it. This means that even where one speaks of the formation of the world, only the form of Jesus Christ is meant.

No Abstract Ethics

The figure of Christ is one and the same at all times and in all places. The church of Christ is also the same over all peoples. Nonetheless, Christ is not a principle according to which all the world must be shaped. Christ is not the promulgator of a single system of what would be good today and at all times. Christ teaches no abstract ethics that must be implemented—whatever the cost. Christ was not essentially a teacher or lawgiver but a human being, a real human being like us. Therefore, he does not want us to be just students, representatives, and defenders of a certain teaching, but human beings, real human beings before God. Christ did not, like an ethicist, love a theory about what is good. Rather, he loved real human beings. He was not, like a philosopher, interested in what is "generally true," but in what serves concrete, real human beings. He was not concerned as to whether the maxims of an action could become the principle of a general law, but whether my present actions help my neighbors to be human beings before God. The point is not that God became an idea, a principle, a program, a general truth, a law, but that God became a human being.

HERE AND NOW

The figure of Christ, as surely as it is and remains one and the same, wants to assume form in real people, and that means in quite different ways. Christ does not abolish human reality in favor of an idea that demands realization against everything that is real. Christ instead sets reality directly into force. He affirms it. Indeed, he himself is the real human being and thus the foundation of all human reality. Formation according to the figure of Christ includes two things. (1) The figure of Christ remains one and the same, not as a general idea, but as what it uniquely is: the incarnate, crucified, and resurrected God. (2) Precisely for the sake of the figure of Christ, the form of the real human being remains preserved, so that the *real human being receives the form of Christ*. With this we are directed away from any abstract ethic and pointed toward a concrete ethic. What can and should be said is not what is good once and for all time, but *how Christ takes shape among us here and now*.

THE CHURCH OF PETER

The church of Peter (Matt. 16:18–19) means the church of the rock, the church of the confession of Christ. The church of Peter does not mean the church of views and opinions, but the church of revelation. It is not the church in which one speaks of "what people say," but the church in which the confession of Peter is repeated ever anew and passed on. It is the church that does nothing but continually pass on the confession through singing, praying, proclaiming, and doing. It is the church that has rock under it only as long as it stands by this confession. . . .

But "the church of Peter" is not something that one can say just like that, with unalloyed pride. Peter, the confessing, believing disciple, denied the Lord on that night in which Judas betrayed him (Matt. 26:69–75); on that night he stood by the fire and was ashamed, while Christ stood before the high priest. Peter is the one of little faith, the fearful one who sank into the sea. He is the disciple whom Jesus rebuked: "Get behind me, Satan!" (Matt. 16:23); he is the one who also repeatedly became weak, repeatedly denied and fell, a weak, vacillating human being with eyes cast down. The church of Peter is the church that shares this weakness of his. . . . The church of Peter is the church of all those who are ashamed of their Lord just when they should be standing up for him.

The Good Shepherd

Jesus, the good shepherd (John 10:11), has nothing to do with shepherd idylls and pastoral poetry. All such ideas spoil the text. "I am" makes it clear that the subject is not shepherds and their work in general but Jesus Christ alone. I am *the* good shepherd—not *a* good shepherd, which might mean that Jesus is comparing himself with other good shepherds and learning from them what a good shepherd is. What a good shepherd is can be learned only from *the* good shepherd, beside whom there is no other, from the standpoint of this "I"—from the standpoint of Jesus.

No other pastoral office in the church of Jesus Christ sets beside *the* good shepherd a second and third shepherd; rather, it lets Jesus alone be *the* good shepherd of the church. He is the "chief shepherd" (1 Pet. 5:4). It is his pastoral office in which the "pastors" participate, or else they spoil the office and the flock. That this is a question of *the* good shepherd himself, and not of one shepherd among many, becomes immediately clear in the unusual activity that he ascribes to himself. He speaks not of pastoring, watering, and helping. Rather, "The (again, note the article!) good shepherd lays down his life for the sheep" (John 10:11). So Jesus calls himself the good shepherd because he dies for his sheep.

WORD OF GOD—
UNITY OF THE CHURCH

Because Jesus alone knows his own, he alone can therefore say that he has sheep of his flock in the midst of the pagan world (John 10:16). The love and the dying of the good shepherd is not only for the chosen people. Jesus, the good shepherd, also has sheep where we might least suspect, where up to now there is nothing but denial of God and idolatry. Jesus does not belong only to us, and he is not dependent on us. That is said to the church for comfort and as a warning against arrogance. . . . The good shepherd must lead all his sheep, so that they will know the right way and be protected from danger and injury. That will be the perfection of Jesus' church: when they all hear his voice. No other voice will then be worth anything or be able to lead the sheep astray. The voice of Jesus will be hidden from no one, and all will live by its command, its instruction, its comfort. The voice of the good shepherd will be the only thing that unites them all. The word of God will be the unity of the church on earth. The unity of the church will consist not in organizations, not in dogmas, not in liturgies, not in pious hearts, but in the word of God, in the voice of Jesus Christ, the good shepherd of his sheep. All division of Christendom will come to an end when they all hear his voice and only his voice, when everything falls away that, apart from this one voice, also demands to be heard and obeyed.

FOOLISH WAYS

God is love" (1 John 4:16). This is no longer a general wisdom of life but, rather, the only real and indestructible ground on which a whole life is built. It is truth and it is reality. It is part of the church's definition that it has to say such things to people who must feel this either as a well-meant phrase and as untruth or as obvious. The saying "God is love" is completely open to this danger. It is extremely easy to take it as a well-meant exaggeration, a phrase used for the purpose of ecclesiastical celebrations, and thus basically to reject it as untrue and rob it of its seriousness. It is, however, just as much a destruction of the seriousness of this statement when one piously takes it for granted. No, when we speak here of the love of God, we are talking about something plainly not obvious, something improbable, indeed something incredible. And yet this plainly improbable thing is true, so true that a person's whole life should be built on it. . . . Those who stay with love do not travel the prescribed way of excellence in the world, but rather their own often incomprehensible, often foolish ways. They lack that last bit of worldly wisdom that is called self-interest. But in these foolish, odd ways, those who have eyes to see, see something shining from the glory of God himself.

WORD AND DEED

What should the word of the church be in a world in which deeds speak their own language so overwhelmingly? Has the church's word become superfluous? Shouldn't we also simply arrange our lives to fit in with these deeds and just cooperate instead of using words? Deeds are believable. Should we complain about how they come into being in the world? That they are self-serving? That the phrase here simply holds true: "God helps those who help themselves"? . . . Standing in the midst of deeds, we must ask about the *word;* we can no longer do anything else.

Deeds have their own momentum. They silently run over everything that is weaker than they are. . . . Only one thing is greater than the deed: the One who gives it. Every deed knows that itself; it is allowed and given. It should praise the One who gives it. Whether it does that or not is decided by its position in regard to the *word of God.* The word of God is there, and it is the only thing over which the deed has no power. Whatever human powers stand around the word of God may be small and weak, so that they may also be broken and annihilated. Only the word remains. It challenges every deed and is not afraid, for it is eternal, invulnerable, and almighty.

CONFESSION — THEOLOGY — FAITH

The essence of the church is not doing theology but *believing* and *obeying* the word of God. But because it has pleased God to reveal himself in the *spoken human word*, and because this word is subject to distortion and contamination by human ideas and opinions, the church needs clarity regarding true and false proclamation. It needs something that is a means of helping, a means of struggling, and not an end in itself. In times of temptation the church is called to such maturity in a special way. The *word of God* is the sole norm and rule of all proper Christian knowledge. A *confession* is an interpretation and witness to the word of God for a particular time or particular danger; it is subject to the word of God. *Theology* is the interpretation of the confession from certain points of view and with the ongoing testing of the confession against Scripture. *Faith* arises solely from the preaching of the word of God (Rom. 10:17); it does not need theology, but proper preaching requires confession and theology. Faith that arises through preaching seeks its confirmation again in the Scripture and the confessions, and thus it does theology itself.

THE CLAIM OF THE AUTHORITIES
ON THE CHURCH

The claim of the authorities to obedience and respect also extends to the church. With regard to the spiritual office, naturally, the authorities can require only that this office not interfere with the secular office but fulfill its own commission, which includes the admonition of obedience to the authorities. Over this commission itself, as it is exercised in the pastoral office and in the office of church leadership, the authorities have no power. To the extent that the spiritual office is a publicly executed office, the authorities have a claim to oversight to assure that everything happens in an orderly fashion, that is, according to public justice. Only in this respect do they also have a claim regarding personnel matters in the office. The spiritual office itself is not subject to the authorities. . . . As a citizen, the Christian does not cease to be a Christian but serves Christ in other ways. This is also already enough to define the genuine claim of authorities in terms of content. They can never lead Christians against Christ. Rather, they can help them serve Christ in the world. In this way the person in authority becomes for the Christian a servant of God.

THE CLAIM OF THE CHURCH
ON THE AUTHORITIES

The church is commissioned to call all the world to the lordship of Jesus Christ. It witnesses the common Lord to the authorities. It calls people in authority to faith in Jesus Christ for the sake of their blessedness. It knows that the commission of the authorities is properly executed in obedience to Jesus Christ. Its aim is not that the authorities make Christian policies, Christian laws, and so on, but that they be proper authorities in the sense of their special commission. It is the church that leads the authorities to an understanding of themselves. For the sake of their common Lord, the church asks for the attention of the authorities, for protection of public Christian proclamation against violence and blasphemy, for protection of ecclesiastical order against arbitrary interference, for the protection of the Christian life in obedience to Jesus Christ. The church can never let go of this claim. It must also let it be heard publicly as long as the authorities themselves claim to recognize the church. Yet where the authorities in words or in deeds set themselves against the church, the time may come when the church—while not giving up its claim—will, nonetheless, no longer waste its words.

THE NEW EARTH AND THE NEW HEAVENS

Christ is not far away from the world or in some distant region of our existence. He went into the deepest depths of the world. His cross is in the middle of the world. And now this cross of Christ calls wrath and judgment over a world of hate and proclaims peace. . . .

No visible divine state will be established in this world, not even if there were international understanding everywhere. Everything that the church does here is temporary and designed only to hold together the collapsing systems of the world and keep them from falling into chaos. This activity of the church is indispensable. All order and all community in the world will have to pass away when God creates his new world and the Lord Christ comes again to judge the old world and establish the new. In this world there is peace only in the struggle for truth and justice, but in the new world there will be the eternal peace of the love of God. That is the new earth and the new heavens that God will create (Isa. 65:17). And because we believe that we will one day be there together in this new kingdom, we should love each other here in all our diversity.

Spiritual Authority

Genuine spiritual authority exists only where the service of hearing, helping, bearing, and proclaiming is fulfilled. Every cult of personality that is based on the important personal characteristics, outstanding abilities, powers, and gifts of another person—even if they are of a spiritual nature—is worldly and has no place in the Christian church. Indeed, it poisons the church. The longing heard so often today for "episcopal figures," for "priestly people," for "authoritative personalities," springs often enough from the spiritually sick need to admire people and for the establishment of visible human authority, because the genuine authority of service appears too rarely. Nothing contradicts such longing more sharply that the New Testament itself in its description of the bishop (1 Tim. 3:1-7). There is nothing here of the charm of human gifts, of the shining characteristics of a spiritual personality. . . .

The question of spiritual confidence, which is so closely connected with the question of authority, is decided by the loyalty with which one stands in the service of Jesus Christ—never by the extraordinary gifts a person may possess. Pastoral authority can come only to the servants of Jesus who seek no authority of their own.

THE RELATIONSHIP OF JESUS CHRIST TO EVIL AND TO GOOD

Where the church has been based on Scripture, it has repeatedly reflected on the relationship of Jesus Christ to evil and to evil people. In the Reformation churches this question had been dominant. Indeed, one of the decisive perceptions of the Reformation is that at this point the gospel word in the New Testament has spoken fully and profoundly. By contrast, the question of the relationship of the good person to Christ remained strangely untouched. Good people were either Pharisees and hypocrites, who had to be convinced of their evil, or people who were converted from their evil to Christ and through him were now enabled to do good works. Accordingly, *the* good was either the "shining vices" of the pagans or the fruit of the Holy Spirit. Now, to be sure, this in no way exhausted the question of the relationship of Jesus Christ to the good; rather, through the neglect of this question, the gospel provided only the call to conversion and solace from sins for drinkers, adulterers, and evildoers of all kinds, and the gospel lost its power for good people. On the conversion of the good person to Christ, the church had little it could say.

FROM THE WORLD TO GOD OR FROM GOD TO THE WORLD?

Who is telling us, actually, that all worldly problems should and can be solved? Perhaps for God the unsolved nature of these problems is more important than their solution—namely, because it points to the original sin of the human race and to God's redemption. Perhaps the problems of humanity are so involved, so wrongly stated, that they really are unsolvable. . . . The thinking that starts with human problems and looks for solutions on that basis must be overcome. It is unbiblical. The way of Jesus Christ goes not from the world to God but from God to the world, and therefore so does the way of all Christian thinking. That means that the nature of the gospel does not consist in solving worldly problems, nor does the essential duty of the church. Yet it does not follow from this that the church has absolutely no duty in this regard. . . . The word of the church to the world can be none other than the word of God to the world, which is Jesus Christ and salvation in his name. God's relationship to the world is defined in Jesus Christ; we know of no relationship of God to the world other than through Jesus Christ. Therefore, for the church, also, there is no relationship to the world other than through Jesus Christ—not from a natural law, a law of reason, or general human law. The proper relationship of the church to the world comes *only* from the gospel of Jesus Christ.

THE LORD'S SUPPER

What is the proper use of the Lord's Supper? What can we expect from receiving the sacrament? What is the gift we share? What did Jesus promise with the institution of the Lord's Supper, and what is the proper preaching that invites us to the Lord's Supper? We cannot escape the conclusion that the Lord's Supper does not concern a vague mystical experience but the clear, incarnate Word of God, the promise and claim of Jesus Christ. Jesus himself did not silently pass the disciples bread and wine; he accompanied them with his word. When the Lutheran church has promoted its teaching of the Lord's Supper so emphatically and seriously, its concern has been the proper retelling of these words of Jesus (which, like all preaching, cannot be simply the repetition and declamation of the biblical words), that is, that the sacrament remain for all times Jesus' own words and actions. In the church, nothing is supposed to be valid or to happen except Jesus' word and deed. . . . Only where the church—despite all mockery and disdain in the modern world—rests on the pure word of God and the sacraments instituted by Christ can it claim the promise that the gates of Hades will not prevail against it (Matt. 16:18).

JULY

CHRISTIANS IN THE WORLD

Christians have
their field of activity
in the world.
There they are to
get involved,
go to work, cocreate,
and do the will of God.

THE ROSES AND LILIES OF THE CHRISTIAN LIFE

Christians cannot take it for granted that they will be allowed to live together with other Christians. Jesus Christ lived in the midst of his enemies. And in the end all the disciples abandoned him. . . .

The degree to which God gives the gift of visible community varies. Christians in the diaspora are comforted by a brief visit from a fellow Christian, a common prayer, and a fraternal blessing. They gain strength from a letter written by the hand of a Christian. The handwritten greeting of Paul in his letters was indeed a sign of such fellowship. Others receive the gift of Sunday fellowship in community worship. Still others may live a Christian life in the fellowship of their family. Among serious Christians in the church today a desire has arisen to gather with other Christians during work breaks for a time to find life together under the Word. Today Christians again understand life together as the grace that it is, as something unusual, as the "roses and lilies" of the Christian life (Luther).

BEING A CHRISTIAN IS NOT A MATTER OF A MOMENT

There is no standing still. Every gift, every perception I receive, only drives me deeper into the word of God. For the word of God I need time to understand God's commandments, and I often have to reflect on the word for a long time. Nothing would be more perverse than an activity or state of emotions that rejects the value of reflecting and pondering. Nor is it the business only of those already especially called; it is the business of anyone who wants to walk in the ways of God. To be sure, God often demands drastic, unreserved action, but he also demands quiet and reflection. Hence I often may and must stay with the same biblical saying for hours or days, until I am enlightened with its proper understanding. No Christians have progressed so far that they no longer have need of reflection. None may exempt themselves from it because of the great and constant demands made on their time. God's word demands my time. God himself entered time and now wants me also to give him my time. Being a Christian is not a matter of a moment. It takes time. God gave us the Scripture, and from it we are to know his will. The Scripture must be read and pondered anew every day. God's word is not the sum of some general statements that I can access at any time. It is instead God's word to me — new every day — in the infinite riches of interpretation.

DEPENDENT ON THE WORD OF GOD

Christians are people who no longer seek their salvation, their rescue, their righteousness in themselves, but through Jesus Christ and through him alone. They know that God's word in Jesus Christ pronounces them guilty, even when they feel nothing of their own guilt, and God's word in Jesus Christ pronounces them free and righteous, even when they feel nothing of their own righteousness. Christians no longer live on their own, by their own indictment and their own justification, but by God's indictment and God's justification. They live entirely by the word of God about them, in faithful submission to God's judgment, whether it pronounces them guilty or righteous. The life and death of Christians are not bound up in themselves. They instead find both only in the word that comes to them from outside, in God's word to them. The Reformers put it this way: our righteousness is a "foreign righteousness," a righteousness from outside (outside of us). By this the Reformers meant that Christians are dependent on the word of God that is spoken to them. They are oriented in an outward direction toward the word that comes to them. Christians live entirely by the truth of the word of God in Jesus Christ.

CHRISTIANS NEED OTHER CHRISTIANS

Christians need other Christians who will speak to them the word of God. They need them again and again when they are uncertain and downcast, for on their own they cannot help themselves without deceiving themselves about the truth. . . . Christians come to each other only through Jesus Christ. Among people there is conflict, but "he is our peace" (Eph. 2:14), says Paul of Jesus Christ, in whom the old, divided humanity has become one. Without Christ there is discord between God and humankind and among people. Christ has become the mediator and has made peace with God and among people. Without Christ we would not know God and could not call upon him or go to him. Without Christ, however, we would not know our fellow human beings, either, and could not go to them. The way to them is blocked by our own ego. Christ opened the way to God and to our sisters and brothers. Now Christians can live together in peace. They can love and serve one another, and they can become one. Only in Jesus Christ are we one. Only through him are we bound to each other.

THE DREAM OF A CHRISTIAN COMMUNITY

Those who love their dream of a Christian community more than the Christian community itself become destroyers of any Christian community, no matter how honest, how serious, and how committed they may personally be.

God hates dreaming, for it makes people proud and demanding. Those who have dreamed up an image of a community demand its fulfillment by God, by others, and by themselves. They come into the fellowship of Christians as demanders and set up their own law. They act as if it is they who have the task of creating the Christian community, as if their dream image is supposed to obligate other people. Anything that does not go according to their will is called failure. When their dream comes to nothing, they see the community falling apart.

Because God has already laid down the only basis for our community, because God—long before we entered into life together with other Christians—has joined us together with them into one body in Jesus Christ, therefore, we come into life together with other Christians not as demanders but as grateful receivers. We thank God for what he has done with us and for us. We don't complain about what God has not given us. Rather, we thank God for what he gives us daily.

BETWEEN THE HUMAN IDEAL AND GOD'S REALITY

The basic existence of every Christian community depends on whether in good time it succeeds in becoming conscious of the distinction between the human ideal and God's reality, between human and spiritual community. It is a question of life and death for a Christian community that at this point it achieve sobriety as soon as possible. In other words, life together under the word will remain healthy only where it does not present itself as a movement, an order, an association, a *collegium pietatis* but instead understands itself as a part of the one, holy, and universal Christian church, where, through working and suffering, it shares in the need, struggle, and promise of the whole church. Every principle of selection, with its concomitant segregation, . . . is extremely dangerous for a Christian community. By the avenue of intellectual or spiritual selection, the human element always creeps in again and robs the community of its spiritual strength and effectiveness for the church. It drives it into sectarianism. The exclusion of the weak and the plain, the seemingly unusable, from a living Christian community can mean, as it were, the exclusion of Christ, who in the poor sister or brother is knocking on the door. At this point, therefore, we should be very much on our guard.

THE DISCIPLINE OF THE TONGUE

Where the discipline of the tongue is practiced (Eph. 4:29), individuals will make an incomparable discovery. They will be able to stop incessantly observing others, judging them, condemning them, relegating them to their particular, controllable positions, and thus doing violence to them. They can let them stand entirely free, just as God placed them in regard to himself. Their vision widens, and for the first time—and to their astonishment—they know the wealth of God's glory as Creator. God did not make others as I would have made them. . . . In their creaturely freedom, others now become for me a reason for joy, whereas earlier they represented only trouble and need. God does not want me to form other people in the image that seems good to me—that is, in my own image. Rather, in his freedom from me, God made others in his own image. I can never know in advance what God's image will look like in others; again and again it has an entirely new form, based solely on God's free creation. . . . The whole variety of individuals in the community will no longer be grounds for talking, judging, condemning—that is, for self-justification. It will become instead the basis for mutual joy.

AN INDISPENSABLE LINK IN A CHAIN

In a Christian community everything depends on each individual becoming an indispensable link in a chain. The chain will be unbreakable only if all links, even the smallest, hold fast. A community that allows a situation in which some members are unused will fail at that point. Therefore it will be good for all individuals to perform definite tasks for the community, so that in hours of doubt they will know that they are not useless and unusable. Every Christian community must know that not only do the weak need the strong, but also the strong cannot do without the weak. The exclusion of the weak means the death of the community. . . .

Because Christians can no longer consider themselves smart, they will therefore also think little of their own plans and intentions. They will know that it is a good thing that their own will is broken when they meet their neighbor. They will be ready to consider their neighbor's will more important and more pressing than their own. What does it matter if their own plans are thwarted? Is it not better to serve your neighbor than to persist with your own will? . . .

Those who seek their own honor are no longer seeking God and neighbor.

HEARING AND SPEAKING

As the love of God begins with us listening to his Word, so the love of our sisters and brothers begins with us learning to listen to them. God's love for us consists not only in giving us his Word but also in lending us his ear. Thus it is his work that we do for our brothers and sisters when we learn to listen to them. Christians, and especially preachers, so often believe that they must always have something to "offer" when they are together with other people and that this is their only service. They forget that listening can be a greater service than speaking. Many people are looking for a willing ear to listen to them, but they don't find it among Christians, because Christians tend to talk when they should be listening. But those who can no longer listen to a sister or brother will soon no longer listen to God either, because even before God they will always be only talking. This is the beginning of the end for the spiritual life, and finally there will be only pious prattle and sanctimonious condescension that suffocate with godly words. Those who cannot listen at length and with patience will always talk past the other person and in the end not even realize it. Those who believe their time is too valuable to spend it listening will never really have time for God and neighbor, but only for themselves and for their own words and plans.

Letting Oneself Be Interrupted by God

One service that a member of a Christian community should offer to another is active readiness to be of assistance. This means, first, simple help in small and outward things. There are a great number of these in the life of every community. No one is too good for the smallest service. Our concern about the loss of time that such small outward assistance can bring usually means that we are taking our own work too seriously. We must be prepared to have God interrupt us. Again and again—and sometimes daily—God will block our path and thwart our plans by putting in our way people with their demands and petitions. We can then pass them by, busy with the important items on our daily agenda, like the priest who—perhaps while reading his Bible—passed by the man who had fallen into the hands of robbers (Luke 10:31). Then we pass by the sign of the cross—visibly erected in our lives—whose purpose is to show us that it is not our way but God's way that counts. It is a strange fact that Christians and theologians are the very ones who often regard their work as so important and urgent that they don't want to let anything interrupt it. They believe that in this way they are doing a service to God and thereby despise the "crooked way" of God, which is nonetheless straight.

Living under Curse and Promise

The eternal enmity in which Adam is placed in regard to the snake and the power of pious godlessness is both a curse and a promise. Human beings in a disturbed world, between God's curse and promise, are challenged human beings. We hear the word of God not in peace and quiet, but again and again in the distortion of the godly question. We hold to God not in peace but in enmity and struggle. With this cursed fate, however, comes the promise of victory won ever anew in struggle, in which the man will strike the head of the snake. Yet he also comes out of this battle as the wounded one, as one whom the defeated snake will still strike in the heel (Gen. 3:15).

The struggle over the word of God leaves him with scars. Adam is not supposed to be a hero but one who is bitten in the struggle, one who wins ever anew and is wounded ever anew; and the whole human race shares his fate. In this struggle, which humankind takes upon itself and fights through as curse and promise, we are allowed to live.

CALL AND CALLING

In their encounter with Jesus Christ human beings experience the call of God and with it a calling to life in the community of Jesus Christ. . . . As Jew or Greek, as slave or free, as male or female (Gal. 3:28), as married or single, people hear the call. Right where they are, people are supposed to hear the call and let themselves be claimed by it. . . . People fulfill the responsibility laid upon them, not in the faithful completion of their earthly vocational duties as citizens, workers, and parents, but in hearing the call of Jesus Christ, which also leads them into earthly duties but is never totally absorbed in them. It instead stands beyond, before, and behind them. . . . Luther's return from the monastery to the world, to his "vocation"—in the genuine New Testament sense—is the strongest attack and offense that was carried out against the world since early Christianity. Now a position against the world is taken *in* the world. One's vocation is the place where the call of Christ is answered and lived responsibly. The task given me in my vocation is a limited one, to be sure, but at the same time, my responsibility to the call of Jesus Christ goes beyond all boundaries.

RESPONSIBILITY IN VOCATION

The question of the place and limit of responsibility has led us to the concept of vocation. This discussion will prove to be correct only when vocation is simultaneously understood in all its dimensions. . . . If I am a physician, for example, I serve not only my patient in a specific case but also, and at the same time, I serve scientific knowledge and thus science and the knowledge of truth in general. Although, practically speaking, I perform this service in my specific situation—for example, at the bedside of my patient—I still keep in mind my responsibility for the whole, and in this way I fulfill my vocation. It can also happen that as a doctor I must recognize and fulfill my concrete responsibility no longer at the bedside but, for example, in making a public appearance against a measure that threatens medical science or human life or science as such. Precisely because vocation is responsibility, and because responsibility is the answer of the whole person to the whole of reality, there is no philistine limiting of oneself to the narrowest vocational duties, for a limitation of this sort would be irresponsible.

GOD GIVES LIFE A SHAPE

Natural life is shaped life. There is a natural shape dwelling within and serving life. If, however, life rids itself of this shape, if life wants to be free from it in order to affirm itself, if it does not want to be served by this natural shape, then it will destroy itself down to its roots. The life that sets itself up as absolute and an end in itself will annihilate itself. Vitalism necessarily ends in nihilism, in the destruction of everything natural. Life in itself—in the logically consistent sense—is nothing, an abyss, a fall. It is movement without end, without aim, a movement into nothingness. It does not rest until it has pulled everything with it into this annihilating movement. This vitalism exists in individual and in community life. It arises from the false absolutization of an insight focused on itself, namely, that life is not only the means to an end but also an end in itself, and that this insight is valid for both individual and community life. God wills life and gives it a shape in which it can live, because left to itself, it can only annihilate itself. At the same time, however, this shape puts life at the service of other life and the world.

RELIGION AND TRUTH

We have gotten used to seeing in religion something that corresponds to a need of the human soul and satisfies this need. Something that is supposed to lead from the unrest of existence to rest, from haste into quietness. Something in which, quite apart from our daily and occupational lives, we come completely to ourselves. Then we say that religion is something beautiful, something valuable, something necessary in life. It is the only thing that can make people profoundly happy.

In this process, however, we forget the decisive question of whether religion is also something that is true, whether it is the truth. For it could be that religion, while beautiful, is not true, and that all of this is an illusion — beautiful and godly, but nonetheless an illusion. And the raging battle against religion was started when people in the church itself often talked as if the truth question is the second question of religion. But whoever talks like that sees religion only from the standpoint of human beings and their needs, and not from the standpoint of God and his claim and demand. And therefore it is important that one thing be quite clear to us and that we let this be said to us by the New Testament: religion essentially comes down to just one thing, namely, being true. Truth is the highest value not only in science but even more — and much more urgently — in the religion on which we claim to base our lives.

ONLY IN LIFE DOES ONE
KNOW THE TRUTH

How do I know that what Christian proclamation talks about is the truth? Here the Bible gives a strange answer: "If you continue in my word, you are truly my disciples; and you will know the truth" (John 8:31)—not through open research, not through disinterested thinking and looking for truth, but only through a free, living effort to base one's life completely on the word of Christ, to live totally with him, to emulate him, to listen to him, to obey him. Only when we commit our lives so completely can we judge whether Christ speaks and is the truth. And Christ makes the promise: whoever dares to do this, will know the truth (John 8:32). Only in life does one know the truth. And, finally, the truth will make you free! That is the gift of the truth. Those who have the power of the truth behind them are the freest of people. They fear nothing; they are bound by nothing. With no prejudgment, no weak surrender to deceptive hopes, they are bound to one thing: to the truth that is the truth of God, which bestows validity on all truth. Those who abide in the truth of God are truly free.

WITHOUT GOD HUMAN BEINGS
LOSE THE EARTH

We do not rule; we are ruled. The thing, the world, rules human beings, who are prisoners and slaves of the world. Our own rule is an illusion. Technology is the power with which the earth reaches for human beings and controls them. And because we no longer rule, we lose the earth. Therefore, the earth is no longer *our* earth, and we are aliens on the earth. We do not rule, however, because we do not know the world as God's creation and because we do not receive our rule from God but grab it for ourselves. There is no "freedom from" without "freedom for"; there is no rule without service to God. Without the one, human beings necessarily lose the other. . . . The freedom of human beings for God and other people and the freedom of human beings from creation in their rule over it constitute the image of God in the first human being.

WHAT IS LOVE?

. . . but do not have love, I gain nothing" (1 Cor. 13:3). Here we have the crucial word on which people basically differ and part ways: love. There is a knowledge of Christ, a powerful faith in Christ. Indeed, there is an attitude and a devotion of love unto death, but without love. That's just it: without this "love" everything falls apart, and everything is reprehensible; in this love everything is united, and everything is pleasing to God. What is this love? There are many differing definitions that claim to understand love: as human behavior, as attitude, as devotion, as sacrifice, as community spirit, as feeling, as passion, as service, as deed. All of this, without exception, can exist without "love." Everything that we usually call love — what lives in the depths of the soul and in the visible deed, and even what comes forth from the godly heart as friendly service to the neighbor — can be without "love." That is not because in every human behavior there is always a "remnant" of self-seeking that totally darkens love. Rather, it is because love is absolutely something entirely different from what is meant by it here.

Love Rejoices in the Truth

Love is not an immediate personal relationship, going into the personal and the individual, in contrast to a law of the objective, of impersonal order. Apart from the fact that here "personal" and "objective" are torn apart in a very unbiblical and abstract way, love here becomes just a human behavior and, moreover, only a partial one. Beside the lower ethos of the purely objective and orderly, "love" is then a higher ethos of the personal that appears as perfection and expansion. This corresponds to a situation in which, for example, one has love and truth in conflict with each other and ranks love as the personal above truth as the impersonal. This puts one in direct contradiction with Paul's statement that love rejoices in the truth (1 Cor. 13:6). Love does not know the conflict by which one might want to define it. Rather, love, by its very nature, is beyond any separation. Luther, with a clear biblical view, calls a love that encroaches on the truth, or even just neutralizes it, a "cursed love," even if it appears in the most pious clothing. A love that comprises only the area of personal human relations, but capitulates before objectivity, can never be the love of the New Testament.

GOD IS LOVE

Thus, if there is no conceivable human behavior that as such could be unambiguously referred to as "love," if "love" is beyond all separation in which people live, and if everything that people can understand and practice as love is conceivable only as human behavior within given separations, then there is still a puzzle here, an open question as to what the Bible could mean by "love." And the Bible does not fail to give us an answer. It's also well enough known to us, but it's just that again and again we misinterpret it. The answer is: "God is love" (1 John 4:16). For the sake of clarity, this sentence must first be read with the emphasis on the word "God," whereas we have been used to emphasizing the word "love." *God* is love. This means that not a human behavior, not an attitude, not a deed, but God himself is love. Only those who know God know what love is, not the other way around. That is, it's not that we first—and from nature—know what love is, and then on that basis also know what God is. Rather, no one knows God, unless God has revealed himself to them (1 John 4:7–9). . . . Love has its origin not in us but in God. Love is not human behavior but the behavior of God (1 John 4:10).

THIS-WORLDLY LIFE—JULY 21, 1944

It is in the complete this-worldliness of life that we must first learn how to believe. When we have fully renounced making something out of ourselves—be it a saint or a converted sinner or a church man or woman (a so-called priestly figure!), a righteous or an unrighteous person, a sick or a healthy person—when we have renounced all of that, we fall completely into God's arms and into what I call this-worldliness, namely, living in an abundance of tasks, questions, successes and failures, experiences, and helplessness. We then take seriously no longer our own suffering, but the suffering of God in the world. We watch with Christ in Gethsemane. This, I think, is faith. This is conversion, and in this way we become human beings and Christians (cf. Jer. 45). How can we get carried away with successes or failures if in the life of this world we empathetically suffer the sufferings of God? . . . I am thankful that I have been able to recognize this, and I know that I have been able to do so only on the path that I am now traveling. Therefore, I think gratefully and peacefully about the past and the present.

May God lead us as a friend through these times, but above all, may he lead us to himself.

Human Love and Spiritual Love

Human love makes itself an end in itself, an occupation, an idol that is worshiped and to which everything must be subordinated. It looks after and promotes itself; it loves itself and nothing else in the world. Spiritual love, however, comes from Jesus Christ; it serves him alone. It knows that it has no direct contact with other people because Christ stands between me and others. I cannot know already in advance what love for others means based on the general concept of love that has grown out of my human longing; to Christ all of that may very well be hate or the most evil self-interest. Only Christ through his word tells me what love is. Spiritual love is bound to the word of Jesus Christ alone. Where Christ tells me to have fellowship for the sake of love, I want to have it. Where his truth orders me to withhold fellowship for the sake of love, there I withhold it, in spite of all the protests of my human love. . . . Human love can never comprehend spiritual love, for spiritual love is from above. To all earthly love it is something completely new, foreign, and incomprehensible.

THE MORAL MEMORY

Something that always puzzles me and others is the forgetfulness we experience in regard to impressions made during a night of bombing. Only a few minutes afterward, almost everything we had been thinking is already gone, as if blown away. For Luther it took only a bolt of lightning to change his whole life for years to come. Where is this "memory" today? Isn't the loss of this "moral memory"—what a dreadful term!—the basis for the ruin of all ties, of love, of marriage, of friendship, of loyalty? Nothing sticks; nothing holds fast. Everything is short-term and short-winded. But good things like righteousness, truth, beauty, and all great accomplishments in general need time, constancy, "memory," or they degenerate. Those who are not inclined to be responsible for the past or to shape the future are "forgetful," and I don't know how to reach them and make them aware. For every word, even if it makes an impression at the moment, is subject to forgetfulness. What is to be done? This is a great problem in Christian pastoral care.

FEELINGS MUST REMAIN ALIVE

Also in recent times I have often been occupied with the question of how one can really explain what we usually call the deadening of strong impressions over the course of time. . . . The answer that this is a self-protection device of nature seems to me inadequate. I believe, rather, that it may also be a matter of a clear, sober comprehension of one's own limited duties and possibilities, and thus of the possibility of real love of neighbor. As long as the imagination is whipped up and excited, love of neighbor remains something very vague and general. Today I can look more calmly at people, at their misery and neediness, and thus serve them better. Instead of deadening, I would rather speak of clarification; naturally, however, it often remains a task of changing the one into the other. But in such situations I don't believe we need to reproach ourselves about the fact that over the course of time feelings are no longer so hot and intense. To be sure, one must always remain conscious of the danger that one will lose sight of the whole thing, and even during clarification, strong feelings must remain alive.

FORGIVENESS WITHOUT BEGINNING OR END

We make it easy for ourselves with other people. We deaden ourselves completely and believe that if we don't harbor any bad thoughts against people, then it's the same as if we have forgiven them—and we completely overlook the fact that we have no *good* thoughts about them. And forgiving could also mean having purely good thoughts about people, *bearing* them whenever we can. And that is just what we avoid—we don't bear other people but walk beside them and get used to their silence, and, in fact, we don't take them seriously at all. But *it is precisely a question of bearing*—bearing others in all respects, in all their difficult and unpleasant aspects, and in their error and sin against me. Being silent, bearing, and loving without ceasing—that would come close to forgiveness. . . . Forgiveness is without beginning or end; it happens daily without ceasing, for it comes from God. It is liberation from everything that is forced in being with our neighbor, for here we are freed from ourselves; here we can give up all of our own rights and only help and serve others.

THE NEWS OF THE SOVEREIGN GOD

Christianity hides within itself an antichurch seed, for it is all too easy for us to want to base our claim to God only on our being Christians and members of the church, and in this way to misunderstand and distort the Christian idea entirely. And yet Christianity needs the church. This is the paradox and the point at which the church has an enormous responsibility to bear. Ethics and religion and church lie in the movement of people toward God, but Christ speaks alone, entirely alone, of the movement of God toward human beings—not of the human way to God, but of God's way to humanity. Therefore, it is fundamentally perverse to look for a new morality in Christianity. In fact, Christ hardly gave ethical precepts that were not already available from contemporary Jewish rabbis or pagan literature. The essence of Christianity lies in the news of the sovereign God, to whom alone honor is due in all the world. It is news of the eternal Other; the One who is apart from the world; the One who in love and out of the ground of his being has mercy on human beings, who give honor to him alone; who undertakes the journey to human beings in order to seek his honor in the vessels where human beings are no longer anything, where they fall silent, where they give way to God alone.

THE GREAT DISTURBANCE
OF OUR ILLUSIONS

The idea that there is something eternal and infinite makes our souls anxious in their mortality. They want to reach beyond themselves to immortality; they themselves want to be immortal but know not where to begin. . . . Out of this disquiet of the soul have come the mighty works of philosophy and art: the systems of Plato and Hegel, the Adam of Michelangelo, the quartets and symphonies of Beethoven, the Gothic cathedrals, the paintings of Rembrandt, and the Faust and Prometheus of Goethe. They were all overpowered by the idea of something eternal and immortal. . . . At the same time, the most grandiose and delicate of all human attempts to strive for the eternal out of the heart's anxiety and restlesness is religion. . . . Human beings have found the way to light, to joy, to eternity. The human race could proudly point to the flourishing of its spirit, were it not for one thing, namely, that God is God and grace is grace (Rom. 11:6). Here comes the great disturbance of our illusions and our blessed culture, the disturbance that God himself causes and that is made graphic in the old myth of the tower of Babel. Our way to the eternal was interrupted, and with our philosophy and art, our morality and religion, we fall into the depths from which we came. For another way has opened up, the way of God to humanity.

THE SUM OF CHRISTIANITY

It is not religion that makes us good before God. Rather, it is God alone who makes us good. It all comes down to what God has done. Before this, all our claims fall. Both culture and religion stand under divine judgment. The themes of our morality and our religion have been exposed; we wanted to be masters of eternity, and now we are slaves. Only one thing can save us: the way of God, which is called grace. . . . Not religion but revelation, grace, love. Not the way to God but the way of God to humanity: that is the sum of Christianity. Here lie the great disappointment and the still much greater hope. Our merit, our pride — our honor — all that is finished. But God's grace, God's glory, and God's honor all begin. Not our religion — not even the Christian religion! — but God's grace: that is the message of all of Christianity. It all depends, not on our outstretched beggar's hand, but on what God puts in it, and that means basically that it's not about us and our doing, but about God and God's doing. It's about our doing only to the extent that our doing makes room for God's doing, to the extent that it lets God's grace be grace. Our hope rests not on ourselves but on God. Where could there be a place where it rests more firmly than on God?

HUMAN BEINGS AS
HUMAN BEINGS BEFORE GOD

The church does not have two kinds of commandment at its disposal, one for the world and another for the Christian church; rather, its commandment is the *one* commandment of God revealed in Jesus Christ, which it proclaims to all the world. The church proclaims this commandment by bearing witness to Jesus Christ as Lord and Savior of his church and of all the world, and in this way it calls them into his community.

Jesus Christ, the eternal Son with the Father in eternity: this means that nothing created can be thought of and comprehended in its essence without Christ, the mediator of the creation. . . .

Jesus Christ, the incarnate God: this means that God has bodily taken on everything that is human; that from now on, divine essence can be found in none other than human form; that in Jesus Christ human beings are free before God to be real human beings. What is "Christian" is now not something beyond what is human, but something that wants to be in the midst of humanity. Being "Christian" is not an end in itself, but consists in the fact that human beings as human beings can and should live before God.

THE SECULAR AND THE CHRISTIAN

The Christian element is not identical with the secular, the natural with the supernatural, the revealed with the reasoned. Rather, between the two there is a unity given only in the reality of Christ, and that means in faith in this ultimate reality. This unity is preserved by the fact that the secular and the Christian mutually forbid any static independence of the one from the other; that is, they behave polemically toward each other and in this very way bear witness to their common reality, to their unity in the reality of Christ. As Luther led the secular polemically into battle against the sacralization of the Roman church, so this secular element—at the same moment in which it stands in danger of asserting its independence, as happened soon after the Reformation and reached its high point in cultural Protestantism—has to be contradicted polemically by the Christian element, by the "sacral." Thus, in both cases, it is a question of exactly the same process, namely, an indication of the divine and worldly reality in Jesus Christ.

RESIGNED PESSIMISTS?

You live in the world. God has placed you in it, and in it you are to do the will of God in the midst of a transitory life. Enjoy whatever you can enjoy, but don't lose your heart to the world. Your heart belongs to eternity. It belongs to God.

You would misunderstand the text (1 John 2:17) if you thought that Christians are pessimists who, with everything they see, think only of its transitory nature and just resign themselves. Certainly, Christians are pessimists in regard to the world; they don't expect very much from the world, and they are not blessed by culture. But they are optimists in regard to the divine in the world, for they know that God gives them eternity. Therefore they are joyful, cheerful people, though it is admittedly a cheerfulness in which, now and then, they experience a little melancholy and world-weariness. Christians have their field of activity in the world. There they are to get involved, go to work, cocreate, and do the will of God. And therefore Christians are not resigned pessimists, but people who admittedly expect little from the world, and therefore are joyful and cheerful in the world. For them the world becomes a field sown for eternity.

AUGUST

ENCOUNTER AND RESPONSIBILITY

People necessarily live
in contact with other people,
and with this contact comes
responsibility for other people.

You Know All Needs

Lord Jesus Christ,
you were poor and miserable, imprisoned and abandoned
    like me.
You know all human needs;
you stay with me when no one stands by me;
you do not forget me, but look for me;
you want me to know you and to come to you.
Lord, I hear your call and follow.
Help me!

Holy Spirit,
give me faith
that will save me from despair and evils.
Give me the love for God and other people
that removes all hate and all bitterness;
give me the hope
that frees me from fear and despondency.
Teach me to know Jesus Christ and to do his will.

CHRISTIAN RESPONSIBILITY — SECULAR ORDERS

All things have been created through him and for him. . . . and in him all things hold together" (Col. 1:16–17). That means that there is nothing that stands outside a relationship with Christ, neither persons nor things; indeed, only in its relationship to Christ does anything created have its essence, not only human beings but also the state, the economy, science, nature, and so on. . . . Because all things were created for Christ's sake and for Christ, they therefore stand under the commandment and claim of Christ. For Christ's sake and for Christ, there is and there should be secular order in the state, the family, and the economy. For Christ's sake the secular order stands under the commandment of God. Here we must note that it is not a question of the "Christian state" or the "Christian economy," but the just state and the just economy as secular orders for Christ's sake. Thus there is a Christian responsibility for the secular orders, and there are related assertions within a Christian ethic.

Responsible Action

People necessarily live in contact with other people, and with this contact comes responsibility for other people. History arises through the perception of responsibility for other people — or for whole communities and groups of communities. Individuals act not only for themselves, but they also unite in themselves the selves of many people, possibly even a great number of people. . . .

At the moment when people make themselves responsible for other people — and only when they do this, do they stand within reality — there arises the genuine ethical situation, which is different from the abstraction in which people otherwise seek to master the realm of ethics. . . .

Concrete responsibility means to act in *freedom,* to decide *for oneself,* without the support of people or principles, to act and take responsibility for the consequences of one's action. Responsibility presupposes the ultimate freedom of judging a given situation, of deciding, and of acting. Responsible action is not fixed beforehand and for all time, but is instead born in the given situation. . . .

Those who act responsibly include the given situation in their action, not just as material on which they want to imprint their ideas, but as a coshaper of the deed.

NECESSARY ACTION

Because responsible action is nourished not by ideology but by reality, it can take place only within the framework of this reality. Responsibility is limited both in scope and in essence, that is, quantitatively and qualitatively. Any crossing of this boundary leads to catastrophe. The task cannot be to lift the world off its hinges, but in a given place to do—with a view to reality—what is objectively necessary, and to truly do this. But even in this given place, responsible action cannot always be the last thing done. It instead must go step-by-step and ask what is possible, and then leave the last step—and thus the ultimate responsibility—in the hands of others. Because God became *human*, responsible action must therefore be weighed, judged, and evaluated in the human realm. Therefore the consequences of the action must also be seriously considered and a look into the immediate future ventured—responsible action will not want to be blind. But because *God* became human, responsible action must therefore, in awareness of the humanity of its decisions, leave the judgment of this action, as well as its consequences, completely to God.

A Mysterious Abyss

The question of how well human activity serves the divine goal of history and thus realizes the good in history cannot be answered by human beings with any ultimate certainty. This is reserved for the hidden counsel of God. Whereas for the ideologue the agreement of a deed with the idea provides an unambiguous standard of good and evil, those who act responsibly "in accordance with reality" and deliver their deed up to God must console themselves with faith in the forgiving and healing grace of God. They cannot prove their correctness, because living reality provides them with no unambiguous standard. Rather, a deeper, more mysterious abyss opens up before them. God uses good and evil in order to reach his goal, and indeed—as far as human eyes can see—in a way that often changes "good" into disaster, but "evil" into salvation. . . . God goes his own way through the good and evil of human beings. He proves to be the One who only wants to do good and to whom every deed must be delivered up for wrath and grace. Does this mean the lifting of the distinction between good and evil? No, but it means that people cannot justify themselves in their own good, since God alone does what is good. The power of the divine guidance of history throws human beings onto divine grace.

CORESPONSIBILITY FOR THE COURSE OF HISTORY

It is certainly not true that success justifies even evil deeds and reprehensible means, nor is it possible to regard success, ethically speaking, as something completely neutral. . . . As long as the good is successful, we can afford the luxury of regarding success as ethically irrelevant. But when evil means lead to success, then we have a problem. Faced with such a situation, we learn that neither theoretically observant criticizing and wanting to be right—that is, the refusal to take one's stand on the basis of the facts—nor opportunism, self-surrender, and capitulation in the face of success, do justice to our task. . . . Those who let nothing take from them their coresponsibility for the course of history, because they know it is laid upon them by God, will find—beyond unfruitful criticism and equally unfruitful opportunism—a fruitful relationship with historical events. Talk of a heroic downfall in the face of an unavoidable defeat is not very heroic, namely because it does not dare to look into the future. The ultimate responsible question is not how I can heroically extract myself from the affair, but how a coming generation is supposed to go on living. Only out of this historically responsible question can fruitful—even though temporarily very humiliating—solutions arise. It is a lot easier to carry a matter through in principle than in concrete responsibility.

THE VIEW FROM BELOW

It is an experience of incomparable value that we have learned to see the great events of world history from below, from the perspective of the excluded, the suspect, the poorly treated, the powerless, the oppressed, and the ridiculed—in short, those who suffer. Only if bitterness and envy have not eaten up our heart, can we then see with new eyes the great and the small, fortune and misfortune, strength and weakness. Our view of greatness, humanity, right, and mercy has become clearer, freer, and more incorruptible. And for observing and actively exploring the world, personal suffering has become a more useful key, a more fruitful principle, than personal fortune. It all depends on our not letting this perspective from below make us biased in favor of the eternally unsatisfied. Rather, out of a higher satisfaction that is actually grounded from beyond—beyond below and above—we must do justice to life in all its dimensions and in that way affirm life.

THE FREEDOM OF OTHERS

First of all, it is the *freedom* of others that is a burden to Christians. It goes against their autonomy, and yet they must recognize it. Christians could rid themselves of this burden by not releasing others but by oppressing them, by stamping them with their own image. But if they allow God to create the others in his own image, they will allow others their freedom and will themselves bear the burden of the freedom that other creatures have. The freedom of others includes everything that we understand by nature, particularity, and disposition; it also includes the weaknesses and quirks that try our patience so severely, as well as everything that brings forth an abundance of frictions, antitheses, and clashes between me and other people. Bearing the burden of others means tolerating the creaturely reality of others, affirming them, and in their suffering finding joy in them. Particularly difficult is the case where the strong and the weak in the faith are bound together in one community. The weak should not judge the strong; the strong should not disparage the weak. The weak should guard themselves against arrogance; the strong against indifference. None should seek their own right. If the strong fall, the weak should keep their hearts from malicious pleasure; if the weak fall, then the strong should cheerfully help them up again. The one group needs patience as much as the other.

THE STRONG AND THE WEAK

Christian love and help for the weak mean the bowing of the strong before the weak, of the healthy before the suffering, of the mighty before the exploited. The Christian relationship of the strong to the weak is that the strong should always look *up* to the weak and never look down on them. Weakness is holy. Therefore we give ourselves to the weak. In the eyes of Christ, weakness is not the imperfect compared to the perfect; rather, strength is the imperfect, and weakness is the perfect. The weak do not have to serve the strong, but the strong the weak—and not out of charity, but out of concern and respect. It is not the mighty who are right, for ultimately the weak are always right. Thus Christianity means a revaluation of all human values and the establishment of a new order of values in the light of Christ.

BREAK ALL THIS WRETCHEDNESS

Lord, our faith and our hope are so weak.
We do not dare to base our lives entirely on your
    promise. We doubt your power.
Lord, forgive the doubters and the hopeless, and give us
    your promise anew today.
Lord God, you let the water rise high around us. Look
    down on your world.
There is terrible torment of hunger and thirst, no home,
    no work, tears and despair;
God, are these the children of your mercy? Is this the
    world that you have created?
Oh, we must be terribly far from you for your creatures
    to have to suffer so. We will soon come to the end.
We no longer believe, and we no longer hope.
Come now, O God, and break all this wretchedness, all
    the misery, and if it is your gracious will that we fall
    still deeper into the water, then do not hide from us
    the promise that you want to create a new heaven and
    a new earth (2 Pet. 3:13), that you have invited the
    poor and wretched, the troubled and suffering into
    your kingdom.
God, make us glad again.

BODILY LIFE

Bodily life, which we receive without our effort, brings with it the right to its sustenance. It is not a right that we stole or acquired, but is in the most real sense a right "we were born with," a received right that was there before our will, that rests on the nature of being itself. Since according to God's will there is human life on earth only as bodily life, the body has a right to sustenance for the sake of the whole person. . . . The human dwelling, unlike an animal's shelter, is not intended only as a protection against the weather and night, and a nursery for the young. It is, rather, the place in which human beings may relish the joys of a personal life in the seclusion of their own family and their own property. Eating and drinking serve not only the purpose of keeping the body sound but also the natural joys of bodily life. Clothing is supposed not only to serve the necessary function of keeping the body covered, but also to be an embellishment of the body. Relaxation not only has the purpose of greater capacity for work, but also gives the body its allotted amount of rest and enjoyment. . . . Where people are robbed of the possibility of bodily joys, when their bodies are used exclusively as a means to an end, there we find an assault on the original right of bodily life.

LIFE WORTH LIVING AND
LIFE NOT WORTH LIVING

Before God there is no life not worth living, for life itself is deemed by God to have value. The fact that God is the creator, sustainer, and redeemer of life makes even the most miserable life worth living before God. Poor Lazarus, who, covered with sores, lay at the gate of the rich man while dogs licked his sores, that man without any social value, that victim of those who judge life only according to it usefulness, is considered by God to be worthy of eternal life (Luke 16:19–31). Where else should the standard for the ultimate value of life lie, except in God? In the subjective affirmation of life? In this, many a genius might be surpassed by an idiot. In the judgment of the community? Here it would soon develop that judgment on the socially valuable or worthless life would be subject to the needs of the moment and thus to arbitrary decision, and that now this, now that group of people would be affected by the judgment to annihilate. The distinction between life worth living and life not worth living sooner or later destroys life itself. We cannot get around the fact that precisely this so-called not-worth-living life of the incurably ill stimulates the greatest degree of willingness on the part of the healthy—doctors, caregivers, and relatives—to make social sacrifices, and that such devotion of healthy life to unhealthy life has produced the highest level of real usefulness for the community.

MISANTHROPY

If we despise other people, we will never be able to make anything out of them. None of what we despise in others is completely foreign to ourselves. How often we expect more from others than we are willing to produce ourselves. Why have we thus far not thought more soberly about people, about their weakness and openness to temptation? We must learn to look less at what people do or don't do and more at what they suffer. The only fruitful relationship with people—and especially with the weak— is love, that is, the will to have fellowship with them. God himself did not despise human beings but became human himself for our sake.

There is also, however, a well-intended love of people that comes close to despising people. It rests on the judging of people according to the values slumbering within them, according to their deepest health, reason, goodness. . . . We love a self-made image of people that hardly bears any resemblance to reality and thus ultimately despises the real person that God loved and whose being God has accepted.

BEING THERE FOR OTHERS

Our relationship to God is not a "religious" one to the highest, mightiest, best conceivable being; this is not genuine transcendence. Rather, our relationship to God is a new life in "being there for others," in participation in the being of Jesus. The transcendent does not consist in infinite, unreachable tasks, but in the currently available, reachable neighbor. God in human form! Not, as in some religions, in animal form as the monstrous, chaotic, distant, horrifying; nor in the conceptual forms of the absolute, the metaphysical, the infinite, and so on; nor in the Greek god-human form of the "man in himself," but "the man for others"—the crucified One. . . . The idea that it doesn't depend on me but on the church can be a sanctimonious excuse and will always be felt as such by others. The situation is similar with the dialectical indication that my faith is not at my disposal, and therefore I cannot simply say what I believe. All of these ideas, as justified as they may be in their place, do not release us from honesty with respect to ourselves. We cannot, like the Catholics, simply identify with the church. . . . The church is only the church when it is there for others.

The Limits and Origin
of Responsible Action

The limits of responsible living and acting include taking into account the responsibility of others whom we meet. This is precisely where responsibility is distinguished from oppression: that it recognizes the responsibility of other people—indeed, that it lets others become aware of their own responsibility. The responsibility of a father or a government leader is limited by the responsibility of the child or the citizen. . . . There can never be an absolute responsibility that does not find its essential limits in the responsibility of other people. . . . God and the neighbor, as they meet us in Jesus Christ, are not only the limits but also the origin of responsible action. Irresponsible action is defined precisely by the fact that it ignores these limits: God and the neighbor. Responsible action gains its unity and ultimately, also its certainty, from this, its limitation by God and the neighbor. Precisely because it is not master of itself, because it is not limitless and high-spirited but creaturely and humble, responsible action can be borne by an ultimate joy and confidence. It can know itself hidden in its origin, essence, and aim, in Christ.

BEING AWAKE

Human beings are not supposed to sleep but to be awake. Being awake means being sober, living not in dreams and wishes but in stark reality. Being awake means loving the day and its work. It means being without illusions, because illusions idolize the world for us and veil our vision of the one God of whom one is to make no idols; illusions let us see the world in the colors of our own wishes and prejudices. Being awake means seeing the world as it is before God, without judging it. Being awake means being open, being ready for the future, looking it in the eye and not fearing it. It means seeing God's clear day as it is, loving his creation and his work, but at the same time seeing the suffering of creation, the misery and helplessness of other people, hearing their petition even where it remains unspoken. And it means knowing about eternal guilt. This being awake is not something we can give ourselves. Rather, God must call us to this being awake. . . . Live before God as the one he has made you to be! But this word "live" cannot be a command; it is the word of God himself as Creator.

Admonition to Do Good

Do not withhold good from those to whom it is due,
   when it is in your power to do it" (Prov. 3:27).
To whom is it due? To each of us.
Who is it who has received from God the power to do
   good? Each of us.
Do not *withhold*—do not immediately look for reasons to
   reject the request (Prov. 3:28)—proper giving means
   passing on *God's gift*, so that it will be seen not as mine
   but as *God's* gift.
The greatest gift of God is Christ.
Do not withhold it.
Do not put off what you can do today; you will make
   your day poorer. Tomorrow may be too late.
Help is help only when it is needed, not when it suits me
   to offer it.
Postponing means not taking seriously the last decision
   of *death*.
Each request may be the last decision about us.
We often justify ourselves with planned good deeds.
We seem righteous to ourselves because we are ready to
   do good, but it all comes down to doing it.

THE MEANING OF HUMAN
RELATIONSHIPS

There is hardly a more gratifying feeling than to sense that one can be something for other people. Here it is not at all a question of quantity but of quality. Ultimately, human relationships are simply the most important thing in life. Not even modern "achievers" can do anything about that, nor can those who know nothing of human relationships. Even God himself lets us serve him in human ways. To be sure, an all-too-conscious cultivation of human relationships and "meaning something to each other" can lead to a cult of the human being that is inappropriate to reality. By contrast, I mean here simply the fact that in life human beings are more important to us than everything else. This certainly does not mean a belittling of the world of things and material achievement. But what is the most beautiful book or picture or house or property to me compared with my wife, my parents, or my friend? Naturally, only those who have really found people in their life can speak. Yet for many people today, a human being is only a part of the world of things. That is because the experience of anything human simply does not interest them.

FIRST THE RIGHTS, THEN THE DUTIES

To an *idealistic* way of thinking, it may sound a little odd that a Christian ethic first speaks of rights and only then of duties. But we follow not Kant but the Holy Scripture, and for that very reason we must first speak of the rights of natural life—that is, of what is given to life—and only then of what is required of it. God gives before he demands. In the rights of natural life, it is not the creature but the Creator who is honored, and the wealth of his gifts is recognized. There are no rights before God, but the things given to human beings in nature become their rights. The rights of natural life are the reflection of God's glory as Creator in the midst of the fallen world. They are not simply what people can sue for in their own interest, but what God himself guarantees. The duties, however, spring from the rights themselves, as the tasks do from the gifts. They are included in the rights. Thus, when in the context of natural life we speak first of the rights and then of the duties, we are making room for the gospel in natural life.

THE BASIC STUFF OF TRAGEDY

All alone the person of conscience fends off the over-powering predicament that requires a decision. But the size of the conflicts in which people must choose—advised and supported by nothing other than their own conscience—tears them apart. . . . The certain path of *duty* seems to lead out of the confusing wealth of possible decisions. Here what is commanded is grasped as the most certain; the responsibility for the order is borne by the one who gives the order, not by the one who carries it out. In the limitation to acting in accordance with duty, however, one never ventures a free deed on one's own responsibility, which alone can hit the heart of evil and overcome it. Ultimately people of duty must also render the devil his due by fulfilling their duty. But those who undertake, in their *own freedom* to stand on their own in the world, who value the necessary deed higher than the purity of their own conscience and reputation . . . need to be on guard that the very freedom they assume not finally cause them to fall. They will easily agree to what is bad, knowing well that it is bad, in order to protect against what is worse, and in doing this they may no longer be able to recognize that the worse that they want to avoid can be the better course. Here lies the basic stuff of tragedy.

The Call of Conscience

Responsibility for the neighbor has its limit in the inviolability of the call of conscience. A responsibility that forces one to act against conscience would condemn itself. It can never be advisable to act against one's own conscience. On this all Christian ethics is united. But what does this mean? The conscience is the call—heard from a depth beyond one's own will and one's own reason—of human existence to unity with itself. It appears as a complaint against the loss of unity and as a warning against the loss of self. It is not directed primarily against a certain action but against a certain being. It protests against an action that endangers this being in unity with oneself. In this formal definition, conscience remains an authority against which one is highly ill-advised to act, for the disregard of conscience must have the destruction of one's own being and a disintegration of human existence as its consequence. Action against conscience is akin to suicidal action against one's own life. A responsible action that would do violence to the conscience in this formal sense would indeed be reprehensible.

THE LIBERATED CONSCIENCE

Not a law, but the living God and living human beings, as I meet them in Jesus Christ, are the origin and focus of my conscience. For the sake of God and humankind, Jesus became the One who broke through the law: he broke the Sabbath law in order to hallow it in love for God and human beings. He left his parents in order to be in the house of his Father and thus to purify his obedience to his parents. He ate with sinners and rejects. And out of love for humankind he fell into godforsakenness in his last hour. As the one who loved sinlessly, he wanted to stand in the fellowship of human guilt. Thus Jesus Christ is the one who liberates the conscience for service to God and neighbor, who also liberates the conscience where human beings enter into the fellowship of human guilt. The conscience liberated from the law will not shy away from entering into foreign guilt for the sake of other people, but in this very way it will prove itself in its purity. The liberated conscience is not anxious like that bound to the law, but wide open to the neighbor and to the neighbor's need.

Conscience and Concrete Responsibility

Because the law is no longer the last word—but Jesus Christ is—in the disagreement between conscience and concrete responsibility, we must make a free decision for Christ. That does not mean an eternal conflict but the gaining of an ultimate unity. For the basis, essence, and aim of concrete responsibility is indeed the same Jesus Christ who is the Lord of the conscience. Thus responsibility is bound by conscience, but conscience is freed by responsibility. Whether we say that the responsible person becomes guilty without sin, or that only the person with a free conscience can bear responsibility, the result is the same. Those who in responsibility take guilt on themselves—and no responsible person can escape it—credit themselves and no one else with this guilt; they accept it and take responsibility for it. They do this not in frivolous overestimation of their own power but in conscious awareness of this very freedom, which is driven by necessity and puts them in need of grace. Before other human beings, people of free responsibility are justified by the urgency of need. Before themselves, they are set free by their conscience. But before God, they must place all their hope in grace alone.

THE QUEST FOR THE GOOD

Human beings—with all their motives and works, with all their fellow humans, with all the surrounding creation, that is, the reality of the whole held in God— are encompassed by the quest for the good. When "God saw . . . it was very good" (Gen. 1:31), this means the whole of creation. The good demands the whole, not only the whole mind but the whole work, the whole human being and all the fellow human beings we are given. What ever should it mean that only a part is called good—say, the motive—whereas the work is bad or vice versa? *Human beings are an indivisible whole, not only as individuals in their person and their work, but also as members of the community of people and creatures,* in which they stand. This indivisible whole—that is, this reality grounded and recognized in God—is focused on the quest for the good. According to its origin, "creation" means this indivisible whole; according to its aim, it means the kingdom of God. Both are equally distant and equally near, for the creation of God and the kingdom of God are present to us solely in God's self-revelation in Jesus Christ. The quest for the good as the quest for the real is the quest for Jesus Christ.

THE GOOD,
PRELUDE TO THE CHRISTIAN

There is justified feeling against a civil complacency that sees the good as simply a prelude to the Christian, in which the transition from the good to the Christian is supposed to occur more or less without a break. In protest against this comfortable distortion of the gospel, an equally dangerous distortion of the gospel in the opposite sense has been offered to us with great passion. In place of the justification of the good we have the justification of the evil. In the place of the idealization of the civil comes the idealization of the uncivil, the disorderly, the chaotic, the anarchistic, the catastrophic. The divine pardoning love of Jesus to the sinner, the adulteress, the tax collector is distorted to a—psychologically or politically motivated—Christian sanctioning of the uncivil "borderline existence" of the prostitute and the traitor. The gospel of sinners, whose power was at stake, became—without anyone wanting it—a recommendation for sin. The good, in its civil sense, fell victim to laughter.

A MORE DANGEROUS
ENEMY OF THE GOOD

Stupidity is a more dangerous enemy of the good than evil is. Against evil, one can protest; it can be exposed and, if necessary, stopped with force. Evil always carries the seed of its own self-destruction, because it at least leaves people with a feeling of uneasiness. But against stupidity, we are defenseless. Neither with protest nor with force can we do anything here; reasons have no effect. Facts that contradict one's own prejudice only need to be disbelieved—in such cases stupid people even become critical, and when facts are unavoidable, they can simply be swept aside as meaningless isolated cases. Stupid people, in contrast to evil ones, are satisfied with themselves. Indeed, they become dangerous in that they may easily be stimulated to go on the attack. Therefore, more care must be taken in regard to stupidity than to evil. . . .

Closer examination reveals that every strong external development of power, whether of a political or religious nature, strikes a large portion of the people with stupidity. . . .

The biblical saying, "The fear of the LORD is the beginning of knowledge" (Prov. 1:7), says that the internal liberation of people for responsible life before God is the only real way to overcome stupidity.

EVIL, THE INTELLIGENT PERSON, AND RIGHTEOUSNESS

One of the most astounding but at the same time most irrefutable facts is that evil turns out to be—often in a surprisingly short time—stupid and impractical. This does not mean that punishment follows closely on the heels of every individual evil deed, but that the abolishing in principle of the divine commandments in the presumed interest of earthly self-preservation can work against this very interest in self-preservation. . . .

In the abundance of the concrete world and the possibilities it contains, the intelligent know the inviolable boundaries of all action that are given by the prevailing laws of human life together, and in this knowledge the intelligent act in a good way and the good act in an intelligent way. . . .

The world *is* simply so arranged that the fundamental observance of the ultimate laws and rights of life is at the same time the most useful way of self-preservation, and that only in quite short, unique, isolated cases do these laws permit a necessary violation, whereas they will, sooner or later—and with irresistible power—strike down those who turn need into a principle and set up their own law beside these laws. The immanent righteousness of history rewards and punishes only the deed, but the eternal righteousness of God tests and judges the heart.

SIMPLICITY AND INTELLIGENCE

Those who can combine simplicity and intelligence can prevail. But what is simplicity? What is intelligence? How can the two become one? Simple is the one who in the transfiguration, confusion, and twisting of all concepts keeps the simple truth of God in focus, who is not double-minded, not a person with two minds (Jas. 1:8), but has an undivided heart. Because such people have and know God, they hold to the commandments, to the judgment and mercy that daily come anew from the mouth of God. Not enslaved to principles but bound by love for God, they have become free from the problems and conflicts of ethical decision. They are no longer weighed down by them. They belong completely and solely to God and God's will. Because simple people do not look past God to the world, they are in a position to look freely and naturally at the reality of the world. Thus simplicity becomes intelligence. Intelligent is the one who sees reality as it is, who sees the foundation of things. Therefore, only those who see reality in God are intelligent. The perception of reality is not the same thing as the knowledge of external processes; it is, rather, seeing the essence of things. The most intelligent are not those who are the best informed.

Proud Calmness

In Lessing I read a short time ago: "I am too proud to think of myself as unfortunate. Just grit your teeth, and let the boat go where wind and waves want to take it. It is enough that I not want to upset it myself"! Should this pride and this gritting of the teeth be completely forbidden and foreign to Christians? Perhaps in favor of a premature, preventive, mild calmness? Is there not also a proud and teeth-gritting calmness, which, however, is something quite different from the stubborn, impassive, rigid, lifeless, and, above all, thoughtless subjecting of oneself to the inevitable? I believe that God is better honored when we know and use and love the life he has given us in all its worth and therefore also strongly and honestly feel pain when life's worth is damaged or lost (some like to complain about this as the weakness and sensitivity of ordinary existence) than when we are impassive regarding life's worth and hence also impassive against its pain. Job's statement, "The LORD gave, and the LORD has taken away; blessed be the name of the LORD" (Job 1:21b), includes this, rather than excluding it, as is seen clearly enough from his teeth-gritting speeches and their divine justification (Job 42:7–9) compared to the false, premature, pious surrender of his friends.

GOD IS NO STOPGAP

We are supposed to find God in what we know, not in what we don't know. God wants to be understood not in the unanswered but in the answered questions. This is true for the relationship between God and scientific knowledge. But it is also true for general human questions about death, suffering, and guilt. Today these questions also have human answers that can totally ignore God. People are, in fact, dealing with these problems without God, as has always been the case, and it is simply not true that only Christianity has an solution for them. In regard to the concept of "solution," the Christian answers are just as unconvincing—or convincing—as other possible solutions. God is no stopgap. God must be known not at the boundaries of our possibilities but in the midst of life, in life and not just in dying, in health and strength and not just in suffering. God wants to be known in action and not just in sin. The reason for this lies in the revelation of God in Jesus Christ. He is in the midst of life. Seen from the midst of life, certain questions disappear, and so do the answers to such questions.

OPTIMISM

By nature optimism is not a view of the present situation but a living power, the power of hope where others are resigned, the power to hold one's head high when everything seems to be going wrong, the power to bear setbacks, the power never to let the future be the enemy but to lay claim to it for oneself. Certainly, there is also a dumb, cowardly optimism that must be scorned. But optimism as the will to the future should not be disparaged by anyone, even if it is wrong a hundred times. It is the health of life, which the sick are not supposed to infect. There are people who don't take hope and preparation for a better earthly future seriously, and Christians who regard this as less than devout. They believe in chaos, disorder, and catastrophe as the meaning of present events and withdraw in resignation or in pious flight from the world and from responsibility for continued life, for new building, for the coming generations. It may be that doomsday will dawn tomorrow. Then we will be glad to lay aside our work for a better future — but not before then.

SEPTEMBER

THE RECONCILING LOVE OF GOD

Either the Sermon on the Mount
is to be regarded as the word
of the world-reconciling love of God
everywhere and at all times,
or it does not seriously concern us at all.

ACTING IN VICARIOUS RESPONSIBILITY

The New Testament words about Christian action encompassed in the Sermon on the Mount (Matt. 5–7) do not come out of bitter resignation over the incurable rift between the Christian and the secular, but out of joy over the accomplished reconciliation of the world with God, out of the peace of the work of salvation completed in Jesus Christ. As God and humankind became one in Jesus Christ, so through him the Christian and the secular become one in the activity of Christians. They do not quarrel with each other like two eternally hostile principles. Rather, the activity of Christians gushes forth from the unity of God and world created in Christ. . . . It is acting in vicarious responsibility, in love for real people, in taking upon oneself the guilt that lies upon the world. What is "Christian" and what is "secular" are no longer fixed ahead of time. The two are instead comprehended only in their unity in the concrete responsibility of action in light of the unity created in Jesus Christ.

The Sermon on the Mount puts what is required in terms of historical action into the context of the world's reconciliation with God in Jesus Christ, and thus into the context of genuine Christian responsibility. This genuine Christian responsibility encompasses the whole of secular activity. There is no way that it can be limited to some isolated religious realm.

THE CALL OF THE
SERMON ON THE MOUNT

Because the individual is always the one placed in responsibility, the old question—whether the Sermon on the Mount (Matt. 5–7) applies to the individual as individual but not to the individual who is responsible for others—is falsely stated. The Sermon on the Mount itself makes people responsible for others and knows no individual only as an individual. It is not satisfied, however, with preparing individuals for their duty in the community; it also lays claim to individuals in their responsible activity itself. It calls them to love that proves itself in acting responsibly toward the neighbor, to love whose origin is the love of God that encloses in itself the whole of reality. Just as there is no limiting the love of God for the world, so also the human love that springs from God's love is not limited to certain areas and relationships of life. Either the Sermon on the Mount is to be regarded as the word of the world-reconciling love of God everywhere and at all times, or it does not seriously concern us at all. . . . The crucifixion of Jesus Christ is the most compelling proof that God's love is at all times equally close and equally distant. Jesus died because God loved the whole world. And in this same love—sealed by the cross of Jesus—we are called into the whole world.

The Decalogue and the Sermon on the Mount

The Decalogue and the Sermon on the Mount are not two different ethical ideals but the *one* call to concrete obedience to the God and Father of Jesus Christ. When in faith in God the institution of property is affirmed and responsibility is taken for it, nothing takes place other than what happens when, in faith in God, property is renounced. Neither the "battle for rights" nor the "renunciation of rights" is anything in itself—a part of the church's proclamation, for example—but in faith both are put under God's sole law. Thus, there is no two-part table of values for the world and for Christians. There is only the *one* word of God requiring faith and obedience that is valid for all people. It would also be wrong in proclamation to the world to emphasize more strongly the battle for rights but in proclamation to the church to stress the renunciation of rights. *Both* apply to world and to church. The assertion that one cannot govern with the Sermon on the Mount comes from a misunderstanding of the Sermon on the Mount. Even a ruling state can, fighting and renouncing, honor God, and this is what the proclamation of the church is all about. It is never the task of the church to preach to the state the natural drive for self-preservation, but only obedience to the law of God.

THE GOSPEL FOR THE POOR

How does a gospel that is brought to the weak, the ignoble, the poor, and the sick (Luke 16:19–31) concern us?

. . . Isn't it downright cynical when we speak of heavenly comfort because we don't want to give earthly comfort? Isn't this gospel for the poor basically a deception and a brainwashing of the people? Doesn't it show that basically the misery is not taken at all seriously, but rather is cynically hidden behind pious phrases? Oh, it has happened untold times — who would deny it? — even in our own time. But one look into the Gospels shows us what is different here. Jesus calls the poor blessed (Luke 6:20). . . . Not a cynical putting off, but the one great hope: the new world, the happy news, the merciful God, Lazarus in the bosom of Abraham, the poor and rejected with God — which indeed may sound frightfully naive and tangible. But what if it nevertheless were true? What if it nevertheless *is* true? Is it then still naive? Is it then still unspiritual? Must we not then open our ears, and hear, and hear again of the unheard-of event that Lazarus — yesterday and today — is carried by angels to the bosom of Abraham? And that the one who is sated, who is full, who lives gloriously and joyfully, the rich man, must suffer eternal thirst?

How Do We See God?

We all know that there are times in life when we grow tired of ourselves, when we become disgusted with ourselves, when we see all the wretchedness and weakness of our way of life. . . . And it is the blessing of such times that in them there breaks through a longing for the face of God, for seeing God. Those who don't know these times, who don't know this longing, won't understand much of what Jesus has to say to us today. Now, like the individual person, the whole world experiences times in which, out of godlessness and godforsakenness, it cries out for the face of God. All of ancient Judaism is one single such cry: "When shall I come and behold the face of God?" (Ps. 42:2). Socrates and Plato, Kant and German philosophy — they all agree in this call. And also in our time the old question resounds: How do we see God? . . . Into these questions comes the saying of Jesus: "Blessed are the pure in heart, for they will see God" (Matt. 5:8). Nothing, absolutely nothing else, enables us to see God except a pure heart, the purity of our being.

MAKERS OF DIVINE PEACE

"Blessed are the peacemakers, for they will be called children of God" (Matt. 5:9). Jesus' followers are called to peace. As Jesus called them, they found their peace. Jesus is their peace. Now they are not only to have peace, but also to create it. This means they *renounce violence and revolution*. These have never helped the cause of Christ. The kingdom of Christ is a kingdom of peace, and members of the church of Christ greet each other with the passing of the peace and the kiss of peace. The disciples of Jesus keep the peace because they would rather suffer themselves than cause others suffering. They preserve fellowship where others break it; they renounce self-assertion and are not provoked by hate and injustice. Thus they overcome evil with good (Rom. 12:21). Thus they are makers of divine peace in the midst of a world of hate and war. Nowhere, however, will their peace be greater than where they meet evildoers in peace and are ready to suffer from them. The peacemakers will carry the cross with their Lord, for peace was made on the cross (Eph. 2:14–16). Because they are thus drawn into Christ's work of peace and called to the work of the Son of God, they themselves will therefore be called children of God.

PEACE ON EARTH

Peace on earth (Luke 2:14) is not a problem but a commandment given with the appearance of Christ himself. There are two ways to respond to the commandment: with the unconditional blind obedience of action or with the hypocritical question of the snake: "Did God say . . . ?" (Gen. 3:1). This question is the mortal enemy of obedience and is therefore the mortal enemy of every genuine peace. Shouldn't God have known human nature better and known that wars must happen in this world, like laws of nature? Did God perhaps mean that we should speak well of peace but not translate it literally into action? Should God have said that we may well work for peace, but for security we should have tanks and poison gas ready? And then the seemingly most serious question: Could God have said, you shall not protect your people? Could God have said, you should turn your neighbor over to the enemy? No, God did not say any of that; he said that there is to be peace among people and that we are to obey him before any further questions, and that's what he meant. Those who call God's commandment into question before obeying it have already denied him.

THE RISK OF PEACE

There is no path to peace by way of security. For peace must be risked. Peace is the opposite of security. Demanding security means having mistrust, and this mistrust gives birth again to war. Seeking security means wanting to protect oneself. Peace means giving oneself totally to the commandment of God, wanting no security. It means in faith and obedience to almighty God placing the history of the nations in God's hands and not selfishly wanting to control it oneself. Battles are not won with weapons but with God. . . .

How does peace come about? Who can issue the call to peace so that this world will hear it, indeed will be forced to hear it, so that all nations have to be happy about it? Individual Christians cannot do it. While all others keep silent, they may well raise their voices and bear witness, but the powers of the world can silently walk away. The individual church can also bear witness and suffer—oh, if they would only do that—but they too are overwhelmed by the power of hate. Only the one *great ecumenical council of the holy church of Christ* from all the world can say it so that the world must grit its teeth, hear the word of peace, and make the nations happy, because the church of Christ in the name of Christ takes the weapons out of the hands of their sons and daughters and forbids them to fight, and calls out the peace of Christ over the raging world.

PEACE WITH EVERYONE

According to the commandment of love (Matt. 22:37–39), we Christians are instructed that we should have peace with everyone, as Christ exemplified when he preached peace to the community, peace with one's brother and sister, with one's neighbor, with the Samaritan. Unless we have this peace, we cannot preach peace to the nations. And most of those who are bothered by the saying about the peace of the nations are already calling into question the love of enemies in regard to a personal enemy. So, when we speak of the things of peace, we will always keep in mind that relationships between two nations have a deep analogy with relationships between two individual people. The things that work against peace in both cases are the desire for power, pride, the drive for fame and honor, arrogance and feelings of inferiority, fear of people, and then quarreling over living space and bread. But what is sin for the individual person is never virtue for a nation. What is proclaimed to the church, to the congregation, and thus to the individual Christian as gospel is said to the world in judgment. But when a nation does not want to hear this commandment, then Christians are called out of this nation as witnesses. We must take care, however, that as miserable sinners we proclaim peace out of love and not out of zeal for security or for a political goal.

THE CALL FOR PEACE

With elementary power, the call for peace breaks through again and again in humankind: it was heard for the first time powerfully and strongly in the ancient prophets, and now again in recent times it is everywhere in the longing for world peace. But as beautiful and seriously intended as all these hopes are, they do not recognize that the peace we need is the peace that comes down from eternity, the peace of God with human beings, with every single one of us. . . .

Having peace means knowing oneself borne, knowing oneself loved, knowing oneself protected; it means being able to be still, quite still. Having peace with people means being able to build unshakably on their faithfulness; it means knowing oneself at one with them, knowing oneself forgiven by them. Having peace means having a homeland in the unrest of the world; it means having solid ground under one's feet. Though the waves may now rage and break, they can no longer rob me of my peace. My peace has made me free from the world, made me strong against the world, made me ready for the other world. But the fact that we are to have such peace with God is something that goes beyond all human comprehension, beyond all reason.

A Peace That Is Higher
than All Reason

The peace of God is a peace that is higher than all reason. . . . The peace of God is the faithfulness of God in spite of our unfaithfulness. In the peace of God we are enclosed, protected, and loved. God does not, to be sure, take away our cares, our responsibility, our unrest completely, but behind all the bustle and care the divine rainbow of peace has risen. We know our life is borne and in unity with the eternal life of God. We know that the rift we have to feel painfully again and again is only an ever renewed indication that God has closed the rift, that he has drawn us into his life as we are, as people of the earth, as people with hearts and minds. In the language of the Bible, that means dealing with the passions and needs, with the impressions of the world. May the peace of God, which surpasses all understanding, keep our hearts and minds in Christ Jesus (Phil. 4:7). May God control our passion; may he discipline our thoughts and our wills and lead us to the peace of Jesus Christ, who has spoken, who has given himself to us in the night on Golgotha: "Peace I leave with you; my peace I give to you. I do not give to you as the world gives. Do not let your hearts be troubled, and do not let them be afraid" (John 14:27).

BEING AN OFFENSE TO THE WORLD

"Blessed are those who are persecuted for righteousness' sake, for theirs is the kingdom of heaven" (Matt. 5:10). This is not about the righteousness of God but about suffering for a just cause, for the sake of the righteous judgment and action of the disciples of Jesus. Judgment and action will distinguish those who follow Jesus in renouncing property, fortune, right, righteousness, honor, and power from the world. They become an offense to the world. For this reason, the disciples are persecuted for righteousness' sake. Not recognition but rejection is the world's reward for their word and work. It is important that Jesus also blesses his disciples when they suffer not directly for the sake of the confession of his name, but for the sake of a just cause. They are given the same promise as the poor. As the persecuted, they are indeed like the poor.

THE DIVINE SALT

"You are the salt of the earth" (Matt. 5:13). The addressees are those who in the Beatitudes (Matt. 5:1–12) are called into the grace of the discipleship of the crucified one. Previously the blessed were worthy of heaven but at the same time apparently had to appear on this earth as totally without value and superfluous. Now they are called the symbol of a good thing that is indispensable on earth. They are the salt of the earth. They are the noblest good, the highest value that the earth possesses. Without them the earth cannot live. The earth is maintained by salt, and for the sake of these very poor, ignoble, and weak, whom the world rejects, the earth lives. It destroys its own life by kicking out the disciples, and—miraculously—precisely for the sake of these rejects, the earth is permitted to live. This "divine salt" proves itself in its effectiveness. It permeates the whole earth. It is its substance. Thus the disciples are not only oriented toward the kingdom of heaven but are reminded of their mission on earth. As those bound to Jesus alone, they are directed to the earth, whose salt they are. When Jesus calls his disciples—not himself—the salt, he is transferring to them his effectiveness on earth. He is including them in his work.

THAT STRANGE LIGHT

Jesus said, "Let your light shine before others" (Matt. 5:16). Naturally, it is the light of the call of Jesus that shines there. But just what kind of a light is that? . . . The good works of the disciples are supposed to be seen in *this* light. People are supposed to see not you, but your good works, says Jesus. What are these good works that can be seen in this light? It can be no works except those that Jesus himself created in the disciples when he called them, when he made them the light of the world under his cross — poverty, gentleness, peacefulness, being a stranger, and finally being persecuted and rejected, and in all of that, bearing the cross of Jesus Christ. The cross is that strange light, the only light that shines where all these good works of the disciples can be seen. In all of this, there is no talk that God becomes visible, but that the "good works" are seen, and the people give glory to God for these works.

THE OATH AND THE LIE

What is an oath (Matt. 5:33–37)? It is a public appeal to God as witness for a statement that I make about something past, present, or future. . . . The oath is the proof of lies in the world. If people could not lie, oaths would not be necessary. Thus, if the oath is a dam against lies, but therefore also promotes them, then where the oath alone claims ultimate truth, the lie is also given room to live and is granted a certain right to life. The Old Testament law rejects the lie through the oath. But Jesus rejects the lie through the prohibition of the oath. . . .

Let your word be "Yes, yes" or "No, no." This does not remove the words of the disciples from responsibility before the all-knowing God. Rather, the very fact that there is no expressed appeal to the name of God means that every word from a disciple is spoken in the understood presence of the all-knowing God. Because there is absolutely no word that is not spoken before God, the disciples of Jesus should, therefore, not swear an oath at all. All of their words should be nothing but the truth, so that none of them require swearing for confirmation. The swearing of an oath puts all of their other words in the darkness of doubt.

TO TELL THE TRUTH

From the time in our lives when we gain the power of language, we are taught that our words must be true. What does that mean? What does it mean "to tell the truth"? . . .

Telling the truth is not just a matter of convictions but also of the proper perception and serious consideration of real conditions. The more complicated people's living conditions are, the more responsible and difficult it is for them "to tell the truth." . . .

Thus, telling the truth must be learned. This sounds horrifying for those who believe that they only have to have convictions, and if these are faultless, everything else is child's play. Since it is true, however, that the ethical cannot be replaced by reality, an ever closer acquaintance with reality is a necessary component of ethical action. In the question that now concerns us, however, the action consists in speaking. *The real is supposed to be expressed in words.* This is what makes speech that is in accord with reality. With this, however, the question of the "how" of the word cannot be avoided. It's always a question of the "right word." To find it is a matter of long, earnest, and ever better effort on the basis of one's experience and perception of the real.

THE APPEARANCE AND ESSENCE OF TRUTH

In order to say how something is real, that is, to speak truthfully, one's views and thoughts must be directed toward what is real in God and through God and for God.

Every word that I speak is governed by the requirement to be true. Quite apart from the truthfulness of its content, the relationship that it expresses between me and another person is already true or untrue. I can flatter, I can be arrogant, or I can be a hypocrite, without speaking a material untruth, and my word will still be untrue, because I am undermining and destroying the truth of the relationship of husband and wife, of superior and subordinate, and so forth. The individual word is always part of a total reality that comes to expression in words. Depending on whom I am speaking to, by whom I am asked, about what I am speaking, my words must vary if they are to be truthful. The truthful word is not something that is constant in itself. Rather, it is as alive as life itself. When it is separated from life and relationships with particular other people, when "the truth is told" without considering the person to whom I am telling it, then it has the appearance but not the essence of truth.

EVERY WORD HAS ITS PLACE

Every word is alive and is at home in a certain place. The word in the family is different from the word in the office or in public. The word that is born in the warmth of personal relationship freezes in the cold air of the public. The word of command, which comes out of public service, would cut the bonds of trust in the family. Every word is supposed to have its place and stay in it. As a consequence of the spread of the public word in newspapers and radio, the nature and boundaries of various words are no longer felt clearly, and indeed the special character of the personal word has been almost destroyed. In place of genuine words, we now have chatter. Words no longer have any weight. There is too much talk. When the boundaries of various words are erased, however, when words become rootless and homeless, then the word loses truth, and this almost necessarily gives rise to the lie. When the various conventions of life are no longer mutually observed, then words become untrue.

THE CONTRADICTION BETWEEN THINKING AND SAYING

The usual definition of a lie, according to which it is a conscious contradiction between thinking and speaking, is totally inadequate. This would include, for example, even the most harmless April Fools' Day joke. . . . Now, if one says that lying is the conscious deception of another to the latter's harm, this would also include, for example, the necessary deception of an enemy in war or analogous situations. . . . If one designates such behavior as lying, then this gives the lie a moral sanctity and justification that the concept contradicts in every way. From this we must conclude that the lie is not to be formally defined as a contradiction between thought and word. This contradiction is not even a necessary component of a lie. There is a kind of speech that in this respect is correct and unassailable, yet is a lie: for example, when a notorious liar tells "the truth" to lead one astray, or when a conscious ambiguity sleeps under the appearance of correctness or a decisive truth is consciously concealed. Even conscious silence can be a lie, though silence might not otherwise be a lie.

THE NATURE OF THE LIE

The nature of the lie is found much deeper than in the contradiction between thought and word. One could say that the person who stands behind the word makes it a lie or the truth. But even this is not enough, for a lie is something objective and must be defined in this way. Jesus calls Satan the "father of lies" (John 8:44). Lying is, first of all, the denial of God as he has shown himself to the world. "Who is the liar but the one who denies that Jesus is the Christ?" (1 John 2:22). A lie is a contradiction of the word of God that he spoke in Christ and upon which the creation rests. Consequently, lying is the negation, the denial, and the knowing and willing destruction of reality as created by God and sustained in God, and this can take place both through words and through silence. Our words have the requirement, in unity with God's word, to assert what is real as it is found in God, and our silence is supposed to be a sign of the boundary that is drawn through what is real as it is found in God.

HOW DOES MY WORD BECOME TRUE?

We find ourselves embedded in various orders of reality, and at the same time our word, which concerns reconciliation and the healing of reality, is repeatedly drawn into the prevailing separation and contradiction. And it can fulfill its requirement to express what is real, as it is found in God, only if it absorbs into itself both the prevailing contradiction and the connection with reality. The human word, if it is to be true, may deny neither the fall through sin nor the creative and reconciling word of God in which all separation is overcome. . . . How does my word become true? By my recognizing who causes me to speak and what entitles me to speak, by my recognizing the place in which I stand, and by my placing the object about which I have something to say into this context. Along with these requirements it is tacitly presupposed that speaking generally occurs under certain conditions; it is not a continuous flow that accompanies the natural course of life, but rather has its time, its place, its commission, and thus its limits.

THE FAILURE OF RATIONAL PEOPLE AND THE FAILURE OF FANATICS

Ethical reality is experienced and recognized not in craftiness, not in knowing all the tricks, but only in simply standing in the truth of God and, in view of it, having an eye that has grown simple and smart. Deeply distressing is the failure of *rational people*, who can see neither the chasm of evil nor the chasm of the holy, who with the best of intentions believe that with a little reason they can reunify a structure that is falling apart. In their lack of vision they want to do justice to both sides and are thus caught in the crossfire between clashing powers, without having accomplished the least bit. . . . Even more distressing is the failure of all ethical *fanaticism*. With the purity of their motives and principles, ethical fanatics believe they can go up against the power of evil. But because it is the nature of fanaticism to lose sight of the whole of evil and like a bull to charge the red cape instead of its bearer, fanatics must ultimately tire and fail. They miss their goal. Whether their fanaticism also serves the high ideal of truth or of justice, they are caught up sooner or later in the trivial and unessential, and in the net of the smarter opponent.

ACTING UNDER GOD'S EYES

The commandment of love is not specifically Christian; in Jesus' time it was already generally recognized and widespread. At first it is remarkable that it occurs only extremely rarely in the Synoptic Gospels. Well known is the passage where Jesus is asked about the greatest commandment and gives the double answer: " 'You shall love the Lord your God . . .' And a second is like it: 'You shall love your neighbor as yourself' " (Matt. 22:37–39). He also speaks of the love of enemy: "Love your enemies" (Matt. 5:44–46). If the proclamation of this commandment had really been the focus of Jesus' entire sermon, he would have started over again at this point, but this is not the case. The situation can also be seen clearly through a comparison of the words of Jesus with the words of Jewish rabbis and pagan philosophers, which are often similar even in their individual formulations. . . . So what now remains of a Christian ethic? Does the Sermon on the Mount really have nothing new to say? Not "new" in the sense of a new demand, but instead something quite different. The sense of all the ethical commandments of Jesus is rather that of saying to humankind: You stand in the presence of God. God's grace rules over you. But you also stand with others in the world. You must act and work so that people can see by your actions that you are acting under the eyes of God, and that God has his will, which he wants to have done.

AND WHO IS MY NEIGHBOR?

The question "And who is my neighbor?"(Luke 10:29) is the last question of despair or self-assurance with which disobedience justifies itself. The answer is: You yourself are the neighbor. Go and be obedient in the act of love. Being a neighbor is not a qualification of others; it is their claim on me, nothing else. At any moment, in any situation, I am the one required to act, to be obedient. There is literally no time left to ask about the qualifications of the other person. I must act and I must obey. I must be the neighbor to others. If you ask me again, alarmed, whether I must not know and consider beforehand how I am to act, then the only answer is that I cannot know or consider things in any way different from the way I have always done; that is, I always know myself as the one who is commanded. I learn what obedience is only by obeying, not by asking questions. Only in obedience do I know the truth. In the dichotomy of conscience and sin, we are met by Jesus' call to the simplicity of obedience. And so the rich man was called by Jesus into the grace of discipleship (Mark 10:21); the testing lawyer was pushed back into the commandment (Luke 10:25–37).

GOD SCOLDS THE PROUD

You scold the proud" (Ps. 119:21, Luther), who are quite satisfied with themselves, who ask about no divine or human law, and for whom mercy is worth nothing. They are despisers of the word of God and the faithful. Pride before God is the root of all disobedience, all violence, all carelessness. Pride is the origin of all outrage, all rebellion, all destruction. Over all pride, however, stands a fearful threat about which the proud comprehend nothing, but the faithful know it: the gospel. "God opposes the proud, but gives grace to the humble" (1 Pet. 5:5). The fact that God is with the weak and humble—in a word, the cross of Jesus Christ—this is the threat of God against the proud. . . . The preaching of the word of God is the only serious threat against a humanity that has become proud. To his word, however, God has added the signs of his power. Here and there in the midst of history, the threat of God is realized, and in this time the church, astonished and shuddering, sees the proud already falling and going to ruin. But it is saved from pharisaical certainty, because it must recognize that innocent people also fall with the proud, and so the visible judgments of God remain hidden and dark even for the faithful.

HAPPINESS AND WELL-BEING

It is God's will that things go well for those who walk in his commandments (Ps. 119:1). It is not the sign of a strong and mature faith when this statement causes us embarrassment, when we say God has greater plans for us than to care for our well-being. There are Christians who want to be more spiritual than God himself. They like to speak of struggle, renunciation, suffering, and cross, but it is almost embarrassing for them that, while the Holy Scripture speaks of those things, it does not speak at all often enough about the good fortune of the pious, the well-being of the righteous. They will probably then say that that is the Old Testament and has been superseded. The true reason for their embarrassment, however, lies in the fact that their hearts are too narrow to grasp the full kindness of God, to honor God also in the abundance of earthly gifts that he shares with those who live in his law. They want to be the schoolmaster of Holy Scripture and thereby deny themselves the full joy of their state as Christians, and fail to give God the thanks they owe for his great kindliness.

RECEIVING FROM THE HAND OF GOD

In the psalms that lament the oppression and suffering of the righteous, it is surprising to note that the praise of God's kindness, which he showers on his own, breaks forth in an especially strong way. The person who prays Psalm 119 has been in misery and temptation. But should not the pious who have fallen in need have special reason to be thankful for all earlier preservation and for each gift that they still have? For "Better is a little that the righteous person has than the abundance of many wicked" (Ps. 37:16). Should not the righteous be the very ones who know that judgment begins with the household of God (1 Pet. 4:17), and that they would have earned nothing but wrath and punishment, if God had wanted to deal with them according to merit and worth? "Happy are . . ." says Psalm 119:1—"Blessed are . . ." says Jesus (Matt. 5:3–12). Luther also translated the same word in this psalm as "blessed" in his first translation of 1521. In the Hebrew it is the same word. Blessed—not because they lack nothing, but because they receive everything out of the hand of God.

OUR LIFE IS NOT THE
MEANS TO AN END

Life is God's bounty. Life is not the means to an end but is fulfillment in itself. God created us so that we may live. He reconciled us and redeemed us so that we may live. . . . Where life itself is turned into an idea, there life, which is really created and redeemed, is more profoundly destroyed than by any other kind of idea. Life is God's aim for us. If it becomes the means to an end, then life steps into a contradiction that makes it a torment. Then the aim, the good, is sought beyond life and can be won only by denying life. . . .

"Deal bountifully with your servant" (Ps. 119:17). Only the life that God gives is bountiful. All other life is torment. Only life in God is goal and fulfillment. Only life in God can overcome the contradiction between what is and what ought to be. Life is a time of grace; death is judgment. Therefore life is God's bounty, because I am given time for the grace of God. Such time is available as long as the word of God is with me. Holding fast to this word is affirmed life from God. The word of God is not beyond life. It does not lower life as the means to an end, but rather protects life from falling into contradiction, into the rule of ideas. God's word is the fulfillment of life, beyond which there is no goal. Therefore I ask God for the bounty of life.

ACTING OUT OF FREEDOM

Christian ethical action is acting out of freedom, out of the freedom of human beings who have nothing in themselves and everything in their God, who ever anew confirms and strengthens his action through eternity. In great words the New Testament speaks of this freedom: "Now the Lord is the Spirit, and where the Spirit of the Lord is, there is freedom" (2 Cor. 3:17). In the Gospel of John we read: "If you continue in my word, you are truly my disciples; and you will know the truth, and the truth will make you free. . . . So if the Son makes you free, you will be free indeed" (John 8:31–32, 36). Christ is the bringer of the freedom to become free from the world and free for eternity. For Christians there is no longer any law but the law of liberty, as it is paradoxically called in the New Testament (Jas. 2:12). There is no generally valid law that can be laid on them by others or that they can lay on themselves. Those who give up freedom, give up their Christianity. Christians stand free before God and before the world without any backing. On Christians alone rests the entire responsibility for how they deal with the gift of freedom. But through this freedom Christians become creative in ethical action.

THE LETTER KILLS, BUT THE
SPIRIT GIVES LIFE

It is the greatest misunderstanding of the commandments of the Sermon on the Mount when one takes them and turns them again into the law, by relating them literally to the present. That is not only a senseless task—because one cannot carry it out—but it is also against the spirit of Christ, who brought freedom from the law. In the New Testament there is no ethical prescript that we literally have to adopt or even could adopt. As Paul famously said (2 Cor. 3:6), "the letter kills, but the Spirit gives life," which means that there is Spirit only in the completion of an action, in the present. The fixed Spirit is no longer the Spirit. So also, there is ethics only in the performance of the deed, not in letters, that is, in the law. But the Spirit that is at work in our ethical action is supposed to be the Holy Spirit. The Holy Spirit exists only in the present, in the ethical decision, not in the fixed moral prescript or in the ethical principle. Therefore, the new commandments of Jesus can never be comprehended as new ethical principles; in their spirit they are not to be understood literally. And that is not an excuse, because things would otherwise be too uncomfortable. Rather, it is required by the idea of freedom and Jesus' idea of God.

OCTOBER

HEAR THE GOSPEL!

We have no more time
for solemn church festivals
in which we present ourselves
to ourselves.
Let us not celebrate the Reformation
this way anymore!
Let the late Luther finally have his rest.
Hear the gospel.
Read his Bible, and
listen there to the very word of God.

Your Steadfast Love Is Better than Life

What is life?
Everything we see, touch, hear, taste, feel;
everything that surrounds us, that we possess,
that we are used to, that we love.
What is God's love?
Everything we do not see,
do not touch, do not understand,
indeed, can hardly believe;
it is something we do not possess,
something quite mysterious, out of this world,
something above and behind everything that happens,
and yet something so intimate, so earnestly exciting.
Who would want to choose here?
It is God's love that wins the victory,
and like something humanly impossible,
we hear it from the lips of the psalmist:
"O God, you are my God . . .
your steadfast love is better than life" (Ps. 63:1, 3).

THE ANSWER TO OUR QUESTIONS

I believe that the Bible alone is the answer to all our questions and that we only need to ask constantly, and with a little humility, to get the answer from Scripture. We cannot simply *read* the Bible like other books. We must be ready to really question it. Only in that way will it open itself. Only when we expect the ultimate answer from it, will the Bible give us that answer. This is due precisely to the fact that in the Bible God is speaking to us. And we cannot simply meditate about God on our own. We must instead question him. Naturally, one can *also* read the Bible like any other book, that is, from the standpoint of text criticism and so on. But that is the usage that does not unlock the essence of the Bible but only its surface. We don't understand the words of a person we love by first dissecting them, but rather by simply receiving such words and letting them echo within us all day long . . . this is how we should treat the words of the Bible. Only when we dare to deal with the Bible in this way, as if here God is really speaking to us, loving us, and does not want to leave us alone with our questions—only then will we find joy in the Bible.

A FOREIGN PLACE IN EVERY WAY

The whole Bible claims to be the word in which God wants us to find him. It's not a place that is pleasant or initially insightful for us, but rather a place that is foreign to us in every way, one that is completely contrary to us. Yet it is the very place where God has chosen to meet us. Now this is how I read the Bible: I ask of each passage, What is God saying to us here? And I ask God to show us what he wants to say. Thus we are no longer *permitted* at all to look for general, eternal truths that correspond to our own "eternal" nature and are to be made evident as such. Rather, we seek the will of God, which is quite foreign and contrary to us—"For my thoughts are not your thoughts, nor are your ways my ways, says the LORD" (Isa. 55:8)— and which is hidden from us under the sign of the cross, where all our ways and thoughts find their end. God is something completely different from so-called *eternal* truth. For that is still the eternity that *we* conceive and wish for. . . . Thus nothing remains except the decision whether or not we want to trust the word of the Bible, whether we want to let ourselves be held by it, as by no other word in life and in death. And I believe we will not be able to find true happiness and peace until we have made this decision.

ANCIENT MATERIAL

That the Bible is the word of God, and a religious poem by Nietzsche is not, is the unsolvable mystery of God's hidden revelation. The biblical text as such, however, binds together the whole Christian church as a unit. It assures us of our family unity not only with the church of Christ of all ages past and future, but also with the entire present-day church. As such, the biblical text is of tremendous unifying, ecumenical importance. This is to be understood not only objectively but also psychologically (unit-unity). The awareness of family unity, however, is clearly reinforced in the hearers of the biblical text, so that they receive everything they—in their deepest knowledge and experience—encounter in such a text as the ancient material of Christian thinking and living, and they thankfully and reverently listen and learn.

The Holy History of God on Earth

The ongoing reading of biblical books forces all who want to hear to commit themselves, to let themselves be found where God acted once and for all for the salvation of human beings. It is precisely in reading in worship that the historical books of the Holy Scripture become quite new for us. We become a part of what once happened for our salvation. Forgetting and losing ourselves, we join in the passage through the Red Sea, through the wilderness, over the Jordan, and into the promised land. With Israel we fall into doubt and disbelief, and through punishment and penance we experience again God's help and faithfulness—and all of that is not dreaming but holy, divine reality. We are torn from our own existence and placed in the middle of the holy history of God on earth. There God acted for us, and there he still acts today for us, for our needs and our sins, through wrath and grace. The important thing is not that God is the observer and participant in our lives today, but that we are the devoted listeners and participants in God's action in holy history, in the history of Christ on earth. And only when we are present in this history is God also present with us today.

WE BECOME ACQUAINTED WITH OUR OWN HISTORY

God's help and presence do not have to be proven in our lives, for God's help and presence have been proven in the life of Jesus Christ. It is indeed more important for us to know what God did in Israel and what he did in his son Jesus Christ than to find out what God has planned for me today. That Jesus Christ died is more important than the fact that I will die, and that Jesus Christ was raised from the dead is the only ground of my hope that I too will be raised on the last day. Our salvation is "outside of ourselves," and I will find it not in my life history but solely in the history of Jesus Christ. Only those who let themselves be found in Jesus Christ, in his incarnation, his cross, and his resurrection, are with God, and God with them. On this basis the whole reading of the Holy Scripture in worship becomes more meaningful and healing for us every day. What we call our life, our needs, and our guilt are not reality at all, for in the Scripture are our life, our need, our guilt, and our redemption. Because it has pleased God to act for us there, we will therefore be helped only there. Only in the Holy Scripture do we become acquainted with our own history.

NOT OUR OWN HEART BUT GOD'S WORD DECIDES

The God of Abraham, Isaac, and Jacob is the God and Father of Jesus Christ and our God. We must once again become acquainted with the Holy Scripture, as the Reformers knew it, as our fathers knew it. We must not be afraid to spend the time and effort required. We must become familiar with the Scripture first of all for the sake of our salvation. Yet there are many other important reasons for us to make this requirement very urgent. How are we supposed, for example, to achieve certainty and confidence in our actions in our personal life and in the church, if we do not stand on solid scriptural ground? Not our own heart but God's word decides our path. But who today still knows, for example, what is right about the necessity of scriptural proof? How often, in laying the foundation of the most important decisions, do we hear untold arguments "from life" and from "experience," but without scriptural proof—precisely where it would perhaps point in the exact opposite direction? It's no wonder that those who try to bring scriptural proof into discredit are the ones who themselves do not seriously read, know, and research the Scripture. Yet those who do not want to learn how to work independently with the Scripture are not Protestant Christians.

KNOWING AND SEEING

I must close the eyes of my mind if I want to see what God is showing me. God makes me blind when he wants to have me see his word (Ps. 119:18). . . . It is a new prayer daily, when we open our eyes in the morning and when we close them at night, that God will give us enlightened eyes of the heart that stay open when the day tries to deceive our natural eyes and when the night deludes us into evil dreams—open, enlightened eyes that are always filled with the wonders of the law of God. . . . When God opens our eyes for his word, we see into a world of miracles. What previously appeared dead to me is full of life, what was contradictory resolves itself in higher unity, and the hard demand becomes the graceful commandment. In the middle of human words I hear God's eternal word; in past history I perceive the present God and his work for my salvation. Merciful words of comfort become a new demand of God; the unbearable burden becomes a gentle yoke. The great miracle in the law of God is the revelation of the Lord Jesus Christ. Through him the Word receives life, what is contradictory gains unity, and what is obvious acquires unfathomable depth. Lord, open my eyes.

FREEDOM IN THE LANGUAGE OF THE BIBLE

In the language of the Bible freedom is not something that we have for ourselves, but something that we have for others. No one has freedom "in itself," that is, in a vacuum, as it were, as one can be musical, intelligent, or blind in itself. Freedom is not a human quality, not some capability, situation, or trait to be discovered deep inside. If we were to examine a person for freedom, we would not find a trace of it. Why? Because freedom is not a quality that can be discovered, not a possession, not something present, something objective, nor is it a form for something present, because freedom is a relationship and nothing else. And it is a relationship between two people. Being free means "being free for others," because others are connected with me. Only in relationship with others am I free. . . . That is the message of the gospel itself: that God's freedom has bound itself to us, that his free grace becomes real only in us, that God does not want to be free for himself, but for human beings.

The Waiting Human Being

"Blessed are those slaves whom the master finds alert when he comes" (Luke 12:37). We live in an age of worldviews. It's already a question of worldview as to how one dresses, how one eats, how one exercises. And seldom have people been so bound, so doctrinaire, so intolerant about their worldviews as today. Now one can naturally smile about all these phenomena and withdraw with an air of superiority. And yet such smiling is not good. It shows that one has not understood what is at stake in these things that seem so curious. And there is doubtless a single great theme around which all our worldview thinking moves. And that is the future of humankind. . . . Whether one thinks of human beings as political beings, as ethical beings, as intellectual beings, as religious beings, as fighting beings, or as peacemakers, there is basically only one great concern, about the human beings of the future. . . .

And now it seems as if the Bible, in this effort to create a new kind of human being, also wants to say something, as if it is proposing its own ideal of the human being who is supposed to meet the future. It is not speaking about the political, not about the ethical, not even about the religious human being, but rather about the human being who is watching and waiting, the waiting human being.

THE SEED IN THE FIELD

When God's word comes to us, it wants to take root in a fertile field. It does not want to remain lying on the path. . . . It does not want to fall among thorns, where it is "choked by the cares and riches and pleasures of life" and bears no fruit (Luke 8:11–15). It is a great wonder that the eternal word of almighty God seeks a dwelling place in me, that it wants to take root in me, like the seed in the field. God's saying is held not in my mind but in my heart (Ps. 119:11). Not to be thought to pieces but to be moved in the heart, as the word of a beloved person lives in our heart, even if we do not consciously think about it: that is the aim of the saying that comes from the mouth of God. If I have God's word only in my mind, then my mind is often busy with other things, and I will transgress against God. Therefore, it is never enough to have read God's word; it must penetrate deep within us, live in us, as in the holy of holies in a shrine, so that we do not go astray in thought, word, and deed. It is often better to read a little and slowly in the Scripture and to wait until it has penetrated our heart, rather than to know a lot about God's word, but not have it take root within us.

REDISCOVERED UNITY

Even to someone who reads the New Testament only superficially, it must be striking that here the world of separation, conflict, and ethical difficulties has faded away. The New Testament speaks not of people at odds with God, with other people, with things, with themselves, but of rediscovered unity. Reconciliation is the foundation of what is said. The life and activity of people is not about something problematical, tormented, dark, but something natural, joyful, certain, clear. It is in Jesus' encounter with the Pharisees that the old and the new are seen the clearest. The proper understanding of this encounter is of great importance for the understanding of the gospel as a whole. Jesus' encounter with the Pharisees is not about an accidental, historically transient phenomenon, but about people in whose whole lives only the knowledge of good and evil has become important. Every distorted image of the Pharisees robs Jesus' exchange with them of its seriousness and importance. The Pharisee is to the highest degree an admirable person, who places his whole life under the knowledge of good and evil and who is just as hard a judge of himself as of his neighbor—to the honor of God, whom he humbly thanks for this knowledge.

THE PHARISEES

For the Pharisee every moment in life becomes a conflict situation in which one must choose between good and evil. To avoid falling, he applies all of his mind day and night to thinking through in advance the infinite number of possible conflicts, bringing them to a decision, and determining his own choice. Life in all its multiplicity is completely drawn into calculations, and special situations and emergencies receive special consideration. . . . These men, with their unimpeachable and distrustful look, cannot meet other people without testing them about their decisions in life's conflicts. So when they met Jesus, they can act no differently than to try to drive him into conflict, too, into alienation, to see how well he survives. . . . Now, the crucial point in all of these confrontations consists in Jesus not letting himself be drawn into a single one of these conflict decisions. With each of his answers he simply left the conflict case beneath him. The Pharisees and Jesus are speaking on completely different levels. Therefore, they so strangely talk past each other; so Jesus' answers appear not to be answers at all, but his own attacks against the Pharisees, which they in fact are.

DID GOD SAY . . . ?

What was played out between Jesus and the Pharisees is only a repetition of that first temptation of Jesus (Matt. 4:1–11), in which the devil tries to bring him a dichotomy in God's word and which Jesus overcame through his essential unity with the word of God. This temptation of Jesus in turn has its prelude in the question with which the snake in paradise brings Adam and Eve to the fall: "Did God say . . .?" (Gen. 3:1). It is the question that hides within it all separation, against which human beings are powerless, because it is part of their essence. It is the question that cannot be answered, but only overcome from beyond the separation. But ultimately all of these temptations are repeated in the questions in which we also confront Jesus, in which we call to him for a decision in conflict situations, and thus in which we draw Jesus into our questions, conflicts, and separations, and demand from him a solution. In the New Testament there is not a single question that people direct toward Jesus that would be answered by Jesus through getting involved in the human either-or that is intended in each question. . . . Jesus does not allow himself to be called as judge in life's questions; he refuses to let himself be bound to human alternatives: "Friend, who sets me to be a judge or arbitrator over you?" (Luke 12:14).

FREEDOM AND SIMPLICITY
IN ALL DOING

Many times Jesus seems not to understand at all what people are asking him. He seems to be answering something quite different from what he was asked and to be talking past the question and speaking directly and totally to the person asking it. He speaks out of a complete freedom that is no longer bound by the law of logical alternatives. Because Jesus tosses all of the distinctions about which the Pharisees are so conscientiously concerned into a heap . . . because Jesus avoids all the clear questions that try to pin him down, he is, for the Pharisees, a nihilist, a man who knows and follows only his own law, an egotist, a blasphemer of God. Yet no one can perceive in Jesus the uncertainty and anxiety of one who acts arbitrarily, for his freedom gives him and his people something peculiarly certain in their actions, something unquestionable, radiant, overcome, and overcoming. The freedom of Jesus is not the arbitrary choice of numerous possibilities but rather consists precisely in the total simplicity of his action, for which there are never several possibilities, conflicts, alternatives. No, there is always only one, and Jesus calls this one the will of God. He calls doing this will his food (John 4:34). He lives and acts not out of the knowledge of good and evil, but out of the will of God.

HUMAN WORD AND DIVINE WORD

The Christian religion stands or falls with faith in the divine revelation that became real, concrete, and visible in history—though only for those who have eyes to see and ears to hear—and thus bears in its inmost being the quest for the relationship of history and spirit or, applied to the Bible, of letter and spirit, writing and revelation, human word and divine word. . . . We cannot prevent anyone from regarding the Bible as one book among many; indeed, we all must do it, for it, like other books, was written by people. But the historian approaches the Bible exclusively from the standpoint that it is one book among others, though it has admittedly acquired a remarkably much greater importance than others. The history of the Christian religion of almost two thousand years rests on this book as its foundation. It is therefore without doubt one document among others, but one of outstanding historical significance. No wonder, then, that historical criticism found here its first and lasting object of interest and that here it learned to sharpen its weapons to the finest degree.

FRAGMENTS AND RUBBLE

The general principles of historical criticism rest on the scientific-mechanical image of the world, and its epistemological methods are basically those of natural science. Every dogmatic connection is excluded. These are the pillars upon which all historical research rests and must rest. Its perceptions—through the separation in principle of perceiving subject and perceived object—are supposed to be "generally valid" and comprehendible by every rational person. The growing interest in psychology cannot bring any decisive change in the understanding of the Bible. Exemplified in the form of the Bible, this procedure means that the concept of the canon is dissolved and meaningless. Text and literary criticism are applied; the sources are separated; and religious-historical and form-historical methods split up even the smallest text units. After this complete smashing of the text, criticism departs from the field of battle, leaving fragments and rubble, its work seemingly finished.

READING THE BIBLE
WITH HUMAN METHODS

In terms of content, the image of the Bible is leveled to contemporary history. Miracle stories are placed in parallel, and the person of Jesus himself is deprived not only of his divine but even of his human majesty. He then disappears, unrecognizable among the numerous rabbis, wise men, and fanatics. To be sure, thinking historians will also recognize that this book concerns especially strange, profound things, that one glimpses figures of special dimensions, and so on—otherwise they would be poor historians, and just as bad as historians if they believed that with such statements they can prove the Bible as the word of God. . . . There is no historical access to the person of Jesus that would be obligatory for faith. Access to the historical Jesus is possible only through the resurrected One, through the word of the risen Christ witnessing to himself. . . . In addition, we must maintain that the witness of Jesus as the resurrected One is none other than what is passed down to us by the Bible. Even as believing people, we remain sober and objective. We must read this book of books with all human methods. . . . But through the fragile Bible, God meets us as the resurrected One.

GOD DOES NOT WANT
TO FRIGHTEN PEOPLE

The Bible never wants to make us fearful. God does not want people to be afraid—not even of the last judgment. Rather, he wants to let human beings know everything, so that they will know all about life and its meaning. He lets people know even today, so that they may already live their lives openly and in the light of the last judgment. He lets us know solely for one reason: so that we may find the way to Jesus Christ, so that we may turn away from our evil way and try to find him, Jesus Christ. God does not want to frighten people. He sends us the word of judgment only so that we will reach all the more passionately, all the more avidly, for the promise of grace, so that we will know that we cannot prevail before God on our own strength, that before him we would have to pass away, but that in spite of everything he does not want our death, but our life. . . . Christ judges, that is, grace is judge and forgiveness and love—whoever clings to it is already set free.

RELIGIOUS CLOTHING

Again and again, my recent activity, which lies so much in the secular realm, gives me much to think about. I am amazed that for days I can and do live without the Bible—if I were to force myself to it, I would then feel it not as obedience but as autosuggestion. I understand that such autosuggestion can be and is a great help, but I am afraid that in this way I might falsify a genuine experience and in the end not receive genuine help. When I then open the Bible again, it is new and gladdening as never before. I know that I only need to open my own books to hear what I have said against all of this. Also, I don't want to justify myself, but I recognize that "spiritually" I have had much richer times. I feel, however, how resistance is growing within me against everything "religious"—often to an instinctive abhorrence—which is certainly not good, either. I am not of a religious nature. But I must continue to think of God and Christ. I place a lot of value on genuineness, on life, on freedom, and on mercy. It's just that I find the religious clothing so uncomfortable.

THE WORD OF GOD NEEDS NO ORNAMENTATION

The word of God, as it comes to us in the Bible and in the proclamation of the gospel, needs no ornamentation; it is its own ornamentation, its own glory, its own beauty. That is certainly true, but like special human beauty, the word of God cannot escape the ornamentation of those who love it. Yet like any ornamentation of true beauty, the ornamentation of the word of God can consist only in letting its own beauty shine all the more gloriously. Such ornamentation can be nothing foreign, nothing false, nothing that is not genuine, no tawdry finery and no makeup, nothing that conceals its own beauty, but what reveals it and makes it visible.

And there are those who have loved this word of God, as it has gone forth for two thousand years, and who have not let anyone stop them from adding their most beautiful contribution to its ornamentation. But the most beautiful could even be something invisible, namely, nothing other than an obedient heart.

GOD NEEDS THE WHOLE HEART

Those who have received God's word must begin to seek God. They can do no other. . . . We can seek God nowhere except in his word, but this word is alive and inexhaustible, for God himself lives in it. If God's word has found us, then we can say: "*With my whole heart* I seek you" (Ps. 119:10). For with half a heart we would seek an idol, but never God himself. God needs the whole heart. He does not want *something* from us. Instead, he wants *us ourselves*, all of us. His word tells us that. Therefore we seek him with our whole heart. There is only one worry left for us: that we will stray from the way we have begun, from the commandments we have heard. When in prayer we say "stray," we are not thinking of an intentional, willful violation of known divine commandments. But how easily we err when evil fogs our vision. We go astray and no longer know up from down or how to find our way back to the commandments of God. We must ask God daily to preserve us from the sin of straying, from unknowing sin (Num. 15:22–28), for if we ever stray unknowingly onto the path of evil, then we often quickly come to enjoy this path, and straying becomes evil intention. But those who seek God with their whole heart will not go astray.

LOVE IS PATIENT

There is no one who lives without love. Everyone has love; we know about its power and its passion. We even know that this love makes up the whole meaning of our life. . . . But this love whose power, passion, and meaning everyone knows is *the love of human beings for themselves*. . . . This self-love sets itself up as love of neighbor, as love of the homeland, as social love, as love of people, and does not want to be recognized. Paul calls self-love to responsibility by sketching before it and before us the image of the love that counts before God. . . . *"Love is patient; love is kind . . ."* (1 Cor. 13:4–7). Love, that is, can wait, wait a long time, wait until the end. It never becomes impatient; it never wants to hurry things up and force them. It deals with long periods of time. Waiting, having patience, continuing to love and be kind, even where it seems entirely to miss the mark—this alone wins people over; this alone breaks the bonds that chain every person, the chains of human fear and anxiety about a radical change, about a new life. Kindness often seems so completely inappropriate, *but love is patient and kind*. It waits, as one waits for those who have gone astray, waits and rejoices when they still come at all.

LOVE WANTS CLEAR RELATIONSHIPS

Love does not bear a grudge. It approaches others anew each day and with new love, and it forgets what has past. In this way it makes itself a fool and the object of people's mockery, but this does not drive it crazy—it just continues to love.

Is love then indifferent to right and wrong? No, it does *not* rejoice in wrongdoing, but rejoices in truth. It wants to see things the way they are. It would rather see hate and wrong and lies clearly, than all kinds of masks of friendliness, which serve only to conceal the hate and make it even more hateful. Love wants to create and see clear relationships. It rejoices over truth, for only in truth can it love anew.

"It bears all things, believes all things, hopes all things, endures all things" (1 Cor. 13:7). Here it all depends on this *all things*; it is uncompromising—*all things* here really means *everything*. Perhaps we say sometimes in a grand moment, "I will do everything for you; I will leave everything for you; I will bear everything with you"—yet in this there is always a big, tacit presupposition: if you will do the same for me. This presupposition is unknown to love. Love's everything has no condition: it is unconditionally *all things*.

WHAT IS REALLY LEFT?

If we ask ourselves in disturbing times what is really left, ultimately, of the back and forth of thoughts and reflections, of all the worries and fears, of all the wishes and hopes that we have, and if we want the Bible to give us the answer, then it will tell us: from all of that, there is ultimately only one thing—namely, love—that we have had in our thoughts, worries, wishes, and hopes. Everything else ends, passes away. Everything we have not thought and longed for out of love—all ideas, all knowledge, all speech—ceases without love. *Only love never ends* (1 Cor. 13:8). . . .

Why must all else cease? Why does love alone never end? Because only in love do people give up themselves and sacrifice their own will for others. Because only love comes not out of my own self, but out of another self, out of God's self. Because, therefore, in love God himself is acting through us, whereas in everything else we ourselves are acting: it is *our thoughts, our speech, our knowledge,* but it is God's love. Everything that is from us must cease—everything—but what is from God remains.

WE KNOW ONLY IN PART

Love wants entry into the world of our thoughts and knowledge. Knowledge is the most like love. It too has others as its object and is directed toward others. It wants to grasp and understand and explain the world and people and the mysteries of God. . . . There are big questions on which we all want to try our knowledge and with which we also quickly learn the boundaries of our knowledge: What is our own way? What are the ways of other people? And what is God's way that goes behind all human ways? . . . All answers are partial and pass away. That was recognized by one of the greatest thinkers of all time as the end and beginning of wisdom: *I know that I know nothing.* That was his final certainty. "For we know only in part, and we prophesy only in part; but when the complete comes, the partial will come to an end" (1 Cor. 13:9–10). The complete, however, is love. Knowledge and love are related to each other as the part to the whole. And the more longing for perfection there is in the knowing person, the more love there will be. *Perfect knowledge is perfect love.* That is a strange but still very profound and true statement of Paul.

THE MIRROR WRITING OF GOD

It is a surprising image when the age of a child is compared with the partial nature of knowledge, and the maturity of adulthood with the perfection of love (1 Cor. 13:11). Knowledge without love is childish, a childish approach, a childish attempt . . . the pride of knowledge without love is like the boasting of youth, which only makes the mature person smile. . . . Paul says that love is the stuff of mature insight, of true knowledge, of age. That clearly distinguishes this love from all fanaticism, from all weakness and sentimentality—love means truth before God. It means perfect knowledge before God.

And yet a second image: "For now we see in a mirror . . ." (1 Cor. 13:12). God's thoughts are found in the world only as if caught in a mirror. We see them only in mirror writing, and the mirror writing of God is hard to read. Indeed, it reads that large is small and small is large, that right is wrong and wrong is right, that hopelessness is promise and the hopeful expect judgment. Indeed, it reads that the cross means victory and death means life. We read the mirror writing of God in Jesus Christ, in his living and speaking and dying.

The Acts of God,
Hidden in the World

A nd now faith, hope, and love abide, these three . . ."
(1 Cor. 13:13). Faith—this means, naturally, that no
person or church can live from the greatness of their own
actions. They instead live solely from the great act that God
himself does and has done. And (this is what is crucial) the
great acts of God remain unseen and hidden in the world.
Things in the church are simply not the way they are in the
world and in the history of nations, where it is ultimately a
question of being able to point to great deeds. The church
that tried to do that would have already long since fallen to
the laws and powers of this world. The *church of success* has
truly not been the *church of faith* for a long time. The act that
God did in this world, and from which all the world has
since lived, is the cross on Golgotha. Such are God's "successes," and the successes of the church and the individual
are like that when they are acts of faith. That faith abides
means that it remains true, *that human beings must live from
what is invisible,* that they live not from their own visible
work but from the invisible act of God. They see error and
they believe truth, they see guilt and they believe forgiveness, they see dying and they believe eternal life, they see
nothing and they believe the act and grace of God. And so
it is with the Reformation church. It never lives from its
deeds or from its acts of love. It instead lives from what it
does not see and yet believes.

HOPE ABIDES

A faith that does not hope is sick. It is like a hungry child who will not eat or a tired person who will not sleep. As certainly as people believe, so certainly do they hope. And it is no shame in hoping, in hoping boundlessly. Who would even want to talk of God and not hope? Who would want to talk of God without hoping one day to see him? Who would want to talk of peace and love among human beings without wanting to experience it once in eternity? Who would want to talk of a new world and a new humanity without hoping that they might one day participate? And why should we be ashamed of our hope? We will one day have to be ashamed, not of our hope, but of our miserable and anxious hopelessness that trusts nothing to God, that in false humility does not grasp where God's promises are given, that is resigned to this life and cannot look forward to God's eternal power and glory. The more people dare to hope, the greater they become with their hope: people grow with their hope—if it is hope only in God and his sole power. Hope abides.

HAVE YOU HEARD MY WORD?

We have no more time for solemn church festivals in which we present ourselves to ourselves. Let's not celebrate the Reformation this way anymore! Let the late Luther finally have his rest. Hear the gospel. Read his Bible, and listen there to the very word of God. On the last day God will certainly not ask us, Have you celebrated your representative Reformation festivals? But rather, Have you heard my word and kept it? Let us therefore say to ourselves: "Nevertheless I have something against thee, because thou hast left thy first love" (Rev. 2:4 KJV). If I could only say this word now so that it would really make us hurt. It is supposed to make us hurt; otherwise it would not be the word of God. But I see how you are already reading the happy ending of the story—even now, as with a bad novel—in order not to be so very disturbed by what goes before, to be able always to say: Oh, it will all come out in the end. "Nevertheless I have something against thee, because thou hast left thy first love." The difference between what is called "first love" here and all others that are customarily so called is very succinct, namely, that beyond this first love there is simply no other love. This first love is absolutely the only love there is, for it is love from God and for God. Outside of this love, this first love, there is only hate, and to abandon that love is to abandon God.

FAITH ALONE JUSTIFIES—
LOVE PERFECTS

Faith alone justifies—our Protestant church is built on this sentence. To the human question, How can I stand before God? Luther found only one answer in the Bible: by believing in his grace and mercy in Jesus Christ. . . . Faith alone justifies, but love perfects.

Faith and hope enter into eternity in the transformed shape of love. Perfection means love, but the sign of perfection in this world is the cross. That is the path that perfecting love must travel in this world, and will travel again and again. But this shows us, first, that this world is ripe for demolition—overripe—and that it is only God's indescribable patience that is still waiting till the end. Second, it shows that the church in this world remains under the cross. Especially the church, which already wants to become here on earth the church of visible glory, this church has denied its Lord on the cross. Faith, hope, and love (1 Cor. 13:13) all lead through the cross to perfection. . . .

Humanity, deceived and disappointed a thousand times, needs faith; wounded and suffering humanity needs hope; humanity that has fallen into discord and distrust needs love. . . .

Let us shout to ourselves on Reformation Day: Believe, hope, and above all love—and you will conquer the world (1 John 5:4).

NOVEMBER

AT THE LIMITS

I would like to speak of God
not at the limits
but in the middle,
not in weaknesses
but in strength,
not in death and guilt
but in life and human goodness.
At the limits it seems
better to me to remain silent
and leave the unsolvable unsolved.

Human Being, You Have a Soul!

"For God alone my soul waits in silence" (Ps. 62:1). Like a song from old times, like a medieval image painted on gold leaf, like the memory of childhood days, the sound of the wonderful word of the soul has grown foreign to us. If there is still in our day—in the age of machines, of economic battles, of the reign of fashion and sports—something like the soul, then it's not just a dear childhood memory like so many others. The little word "soul" sounds just so wonderful and strange in the confusion and shouting of voices that extol it; the language is so soft and still that we hardly hear it anymore over the raging and roaring going on within us. But the word speaks a language that is full of the greatest responsibility and deepest seriousness. Hey, you! Human being! You have a soul! See that you don't lose it, that you don't wake up one day from the frenzy of life—professional and private life—and see that you have become hollow inside, a plaything of events, a leaf driven back and forth and blown away by the wind: that you are without a soul. Human being, pay attention to your soul! What are we to say about that soul? It is the life that God has given us; it is what God has loved about us, what he—from his eternity—has touched. It is love in us and longing and holy restlessness and responsibility and happiness and pain; it is divine breath breathed into mortal being. Human being, you have a soul!

Prayer in Special Need

Lord God,
great misery has come over me.
My cares want to press me down;
I no longer know in from out.
God, be graceful and help;
Give me strength to bear what you send.
Do not let fear rule over me.
Take fatherly care of those close to me,
especially my family;
protect them with your strong hand
from all evil and from all danger.
Merciful God,
forgive me for everything I have done
against you and other people.
I trust your grace
and place my life entirely in your hands.
Do with me as you please and as is good for me.
Whether I live or die,
I am with you and you are with me, my God.
Lord, I await your salvation and your kingdom.
Amen.

TIME MARCHES ON

So even to old age and gray hairs, O God, do not forsake me, until I proclaim your might to all the generations to come" (Ps. 71:18).

With wonder we stand at the end of the year. For some time now we have become accustomed to not counting on long periods of time, as we neither can nor should. It is enough for us that on each new day we learn obedience. But time marches on, and our text today speaks to us of getting old. So, in spite of everything, it is also good to keep in mind that perhaps a long lifetime still lies before us, that the last day will perhaps not come tomorrow or the day after tomorrow.

"Houses and fields and vineyards shall again be bought in this land" (Jer. 32:15).

New generations will bear new burdens on their shoulders. And so we ask God, for whom a thousand years are like a day (Ps. 90:4), for the grace that he will let us remain proclaimers of his power through the years.

Years and generations pass away, but the word of God will stand forever (Isa. 40:8).

We are only links in the chain. Yet the anxious and joyous question remains, Which generation will experience the last day?

IN A SPECIAL WAY, DISEASE
BELONGS TO GOD

In the Bible we find a strange statement: "Yet even in his disease he did not seek the LORD, but sought help from physicians" (2 Chr. 16:12). The passage refers to a pious man whom the Bible otherwise gives high praise for his zeal for God. Yet with all his piety this man was thinking in a very modern way, because he made a strict distinction between matters of religion, in which one turned to God, and earthly matters, in which one sought help in earthly places. Diseases, especially bodily diseases, are earthly matters with earthly causes and earthly remedies. Diseases therefore are the doctor's business, not God's. That is thought out very reasonably and perhaps even very religiously. But it is wrong. Certainly diseases have their earthly causes and earthly remedies, but this falls far short of telling us everything and does not give the most crucial information about the nature of illness. Certainly someone who is sick should go to the doctor and seek help there. But with this alone, the most important thing has not been done or even recognized. Behind the earthly causes and remedies of disease stand supernatural causes and supernatural remedies. As long as we pass them by, we miss the truth about our own illness and do not meet it face-to-face. Its curse and its blessing remain unknown.

WHO BEARS OUR BURDEN?

When we some day reach the end of our inner strength, when we ourselves become a burden, then no words can help us, nor any ideals or future dreams that might be put before us. Then we will need only one thing: we will need someone we can trust completely and without reservation, someone who understands everything, who hears everything, who endures everything, who believes everything, who hopes everything, who forgives everything. . . . Where is there such a person? Now the miracle of all miracles is that every human being has this person and can find him, for this person calls us to himself of his own accord, offers himself, and invites us: Jesus Christ alone—he who alone is human. . . . There are two possible ways to help people who are pressed down by a burden. Either we remove the whole burden, so that from now on they no longer have to carry anything, or we help them carry it by making the burden lighter for them. Jesus does not want to go the first way with us. Our burden is not removed. Jesus, who himself bore his cross, knows that human beings by their nature must be burden bearers, bearers of their own cross, and that only under this burden—and not without it—will human beings be saved. Jesus does not remove the burden that God lays upon us but makes the burden lighter for us by showing us how we must bear it.

NO TEAR FLOWS IN VAIN

Christ did not come into the world so that we might comprehend him, but so that we might cling to him, so that we might let him simply pull us into the tremendous story of the resurrection. He came so that we might simply let him tell us in total incomprehensibility: You are dead—and yet you have risen! You are in the dark—and yet you are in the light. You are afraid—and yet you can rejoice. These totally incompatible things are side by side only a hair's breadth apart. Just like the two worlds, our world and God's world, they are side by side only a hair's breadth apart. . . .

Our visible life with its joys and successes, with its worries and its trouble and its painful disobedience stands holy and innocent and perfect for Jesus Christ's sake in that hidden world of God before the eyes of the Almighty, today and tomorrow and forever. And no tear flows in vain and no sigh goes unheard; no pain is disparaged and no jubilation is lost. The visible world brutally and heartlessly and violently marches over all of that. But out of grace and mercy and great love, God gathers up our burning, blazing life. . . . Our true life is hidden—but it is solidly grounded in eternity.

THE TALK OF HUMAN LIMITS

Religious people speak of God when human knowledge (often out of mental laziness) has reached its limits or when human powers fail. Actually, it is always the deus ex machina that they trot out, either as the apparent solution to unsolvable problems or as strength in human failure, and thus always in the exploitation of human weakness or at human limits. This necessarily holds only until human beings, by their own strength, push the limits a little farther and God as deus ex machina becomes superfluous. The talk of human limits has in general become questionable to me. . . . It always seems to me that we are only anxious to save room for God. I would like to speak of God not at the limits but in the middle, not in weaknesses but in strength, not in death and guilt but in life and human goodness. At the limits it seems better to me to remain silent and leave the unsolvable unsolved.

GOD, WHY ARE YOU SO NEAR TO US?

God, you started it with me.
You hunted me and would not let me loose;
repeatedly — now here, now there — you have suddenly
   stepped in my way;
you have captivated me, enticed me, and made my heart
   pliable and willing;
you have spoken to me of your longing and eternal love,
   of your faithfulness and might;
when I sought strength, you strengthened me;
when I sought support, you supported me;
when I sought forgiveness, you forgave me my guilt.
I did not want it, but you overcame my will, my
   resistance, my heart.
God, you have drawn me irresistibly, and I have given
   myself to you.
Lord, you have persuaded me, and I have let myself be
   persuaded.
You have grabbed me as one without a clue —
and now I cannot get away from you anymore.
You are too strong for me; you have won.

I Am a Guest on Earth

I am a guest on earth" (Ps. 119:19, Luther) — with this I confess that I cannot remain here, that my time here is short. Also, I have no right here to a house and possessions. I must receive with gratitude everything good that comes my way, but I must suffer injustice and violence without anyone interceding for me. I have a firm hold on neither people nor things. As a guest I am subject to the laws of my dwelling place. The earth, which feeds me, has a right to my work and my strength. It is not my place to disparage the earth on which I live my life. I owe it loyalty and gratitude. I cannot avoid my lot of having to be a guest and an alien — and with it the call of God into this alien status — by dreaming away my earthly life with thoughts about heaven. There is a very godless homesickness for the other world, which will certainly not be granted a homecoming. . . . Because on earth I am nothing but a guest without rights, without support, without security, because God himself makes me so weak and small, he has therefore given me only one solid pledge for my goal: his word. This one certainty he will not take away. He will keep this word for me, and in it he will let me feel his power. Where the word is at home in me, I will find my way in a foreign land, my rights in injustice, my support in uncertainty, my strength in work, and patience in suffering.

ONE DOES NOT MEET
GOD ON THE SPOT

God's ways are ways that he himself traveled and that we are now supposed to travel with him. God does not let us go any way that he himself has not gone and on which he does not go before us. The way to which God calls us is the way cleared by God and protected by God. Thus it is really his way. . . .

One does not meet God on the spot. Rather, one follows a way. And the way moves forward, or one is not with God. God knows the whole way, while we know only the next step and the ultimate goal. There is no stopping. Every day, every hour, it goes on. . . .

As a way, it also cannot remain hidden from the eyes of other people. It will be obvious whether good or evil takes place on this way. Nor can we be indifferent as to whether evil is occasionally done on this way, as if, for example, one could withdraw from faulty reality to the perfect ideal, or if one were to be satisfied with knowing the right way and possessing the right faith, even if one cannot always act accordingly. Those who walk in his way do no evil (Ps. 119:3). Knowing the way and being on the right path never make responsibility and guilt easier. Rather, they become more difficult. God's children have no special right—except knowing God's grace and way and how to do no evil.

IN THE CHANGING OF THE TIMES

Deep roots in the soil of the past make life more difficult, but also richer and more powerful. There are basic human truths to which life sooner or later returns again and again. Therefore, we cannot be in a hurry; we must be able to wait. "God seeks out what has gone by," says the Bible (Eccl. 3:15). . . .

We have grown up with the experience of our parents and grandparents that people can and must plan, build, and shape their lives. There is a life's work that people must choose and then carry out with all their power. But it has become our experience that we cannot plan even for the coming day, that what has been built up can be destroyed overnight; our lives, in contrast to those of our parents, have become formless and fragmentary. . . . We have lived and believed too strongly the idea that it is possible, by considering all possibilities in advance, to make life so certain that it then happens completely automatically. Only too late have we learned that the source of action is not the idea, but readiness for responsibility. . . .

Our being Christian today will consist in only two things: in praying and in doing justice among people. All thinking, speaking, and organizing in the things of Christianity must be reborn out of this prayer and this action.

MERIT AND GRACE

B ut if it is by grace, it is no longer on the basis of works,
otherwise grace would no longer be grace" (Rom.
11:6)—an unlikely text that one can easily overlook. . . .
Our text draws for us two powerful lines, two possibilities
that belong together and yet are contradictory. One is
called merit; the other is called grace. In other words, the
one line leads from human beings up to God; the other
leads from God down to human beings. The two are mutually exclusive—and yet belong together. That is the miracle of the Christian faith. . . . The great church father
Augustine began his *Confessions* with the statement: "You
have made us for yourself, and our hearts are *restless*
within us, until they find rest in you." "Restless": it all
comes down to this word. . . . Restlesness not in what is
human and transitory, where there is only nervousness
and impatience, but restlessness in the direction of the
eternal. Instead of restlessnness we could say horror, fear,
longing, love. In the human soul—as far as it is only
human—there is something that makes it restless, that
turns it toward the infinite, the eternal.

THE LASTING WORRY

Not to be able to get away from God anymore—that is the lasting worry of every Christian life. Those who once get involved with God, who let themselves be persuaded by him, cannot get away from God anymore (Jer. 20:7). Those to whom he has spoken can no longer forget him; he accompanies them from now on, in the good and in the bad. Like their shadow, he pursues them. And this lasting nearness of God becomes too much, too great for them. It goes beyond their strength, and they often think: Oh, if only I had never gotten started with God. It's too hard for me. It destroys the peace of my soul and my happiness. And if they believe they can no longer endure it and have to put an end to it, then they also realize once again that they will not get away from God in this way, either—not from the God with whom they got involved, by whom they let themselves be persuaded. They remain his victims and in his hands. But just here, where we believe we can no longer go the distance with God because it is too hard—and such hours do come over everyone in our time—where God is too strong for us, where Christians under God collapse and despair: there God's nearness, God's faithfulness, and God's strength become our consolation and our help, there we first know God aright and perceive the meaning of our Christian life.

LIFE IS NOT A THING, AN ESSENCE, A CONCEPT

Since Jesus Christ said of himself, "I am . . . the life" (John 14:6), no Christian thinking—nor any philosophical thinking—can get past this claim and the reality it contains. This self-assertion of Jesus declares that every attempt to express the essence of life as something in itself is futile and has already failed. How should we—as long as we live and do not know death, the boundary of our life— be able to say what life is in and of itself? We can only live life, not define it. Jesus' saying binds every thought about life to his person. "I am the life." There is no question about life in response to this "I am." Here the question, *what* is life, becomes the answer, *who* is life. Life is not a thing, an essence, a concept, but a person and indeed a particular and unique person—particular and unique not in what he among other people might have, but in his very self—the self of Jesus. Jesus sets his own self in the sharpest contrast to all thoughts, concepts, and ways that claim to make up the essence of life.

THE DOUBLE DECEPTION

We people of today, who live and think in unChristian ways, have come to terms with a double deception in our lives that makes it possible for us to live with a certain kind of peace. The first deception is that we think what has happened, the past, what we have done, sinks into the dark abyss of forgetfulness and is totally forgotten, since we and others have more or less forgotten it. In other words, we live with faith in the strong, final power of forgetting. Eternity means oblivion! The second deception with which we live is that we think we can distinguish between hidden and revealed, secret and public. We live a public, visible, apparent life and, on the side, a hidden, secret life of thoughts, feelings, and hopes that no other person ever experiences. It would give us a terrible fright if we knew that all the thoughts and feelings we have had in only one day were suddenly to lie open and visible for every one. We live under the natural presupposition that what is hidden remains hidden. . . . But eternity is not forgetting. Rather, eternity is memory, eternal memory. . . . For this the ancients coined the image of the book of life, in which our lives are recorded.

WE MUST NOT SPEAK THE ULTIMATE WORD BEFORE THE PENULTIMATE

By the way, I feel more and more how Old Testament-like my thoughts and feelings are. Thus in the past months I have also read rather more Old Testament than New Testament. Only if one knows the inexpressibility of the name of God, may one also express the name Jesus Christ. Only if one loves life and the earth so much that with it everything seems to be lost and at an end, may one believe in the resurrection of the dead and a new world. Only when one lets the law of God hold sway, may one even say the word of grace. And only when the wrath and rage of God fall on one's enemies as valid realities, can something like forgiveness and love of enemies touch our heart. Those who want too quickly and too directly to be and feel New Testament-like are, in my estimation, not Christians. We cannot and must not speak the ultimate word before the penultimate. We live in the penultimate and believe in the ultimate.

GOD WILLS THE CONQUEST OF DEATH

When faced with death, we cannot say in a fatalistic way, "It is God's will." We must also add the opposite: "It is not God's will." Death indicates that the world is not the way it should be and that it requires redemption. Christ alone is the conquest of death. Here the conflict between "God's will" and "not God's will" comes to its sharpest intensification and to its resolution. God agrees to what God does not will. Nevertheless, from now on, death must serve God. From now on, "God wills it" also encompasses "God does not will it." God wills the conquest of death through the death of Jesus Christ. Only through the cross and resurrection of Jesus Christ has death come into God's power; it must serve the aims of God. Not a fatalistic surrender, but only living faith in the Jesus Christ who for us died and rose again, can seriously deal with death.

LOVE IS AS STRONG AS DEATH

There is a battle in the world that is without comparison, a war of the highest powers in which everyone is involved: the war of death against love, of love against death, two opponents that in their majesty are worthy of each other. But love is as strong as death (Song 8:6b), for love is from God. Death is also from God; it has its power not from itself but through God. Therefore it can only defy love, but it must also lose to love, because death is only the temporary before the ultimate, and because God is not death but love. Death is strong in the world; it tears open wounds that never completely heal. . . . It can do the most powerful things possible, for it can separate loving hearts. It can defeat love in this world. But love is as strong as death. Death is strong in the world, but love is strong in eternity. . . . God created human beings for each other in eternity. Friend and friend, husband and wife—he created them so that they may find and purify their souls through each other, so that out of love they may no longer live two lives but one.

A PRECIOUS GIFT

There is nothing that can replace the loss of someone dear to us, and no one should even try. We simply have to hold on and hold ourselves together. At first, that sounds harsh, and yet it is at the same time a great comfort, for when the gap really remains unfilled, it connects us with each other. It's crazy to say that God fills the gap; he doesn't fill it at all. Rather, he keeps it unfilled and in this way helps us to preserve our genuine fellowship—even if in pain. Moreover, the more beautiful and full the memories, the more difficult the separation. But thankfulness transforms the torment of remembering into quiet joy. One bears the past beauty, not like a thorn, but like a precious gift within. One must guard against rummaging around in memories and surrendering oneself to them—just as one doesn't look constantly at a precious gift, but only in special hours, and otherwise simply possesses it like a hidden treasure of which one is certain. A lasting joy and strength then emanate from the past. . . . From waking up until falling asleep, we must commend and turn the other person over to God completely, and out of our cares let there be prayer for the other person.

TIME AND DEATH

Guilt remains guilt; failure remains failure. This is the one reality that in our life has cost and will still cost all of us the most tears. What has happened has happened for all time. The second fearful thing, however, is that there is no moment of standing still, that everything is going forward in eternal change and to a particular goal, to death. . . . Unmercifully, time moves beyond the moment: the moment of bliss, of joy, of blessedness, of desire. . . . Desire in the world is passing away, because the world is passing away (1 John 2:17). . . . What are a few centuries of fame in the history of God's world, in view of the primeval stars? What are all the culture, all the beauty, and all the power of human beings before the eternal beauty and infinite power of God? Dust, a drop in the ocean, a leaf blown by the wind, a nothing. . . . The earth is passing away and the world is passing away; time rules over them both—that is, to say it quite clearly: death rules over everything. *Time and death are the same.* The world is a world of dying and death. Everything that happens in it is only a penultimate compared to the ultimate: death. Therefore, the last word about the world is not life and joy and desire, but transition and death.

LETTING GOD BE GOD

Remember then from what you have fallen; repent . . ."
(Rev. 2:5a).

It was nothing except this call that drove Luther to his action. You should burn, and you are cold. You should be alert, and you are lethargic. You should be hungry, and you are stuffed. You should believe, and you are afraid. You should hope, and you reach for power. You should love, and you can't get away from yourself. You should let Christ be the Lord, and you interrupt him. You should do miracles in him, and you don't even do everyday things. The Reformation church is the church of those who subject themselves to this call, who let God be God, who know that those who stand should see to it that they not fall, that is, that they not brag about their standing. Our church stands in God's word alone, and in his word alone we are the ones judged. The church that stands in repentance, the church that lets God be God, is the church of the apostles and of Luther.

". . . and do the works you did at first" (Rev. 2:5b). This last part of the verse absolutely belongs to the first. Without it, the preceding makes no sense. It is a terrible misunderstanding of the gospel to think that faith and repentance are something for pious evening and morning hours. Faith and repentance mean letting God be God also in our actions and being obedient to him precisely in our deeds.

WHATEVER THIS DAY MAY BRING

Triune God,
my Creator and my Savior,
this day belongs to you. My time is in your hands.
Holy, merciful God,
my Creator and my Savior,
my Judge and my Redeemer,
you know me and all my ways and doings.
You hate and punish evil in this and in that world
without regard for the person;
you forgive the sins
of those who ask you sincerely,
and you love the good and reward it
on this earth with the comfort of conscience
and in the world to come with the crown of righteousness
    (2 Tim. 4:8).
Before you I think of all of my own . . .
Lord, have mercy on me. . . .
Lord, whatever this day may bring, may your name be
    praised.

THE YOKE THAT MAKES THE
BURDEN LIGHT

Take my yoke upon you, and learn from me . . ." (Matt.
11:28–30). A yoke is itself a burden, one burden added
to another, and yet it has the peculiar nature of making
another burden light. A burden that would simply push a
person down to the ground becomes bearable through the
yoke. . . . Jesus wants to put us human beings under such
a yoke, so that our burden will not become too heavy for
us. "My yoke" he calls it—that is, the yoke under which he
has learned to carry his burden, which is a thousand times
heavier than our burden, precisely because it is indeed all
of our burdens that he bears. . . .

"Learn from me . . .": see how I carry this yoke, and you
carry it in the same way.

"Learn from me, *for I am gentle and humble in heart.*"

So that is the yoke he carries, *his gentleness and his
humility.* That is the yoke that we are to take upon ourselves, the yoke that Jesus knows will help us to make our
load light. . . . Those who carry this yoke, and thus learn
from him, have a great promise: ". . . *you will find rest for
your souls.*"

That is the end. This rest is the last thing, and it is already
here under the yoke of Jesus. It is yoked together with him
in gentleness and humility. But only there where all burdens
fall will we find the complete rest that we long for.

IT IS NOT GOOD TO DECEIVE YOURSELF ABOUT THE TRUTH

There are people who cannot go to a funeral — or rather don't want to. Why not? Because they are afraid of the distress caused by immediate contact with death. They don't want to see this side of human life and think that by not looking at such things they can banish them from their world. There are even those who think that it is especially *godly* not to see the dark, black side of life, to shut oneself off from the catastrophes of this world, and to lead one's own self-contemplative, godly life in peaceful optimism.

It can never be good, however, to deceive yourself about the truth, for if we deceive ourselves about the truth of our own life, we will certainly also deceive ourselves about the truth of God. And it's certainly never godly to close our eyes — which God gave us so that we can see our neighbors and their needs — when they have to see sadness and horror. It is certainly never right, therefore, to avoid the things that frighten us and depress us.

AT THE BOUNDARY OF TIME

The seriousness of the world is death. Seriousness begins where the world stops, where it dies, where the world has a boundary. Seriousness also begins where our life stops, where we are no more, at the boundary of time. *The frivolity of the world is in the moment,* the penultimate, the desire of the world, as John says (1 John 2:17). Now it's up to individual people whether they want to live seriously or frivolously in the world; whether they want to stay with the penultimate or press through to the ultimate; whether they regard the desire of the world as ultimate or transitory. With Old Testament power the word proclaims to us a memento mori: think about the fact that one day the world will come to an end, and you will have to render an account of your life. Then the moment of death will come over you with the certainty that the world is a world of death, and that nothing can stand up to the power of time—except the one thing: eternity—and that it's all over for you and me. . . . Let us think about the boundary of the world and of time, and something wonderful will happen. Our eyes will be opened up to the fact that the boundary of the world, the end of the world, is the beginning of a new one, of eternity. Here time loses its power to eternity, and the ultimate thing in the world, death, becomes the penultimate.

DEATH OUTSIDE OF US AND WITHIN US

Death from the outside is the scary enemy that meets us when it will. It is the man with the scythe, by whose strokes the flowers fall. . . . We can do nothing to stop him; he "has power from God on high." He is the death of the whole human race, the wrath of God, and the end of all life. But the other is death within us; it is our own death. We die it daily in Jesus Christ, or we refuse him. This death within us has something to do with our love for Christ and for other people. . . . This death is grace and the completion of life. That we may die this death, that it may be given to us, that the death from the outside will not find us before we are made ready for it through this death of our own: let this be our prayer. Then our death is really only the passageway to the perfect love of God. When strife and death exercise their wild dominion all around us, then we are called not only through words and ideas, but also through God's act to bear witness to love and the peace of God. Daily we want to ask ourselves where, through deeds, we can bear witness to the kingdom in which love and peace reign. Only from peace between two and three people can the great peace for which we hope ever grow.

DREAMERS AND CLOUD WALKERS?

Remain true to the earth! Strive for what is on earth! For countless people that is a holy concern, and we understand their zeal. We understand the jealousy with which they want to chain together the plans and works and strivings of people on this earth. For, indeed, we are chained to this earth. It is the place where we stand or fall. We must account for what happens on earth. And woe to us Christians if we should be put to shame here. . . .

Today powerful forces decide whether we Christians have enough strength to witness to the world, that we are not dreamers and cloud walkers, that we will not allow things to happen as they do now, that our faith is not really the opium that lets us be satisfied in the midst of an unjust world. Rather, precisely because we set our minds on things that are above and not on things that are on earth (Col. 3:2), we protest all the more stubbornly and purposefully on this earth—protest with word and deed in order to press on at any price. Then, does it have to be that Christianity, which once began in such a tremendously revolutionary fashion, is now conservative for all time? That every new movement must make its own way without the church? That the church does not see what is actually happening until twenty years later? Does it really have to be that way?

DEATH AND LIFE ALONG ONE LINE

Seek the things that are above, where Christ is, seated at the right hand of God. . . . your life is hidden with Christ in God" (Col. 3:1–3). And as we zealously press forward with all sound human understanding—and perhaps also with a lot of human wisdom, to fathom what then this "hidden with Christ in God" could mean—there standing like a cherub with flashing sword is that other saying in the middle of the text: "you have died." It is eerie that where the talk is of the living God, this dying always stands in the middle. . . .

To see death and life along one line—and indeed along the line of death—we could do this only if we could look with God's own eyes. For us human beings, the differences between death and life are tremendously great—for God, they come together as one. For God, whether human beings live or die does not make them more or less; it does not make them nearer or farther. But if we should talk in human words and for human understanding about whether human beings live or die, and whether in God's eyes human death may well be a continuation of life, then our text definitely urges us to consider the very opposite.

LOST THOUGHT

You have died" (Col. 3:3), says the apostle, and he knows it well: if it is really true that our living or dying makes no difference before God, then our thinking also makes no difference. Then we could have a thousand thoughts about how much more beautiful and simple and edifying it would be to have a god with whom we could not get lost, yet these thousand thoughts would all be wrong. If it is true that we have died, then we must have this—that we have died—said to us by God himself. For a lost thought does not even know that it is lost. Neither the apostle Paul nor we would know anything of this line of death, this boundary, this lost condition, if God himself did not tell us about all of this. God himself talks with us. God himself comes to us. And God himself informs us that we are lost. When he does that, however, he whom we have lost is, of course, already with us, and we are the ones who have also long since been helped. Indeed, God makes fun of this, our whole lost condition, and triumphs over everything that could separate us from him. His love has drawn us to him, and no worldly power can pull us out of his hand. This is the incomprehensibly wonderful thing that the apostle wants to say to us. He does not say, "You have died," to torment us or to plunge us into gloom, but solely because he can continue in the same breath: "and your life is hidden with Christ in God."

A New Song

Tolstoy once said that the czar would have to forbid Beethoven to be played by good musicians, for he would excite the passions of the people too deeply and put them in danger.

Luther, by contrast, often said that, next to the Word of God, music is the best thing that human beings have. The two had different things in mind: Tolstoy, music to honor people; Luther, music to honor God. And regarding music, Luther knew that it has dried an infinite number of tears, made the sad happy, stilled desires, raised up the defeated, strengthened the challenged, and that it has also moved many a stubborn heart to tears and driven many a great sinner to repentance before the goodness of God.

"O sing to the Lord a *new* song" (Ps. 98:1). The emphasis is on the word *new*. What is this new song, if not the song that makes people *new*, the song that brings people out of darkness and worry and fear to new hope, new faith, new trust? The new song is the song that God himself awakens in us anew—even if it is an ancient song—the God who, as it says in Job, "gives songs in the night" (Job 35:10 RSV).

DECEMBER

CELEBRATING CHRISTMAS CORRECTLY

Who will celebrate Christmas correctly?
Whoever finally lays down
all power, all honor,
all reputation, all vanity,
all arrogance, all individualism
beside the manger.

LIBERATION FROM INCESSANT BEGINNINGS

On the basis of God's beginning with us, which has already happened, our life with God is a path that is traveled in the law of God. Is this human enslavement under the law? No, it is liberation from the murderous law of incessant beginnings. Waiting day after day for the new beginning, thinking countless times that we have found it, only in the evening to give up on it again as lost—that is the perfect destruction of faith in the God who set the beginning once and for all time. . . . God has set the beginning: this is the joyous certainty of faith. Therefore, beside the "one" beginning of God, I am not supposed to try to set countless other beginnings of my own. This is precisely what I am now liberated from. The beginning—God's beginning—lies behind me, once and for all time. . . . Together we are on the path whose beginning consists in the fact that God has found his own people, a path whose end can consist only in the fact that God is seeking us again. The path between this beginning and this end is our walk in the law of God. It is life under the word of God in all its many facets. In truth there is only one danger on this path, namely, wanting to go behind the beginning. In that moment the path stops being a way of grace and faith. It stops being God's own way.

GOD BECOMES HUMAN

God becomes human, really human. While we endeavor to grow out of our humanity, to leave our human nature behind us, God becomes human, and we must recognize that God wants us also to be human — really human. Whereas we distinguish between the godly and the godless, the good and the evil, the noble and the common, God loves real human beings without distinction. . . . God takes the side of real human beings and the real world against all their accusers. . . . But it's not enough to say that God takes care of human beings. This sentence rests on something infinitely deeper and more impenetrable, namely, that in the conception and birth of Jesus Christ, God took on humanity in bodily fashion. God raised his love for human beings above every reproach of falsehood and doubt and uncertainty by himself entering into the life of human beings as a human being, by bodily taking upon himself and bearing the nature, essence, guilt, and suffering of human beings. Out of love for human beings, God becomes a human being. He does not seek out the most perfect human being in order to unite with that person. Rather, he takes on human nature as it is.

LOOK UP!

Let's not deceive ourselves. "Your redemption is drawing near" (Luke 21:28), whether we know it or not, and the only question is: Are we going to let it come to us too, or are we going to resist it? Are we going to join in this movement that comes down from heaven to earth, or are we going to close ourselves off? Christmas is coming—whether it is with us or without us depends on each and every one of us.

Such a true Advent happening now creates something different from the anxious, petty, depressed, feeble Christian spirit that we see again and again, and that again and again wants to make Christianity contemptible. This becomes clear from the two powerful commands that introduce our text: "Look up and raise your heads" (Luke 21:28 RSV). Advent creates people, new people. We too are supposed to become new people in Advent. Look up, you whose gaze is fixed on this earth, who are spellbound by the little events and changes on the surface of the earth. Look up to these words, you who have turned away from heaven disappointed. Look up, you whose eyes are heavy with tears and who are crying over the fact that the earth has gracelessly torn us away. Look up, you who, burdened with guilt, cannot lift your eyes. Look up, your redemption is drawing near. Something different from what you see daily will happen. Just be aware, be watchful, wait just another short moment. Wait and something quite new will break over you: God will come.

THE ADVENT SEASON IS A
SEASON OF WAITING

J esus stands at the door knocking (Rev. 3:20). In total reality, he comes in the form of the beggar, of the dissolute human child in ragged clothes, asking for help. He confronts you in every person that you meet. As long as there are people, Christ will walk on the earth as your neighbor, as the one through whom God calls you, speaks to you, makes demands on you. That is the great seriousness and great blessedness of the Advent message. Christ is standing at the door; he lives in the form of a human being among us. Do you want to close the door or open it?

It may strike us as strange to see Christ in such a near face, but he said it, and those who withdraw from the serious reality of the Advent message cannot talk of the coming of Christ in their heart, either. . . .

Christ is knocking. It's still not Christmas, but it's also still not the great last Advent, the last coming of Christ. Through all the Advents of our life that we celebrate runs the longing for the last Advent, when the word will be: "See, I am making all things new" (Rev. 21:5).

The Advent season is a season of waiting, but our whole life is an Advent season, that is, a season of waiting for the last Advent, for the time when there will be a new heaven and a new earth.

WAITING IS AN ART

Celebrating Advent means being able to wait. Waiting is an art that our impatient age has forgotten. It wants to break open the ripe fruit when it has hardly finished planting the shoot. But all too often the greedy eyes are only deceived; the fruit that seemed so precious is still green on the inside, and disrespectful hands ungratefully toss aside what has so disappointed them. Whoever does not know the austere blessedness of waiting—that is, of hopefully doing without—will never experience the full blessing of fulfillment.

Those who do not know how it feels to anxiously struggle with the deepest questions of life, of their life, and to patiently look forward with anticipation until the truth is revealed, cannot even dream of the splendor of the moment in which clarity is illuminated for them. And for those who do not want to win the friendship and love of another person—who do not expectantly open up their soul to the soul of the other person, until friendship and love come, until they make their entrance—for such people the deepest blessing of the one life of two intertwined souls will remain forever hidden.

For the greatest, most profound, tenderest things in the world, we must wait. It happens here not in a storm but according to the divine laws of sprouting, growing, and becoming.

An Un-Christmas-Like Idea

Not everyone can wait: neither the sated nor the satisfied nor those without respect can wait. The only ones who can wait are people who carry restlessness around with them and people who look up with reverence to the greatest in the world. Thus Advent can be celebrated only by those whose souls give them no peace, who know that they are poor and incomplete, and who sense something of the greatness that is supposed to come, before which they can only bow in humble timidity, waiting until he inclines himself toward us—the Holy One himself, God in the child in the manger. God is coming; the Lord Jesus is coming; Christmas is coming. Rejoice, O Christendom! . . . When the old Christendom spoke of the coming again of the Lord Jesus, it always thought first of all of a great day of judgment. And as un-Christmas-like as this idea may appear to us, it comes from early Christianity and must be taken with utter seriousness. . . . The coming of God is truly not only a joyous message, but is, first, frightful news for anyone who has a conscience. And only when we have felt the frightfulness of the matter can we know the incomparable favor. God comes in the midst of evil, in the midst of death, and judges the evil in us and in the world. And in judging it, he loves us, he purifies us, he sanctifies us, he comes to us with his grace and love. He makes us happy as only children can be happy.

RESPECT FOR THE MYSTERY

The lack of mystery in our modern life is our downfall and our poverty. A human life is worth as much as the respect it holds for the mystery. We retain the child in us to the extent that we honor the mystery. Therefore, children have open, wide-awake eyes, because they know that they are surrounded by the mystery. They are not yet finished with this world; they still don't know how to struggle along and avoid the mystery, as we do. We destroy the mystery because we sense that here we reach the boundary of our being, because we want to be lord over everything and have it at our disposal, and that's just what we cannot do with the mystery. . . . Living without mystery means knowing nothing of the mystery in our own life, nothing of the mystery of another person, nothing of the mystery of the world; it means passing over our own hidden qualities and those of others and the world. It means remaining on the surface, taking the world seriously only to the extent that it can be *calculated* and *exploited*, and not going beyond the world of calculation and exploitation. Living without mystery means not seeing the crucial processes of life at all and even denying them.

THE MYSTERY OF LOVE

The mystery remains a mystery. It withdraws from our grasp. *Mystery, however, does not mean simply not knowing something.*

The greatest mystery is not the most distant star; on the contrary, the closer something comes to us and the better we know it, then the more mysterious it becomes for us. The greatest mystery to us is not the most distant person, but the one next to us. The mystery of other people is not reduced by getting to know more and more about them. Rather, in their closeness they become more and more mysterious. And the final depth of all mystery is when two people come so close to each other that they *love* each other. Nowhere in the world does one feel the might of the mysterious and its wonder as strongly as here. When two people know everything about each other, the mystery of the love between them becomes infinitely great. And only in this love do they understand each other, know everything about each other, know each other completely. And yet, the more they love each other and know about each other in love, the more deeply they know the mystery of their love. Thus knowledge about each other does not remove the mystery, but rather makes it more profound. *The very fact* that the other person is so near to me is the greatest mystery.

THE WONDER OF ALL WONDERS

God travels wonderful ways with human beings, but he does not comply with the views and opinions of people. God does not go the way that people want to prescribe for him; rather, his way is beyond all comprehension, free and self-determined beyond all proof.

Where reason is indignant, where our nature rebels, where our piety anxiously keeps us away: that is precisely where God loves to be. There he confounds the reason of the reasonable; there he aggravates our nature, our piety—that is where he wants to be, and no one can keep him from it. Only the humble believe him and rejoice that God is so free and so marvelous that he does wonders where people despair, that he takes what is little and lowly and makes it marvelous. And that is the wonder of all wonders, that God loves the lowly. . . . God is not ashamed of the lowliness of human beings. God marches right in. He chooses people as his instruments and performs his wonders where one would least expect them. God is near to lowliness; he loves the lost, the neglected, the unseemly, the excluded, the weak and broken. Where human beings say, "Lost," God says, "Found"; where people say, "Condemned," God says, "Saved"; where people say, "No!" God says, "Yes!"

HUMAN BEINGS BECOME HUMAN BECAUSE GOD BECAME HUMAN

The figure of Jesus Christ takes shape in human beings. Human beings do not take on an independent form of their own. Rather, what gives them form and maintains them in their new form is always and only the figure of Jesus Christ himself. It is therefore not an imitation, not a repetition of his form, but their own form that takes shape in human beings. Human beings are not transformed into a form that is foreign to them, not into the form of God, but into their own form, a form that belongs to them and is essential to them. Human beings become human because God became human, but human beings do not become God. They could not and cannot bring about that change in their form, but God himself changes his form into human form, so that human beings—though not becoming God—can become human.

In Christ the form of human beings before God was created anew. It was not a matter of place, of time, of climate, of race, of the individual, of society, of religion, or of taste, but rather a question of the life of humanity itself that it recognized in Christ its image and its hope. What happened to Christ happened to humanity.

WITH GOD THERE IS JOY

Everlasting joy shall be upon their heads" (Isa. 35:10). Since ancient times, in the Christian church, acedia—sadness of heart, resignation—has been considered a mortal sin. "Serve the Lord with gladness!" (Ps. 100:2 RSV), urges the Scripture. For this, our life has been given to us, and for this, it has been sustained for us to this present hour. The joy that no one can take from us belongs not only to those who have been called home, but also to us who are still living. In this joy we are one with them, but never in sadness. How are we supposed to be able to help those who are without joy and courage, if we ourselves are not borne by courage and joy? What is meant here is not something made or forced, but something given and free. With God there is joy, and from him it comes down and seizes spirit, soul, and body. And where this joy has seized a person, it reaches out around itself, it pulls others along, it bursts through closed doors. There is a kind of joy that knows nothing at all of the pain, distress, and anxiety of the heart. But it cannot last; it can only numb for a time. The joy of God has gone through the poverty of the manger and the distress of the cross; therefore it is invincible and irrefutable.

NOTHING GETS LOST

A verse is going around repeatedly in my head: "Brother, come; from all that grieves you / you are freed; / all you need / I again will bring you." What does this mean: "All you need I again will bring you"? Nothing is lost; in Christ everything is lifted up, preserved—to be sure, in a different form—transparent, clear, freed from the torment of self-seeking desire. Christ will bring all of this again, and as it was originally intended by God, without the distortion caused by our sin. The teaching of the gathering up of all things, found in Ephesians 1:10, is a wonderful and thoroughly comforting idea. "God seeks out what has gone by" (Eccl. 3:15) receives here its fulfillment. And no one has expressed that as simply and in such a childlike way as Paul Gerhardt in the words that he places in the mouth of the Christ child: "All you need I again will bring you." Moreover, for the first time in these days I have discovered for myself the song, "Beside your cradle here I stand." Until now I had not thought much about it. Apparently you have to be alone a long time and read it meditatively to be able to perceive it. . . . Beside the "we" there is also still an "I" and Christ, and what that means cannot be said better than in this song.

CHRISTMAS, FULFILLED PROMISE

Moses died on the mountain from which he was permitted to view from a distance the promised land (Deut. 32:48–52). When the Bible speaks of God's promises, it's a matter of life and death. . . . The language that reports this ancient history is clear. Anyone who has seen God must die; the sinner dies before the promise of God. Let's understand what that means for us so close to Christmas. The great promise of God—a promise that is infinitely more important than the promise of the promised land—is supposed to be fulfilled at Christmas. . . . The Bible is full of the proclamation that the great miracle has happened as an act of God, without any human doing. . . . What happened? God had seen the misery of the world and had come himself in order to help. Now he was there, not as a mighty one, but in the obscurity of humanity, where there is sinfulness, weakness, wretchedness, and misery in the world. That is where God goes, and there he lets himself be found by everyone. And this proclamation moves through the world anew, year after year, and again this year also comes to us.

A Love for Theology

No priest, no theologian stood at the manger of Bethlehem. And yet all Christian theology has its origin in the wonder of all wonders: that God became human. Holy theology arises from knees bent before the mystery of the divine child in the stable. Without the holy night, there is no theology. "God revealed in flesh," the God-human Jesus Christ—that is the holy mystery that theology came into being to protect and preserve. How we fail to understand when we think that the task of theology is to solve the mystery of God, to drag it down to the flat, ordinary wisdom of human experience and reason! Its sole office is to preserve the miracle as miracle, to comprehend, defend, and glorify God's mystery precisely as mystery. This and nothing else, therefore, is what the early church meant when, with never flagging zeal, it dealt with the mystery of the Trinity and the person of Jesus Christ. . . . If Christmas time cannot ignite within us again something like a love for holy theology, so that we—captured and compelled by the wonder of the manger of the Son of God— must reverently reflect on the mysteries of God, then it must be that the glow of the divine mysteries has also been extinguished in our heart and has died out.

THANKFUL REMEMBRANCE

Dear parents . . . I don't need to tell you how much I long for freedom and for you all. But over the decades you have provided for us such incomparably beautiful Christmases that my thankful remembrance of them is strong enough to light up one dark Christmas. Only such times can really reveal what it means to have a past and an inner heritage that is independent of chance and the changing of the times. The awareness of a spiritual tradition that reaches through the centuries gives one a certain feeling of security in the face of all transitory difficulties. I believe that those who know they possess such reserves of strength do not need to be ashamed even of softer feelings—which in my opinion are still among the better and nobler feelings of humankind—when remembrance of a good and rich past calls them forth. Such feelings will not overwhelm those who hold fast to the values that no one can take from them.

What Is a Prophet?

A prophet is a man who in a particular, earthshaking moment in his life knows himself seized and called by God, and now he can do no other than go among people and proclaim the will of God. His calling has become the turning point of his life, and there is only one thing left for him to do: to follow this calling, even if it may lead him into misfortune or into death. . . . The genuine prophet is not the one who always cries peace, peace, and victory, but the one who has the courage to proclaim disaster, says Jeremiah (Jer. 23:9ff.). . . . The central point from which one gains an understanding of the prophetic soul is the fact that the prophet knows himself in covenant with God, and this covenant makes his life a tragedy for him; because it is a covenant with God, the tragedy has an incomparable seriousness. The fact that the prophet is in covenant with God puts such amazing words on his lips; it makes him so fearsome, so unrelenting and raises him above everything that is understandable in human psychological terms. . . . God tears up, breaks apart, and annihilates the spiritually harmonic image of human beings through which they let themselves be proclaimed. . . . God himself effects the tragedy of the prophetic life, so that in this defeat of the human the power, the claim, and the burden of the divine demand is brought clearly into the light.

A Soft, Mysterious Voice

In the midst of the deepest guilt and distress of the people, a voice speaks that is soft and mysterious but full of the blessed certainty of salvation through the birth of a divine child (Isa. 9:6–7). It is still 700 years until the time of fulfillment, but the prophet is so deeply immersed in God's thought and counsel that he speaks of the future as if he saw it already, and he speaks of the salvific hour as if he already stood in adoration before the manger of Jesus. "For a child has been born for us." What will happen one day is already real and certain in God's eyes, and it will be not only for the salvation of future generations but already for the prophet who sees it coming and for his generation, indeed, for all generations on earth. "For a child has been born *for us*." No human spirit can talk like this on its own. How are we who do not know what will happen next year supposed to understand that someone can look forward many centuries? And the times then were no more transparent than they are today. Only the Spirit of God, who encompasses the beginning and end of the world, can in such a way reveal to a chosen person the mystery of the future, so that he must prophesy for strengthening believers and warning unbelievers. This individual voice ultimately enters into the nocturnal adoration of the shepherds (Luke 2:15–20) and into the full jubilation of the Christ-believing community: "For a child has been born for us, a son given to us."

THE GREAT TURNING POINT
OF ALL THINGS

The topic here is the birth of a child—not the revolutionary deed of a strong man, not the bold discovery of a wise person, not the godly work of a saint. It really goes beyond all comprehension: the birth of a child is supposed to lead to the great turning point of all things and to bring the salvation and redemption of all humanity. What kings and leaders of nations, philosophers and artists, founders of religions and teachers of morals have tried in vain to do—that now happens through a newborn child. Putting to shame the most powerful human efforts and accomplishments, a child is placed here at the midpoint of world history—a child born of human beings, a son given by God (Isa. 9:6). That is the mystery of the redemption of the world; everything past and everything future is encompassed here. The infinite mercy of the almighty God comes to us, descends to us in the form of a child, his Son. That this child is born *for us*, this son is given *to us*, that this human child and Son of God belongs to me, that I know him, have him, love him, that I am his and he is mine—on this alone my life now depends. A child has our life in his hands. . . .

A shaking of heads, perhaps even an evil laugh, must go through our old, smart, experienced, self-assured world, when it hears the call of salvation of believing Christians: "For a child has been born for us, a son given to us."

On the Weak Shoulders of a Child

Authority rests upon his shoulders" (Isa. 9:6). Authority over the world is supposed to lie on the weak shoulders of this newborn child! One thing we know: these shoulders will come to carry the entire burden of the world. With the cross, all the sin and distress of this world will be loaded on these shoulders. But authority consists in the fact that the bearer does not collapse under the burden but carries it to the end. The authority that lies on the shoulders of the child in the manger consists in the patient bearing of people and their guilt. This bearing, however, begins in the manger; it begins where the eternal word of God assumes and bears human flesh. The authority over all the world has its beginning in the very lowliness and weakness of the child. As a sign of authority over a house, there was a custom of hanging the key across the shoulder of the master of the house. That meant that he had the power to open up and to close up, to let in and to turn away whomever he wanted. This is also the manner of the authority of the one who carried the cross on his shoulders. He opens up because he forgives sin, and he closes up because he casts out the proud. That is the authority of this child: that he accepts and carries the humble, the lowly, and sinners, but he rejects and brings to nothing the proud, the haughty, and the righteous (Luke 1:51–52).

THE UNFATHOMABLY WISE COUNSELOR

Wonderful Counselor" (Isa. 9:6) is the name of this child. In him the wonder of all wonders has taken place; the birth of the Savior-child has gone forth from God's eternal counsel. In the form of a human child, God gave us his Son; God became human, the Word became flesh (John 1:14). That is the wonder of the love of God for us, and it is the unfathomably wise Counselor who wins us this love and saves us. But because this child of God is his own Wonderful Counselor, he himself is also the source of all wonder and all counsel. To those who recognize in Jesus the wonder of the Son of God, every one of his words and deeds becomes a wonder; they find in him the last, most profound, most helpful counsel for all needs and questions. Yes, before the child can open his lips, he is full of wonder and full of counsel. Go to the child in the manger. Believe him to be the Son of God, and you will find in him wonder upon wonder, counsel upon counsel.

GOD BECAME A CHILD

Mighty God" (Isa. 9:6) is the name of this child. The child in the manger is none other than God himself. Nothing greater can be said: God became a child. In the Jesus child of Mary lives the almighty God. Wait a minute! Don't speak; stop thinking! Stand still before this statement! God became a child! Here he is, poor like us, miserable and helpless like us, a person of flesh and blood like us, our brother. And yet he is God; he is might. Where is the divinity, where is the might of the child? In the divine love in which he became like us. His poverty in the manger is his might. In the might of love he overcomes the chasm between God and humankind, he overcomes sin and death, he forgives sin and awakens from the dead. Kneel down before this miserable manger, before this child of poor people, and repeat in faith the stammering words of the prophet: "Mighty God!" And he will be your God and your might.

EVERLASTING FATHER AND PRINCE OF PEACE

"Everlasting Father" (Isa. 9:6)—how can this be the name of the child? Only because in this child the everlasting fatherly love of God is revealed, and the child wants nothing other than to bring to earth the love of the Father. So the Son is one with the Father, and whoever sees the Son sees the Father. This child wants nothing for himself. He is no prodigy in the human sense, but an obedient child of his heavenly Father. Born in time, he brings eternity with him to earth; as Son of God he brings to us all the love of the Father in heaven. Go, seek, and find in the manger the heavenly Father who here has also become your dear Father.

"Prince of Peace"—where God comes in love to human beings and unites with them, there peace is made between God and humankind and among people. Are you afraid of God's wrath? Then go to the child in the manger and receive there the peace of God. Have you fallen into strife and hatred with your sister or brother? Come and see how God, out of pure love, has become our brother and wants to reconcile us with each other. In the world, power reigns. This child is the Prince of Peace. Where he is, peace reigns.

THE MYSTERIOUS, INVISIBLE
AUTHORITY

The authority of this poor child will grow (Isa. 9:7). It will encompass all the earth, and knowingly or unknowingly, all human generations until the end of the ages will have to serve it. It will be an authority over the hearts of people, but thrones and great kingdoms will also grow strong or fall apart with this power. The mysterious, invisible authority of the divine child over human hearts is more solidly grounded than the visible and resplendent power of earthly rulers. Ultimately all authority on earth must serve only the authority of Jesus Christ over humankind.

With the birth of Jesus, the great kingdom of peace has begun. Is it not a miracle that where Jesus has really become Lord over people, peace reigns? That there is one Christendom on the whole earth, in which there is peace in the midst of the world? Only where Jesus is not allowed to reign—where human stubbornness, defiance, hate, and avarice are allowed to live on unbroken—can there be no peace. Jesus does not want to set up his kingdom of peace by force, but where people willingly submit themselves to him and let him rule over them, he will give them his wonderful peace.

LIVING BY GOD'S MERCY

We cannot approach the manger of the Christ child in the same way we approach the cradle of another child. Rather, when we go to his manger, something happens, and we cannot leave it again unless we have been judged or redeemed. Here we must either collapse or know the mercy of God directed toward us.

What does that mean? Isn't all of this just a way of speaking? Isn't it just pastoral exaggeration of a pretty and pious legend? What does it mean that such things are said about the Christ child? Those who want to take it as a way of speaking will do so and continue to celebrate Advent and Christmas as before, with pagan indifference. For us it is not just a way of speaking. For that's just it: it is God himself, the Lord and Creator of all things, who is so small here, who is hidden here in the corner, who enters into the plainness of the world, who meets us in the helplessness and defenselessness of a child, and wants to be with us. And he does this not out of playfulness or sport, because we find that so touching, but in order to show us where he is and who he is, and in order from this place to judge and devalue and dethrone all human ambition.

The throne of God in the world is not on human thrones, but in human depths, in the manger. Standing around his throne there are no flattering vassals but dark, unknown, questionable figures who cannot get their fill of this miracle and want to live entirely by the mercy of God.

WORLD JUDGMENT AND
WORLD REDEMPTION

When God chooses Mary as the means when God himself wants to come into the world in the manger of Bethlehem, this is not an idyllic family affair. It is instead the beginning of a complete reversal, a new ordering of all things on this earth. If we want to participate in this Advent and Christmas event, we cannot simply sit there like spectators in a theater and enjoy all the friendly pictures. Rather, we must join in the action that is taking place and be drawn into this reversal of all things ourselves. Here we too must act on the stage, for here the spectator is always a person acting in the drama. We cannot remove ourselves from the action.

With whom, then, are we acting? Pious shepherds who are on their knees? Kings who bring their gifts? What is going on here, where Mary becomes the mother of God, where God comes into the world in the lowliness of the manger? World judgment and world redemption—that is what's happening here. And it is the Christ child in the manger himself who holds world judgment and world redemption. He pushes back the high and mighty; he overturns the thrones of the powerful; he humbles the haughty; his arm exercises power over all the high and mighty; he lifts what is lowly, and makes it great and glorious in his mercy.

THE POWER AND
GLORY OF THE MANGER

For the great and powerful of this world, there are only two places in which their courage fails them, of which they are afraid deep down in their souls, from which they shy away. These are the manger and the cross of Jesus Christ. No powerful person dares to approach the manger, and this even includes King Herod. For this is where thrones shake, the mighty fall, the prominent perish, because God is with the lowly. Here the rich come to nothing, because God is with the poor and hungry, because he fills the hungry, but the rich and satisfied he sends away empty. Before Mary, the maid, before the manger of Christ, before God in lowliness, the powerful come to naught; they have no right, no hope; they are judged. . . .

We must be clear about how—facing the manger—we want to think in the future about what is high and low in human life. . . .

Who among us will celebrate Christmas correctly? Whoever finally lays down all power, all honor, all reputation, all vanity, all arrogance, all individualism beside the manger; whoever remains lowly and lets God alone be high; whoever looks at the child in the manger and sees the glory of God precisely in his lowliness.

ONLY ONE REAL WAY

Our life is not a simple straight line that our will and reason draw. Rather, life is something that is formed from two different lines, two different elements, two different powers. Life is composed of human ideas and God's ways, and in truth there is no human way at all, for "the human mind plans the way" (Prov. 16:9)—meaning that it's only a sketch of a way, an idea of a way, a way in theory, in illusion. But there is only one real way that we inevitably have to go, and that is God's way. The difference between the two lives is that human beings would like to foresee the whole of their life at one time, but God's way goes just step-by-step. "The human mind plans the way, but the LORD directs the steps." . . . God would like for people to go step-by-step, led not by their own ideas about life but by God's word, which comes to them at each step, whenever they ask. There is no word from God for the whole of our life. God's word is new and open today and tomorrow, and it can only be related to the moment in which we hear it.

GOD CAN WAIT

Human beings are the losers; God is the winner. God lets human beings start; he lets them make progress, have success, and seems himself to be totally passive. His countermoves seem rather insignificant, and we seldom notice them at all. So we march forward, proud and self-confident and certain of our success and ultimate victory. But God can wait; sometimes he waits year after year. . . . God waits in the hope that people will finally understand his moves and want to turn their life over to him. But once in every life—perhaps it will not be until the hour of death—God crosses our way, so that we can no longer take a step. We must stop and in fear and trembling recognize God's power and our own weakness and wretchedness. . . . Only in these great moments in our life do we understand the meaning of God's guidance in our life; only then do we understand God's patience and God's wrath. And only now do we recognize that these hours in which God crossed our way are the only hours of real importance in our life. They alone make our life worth living.

THE RULE OF GOD IN HISTORY

I believe
that God can and will produce good out of all things,
   even out of the most evil.
For this he needs people who let themselves serve all
   things the best they can.
I believe
that in every plight God wants to give us as much power
   of resistance as we need.
But he does not give it in advance, so that we will rely
   not on ourselves, but on him alone.
In such faith all anxiety about the future would have to
   be overcome.
I believe
that even our errors and mistakes are not in vain, and
   that it is not harder for God to deal with them than
   with our presumed good deeds.
I believe
that God is not timeless fate, but that he waits for and
   answers sincere prayers and responsible deeds.

He Has Done Everything Well

So at the end of this year we want to talk about every week, about every hour that has passed. We want to go to prayer with this word until there is no longer an hour about which we do not want to say: "He has done everything well" (Mark 7:37). The days that were heavy for us, that tormented us and made us anxious, days that have left us with a trace of bitterness, are the very days that we do not want to leave behind us today, before we also confess about them, thankfully and humbly: "He has done everything well." We are not to forget but to overcome. That happens through gratitude. We are not supposed to solve the unsolved puzzle of the past and fall into tortuous brooding, but to let even the incomprehensible stand and return it peacefully to God's hand. This happens through humility. "He has done everything well." But the most terrible thorn still remains: mea culpa, mea culpa! . . . The evil fruit of my sin keeps working without end. How can I bring it to an end? And yet you are no Christian—rather, you become hardened in your sin—if you cannot also say about your guilt: "*He* has done everything well!" One thing it does not say is: we have done everything well. . . .

That is the last and most astonishing perception of Christians, that they may finally say even about their sin: "He has done everything well."

Surrounded by Good Powers

Surrounded by good powers, faithful and still,
wonderfully protected and comforted —
in this way I want to live these days with you
and go with you into a new year.

The old year still wants to torment our hearts;
the heavy burden of evil days still holds us down.
O Lord, give our frightened souls
the salvation for which you created us.

And if you hand us the heavy cup, the bitter one,
of sorrow, filled to the highest brim,
then we take it thankfully, without trembling,
from your good and loving hand.

Yet if you want to give us joy once again
in this world and its sun's bright light,
then we want to remember what has passed,
and then our life belongs fully to you.

Today, let the candles glow warm and bright
that you brought into our darkness,
and if it can be, bring us together again!
We know your light shines in the night.

When now the profound stillness spreads round us,
let us hear that full sound of the world
that widens invisibly all around us,
the high hymn of praise of all your children.

Wonderfully secured by good powers,
we confidently await what may come.
God is with us in the evening and the morning,
and most certainly in each new day.

A SHORT BIOGRAPHY
OF DIETRICH BONHOEFFER

———— ⟨∘⟩⟨∘⟩ ————

February 4, 1906	Born in Breslau, Germany (now Wroclaw, Poland)
1923–27	Study of Evangelical Theology in Tübingen, Rome, and Berlin, followed by a doctoral degree and qualification for university lecturing (1930)
1928–29	Vicar in Barcelona
1930–31	Year of study at Union Theological Seminary, New York
1931	*Privatdozent* and university pastor in Berlin, ecumenical work
1933	Beginning of ecclesiastical resistance work, pastor in London
1935	Leadership of an illegal seminary for preachers in Finkenwalde
1937	Closing of the seminary by police, continued illegal work
1939	Trip to New York in summer, return to Berlin before start of war
1940	Beginning of service as an informer for the Resistance
	Beginning of work on his book *Ethik* (*Ethics*)
1941–42	Conspiratorial trips to Switzerland, Norway, Sweden, and Italy
1943	Engagement to Maria von Wedemeyer in January

April 5, 1943	Arrest and incarceration in the Berlin-Tegel prison, lively correspondence with Eberhard Bethge, foundations for his work *Widerstand und Ergebung* (*Letters and Papers from Prison*)
October 8, 1944	Transfer to the main prison of the Gestapo
February 7, 1945	Deportation to the concentration camp Buchenwald
April 5, 1945	Condemnation to death by Adolf Hitler
April 8, 1945	Transfer to the concentration camp Flossenbürg
April 9, 1945	Death sentence carried out

SOURCES

All readings listed in the "Sources of Daily Readings" come from *Dietrich Bonhoeffer Werke* (*DBW*), edited by Eberhard Bethge (†), Ernst Feil, Christian Gremmels, Wolfgang Huber, Hans Pfeifer, Albrecht Schönherr, Heinz Eduard Tödt (†), and Ilse Tödt (Gütersloh: Chr. Kaiser/Gütersloher Verlagshaus).

Vol. 1: *Sanctorum Communio: Eine dogmatische Untersuchung zur Soziologie der Kirche.* Ed. Joachim von Soosten. 1986. Written 1927.

Vol. 2: *Akt und Sein: Transzendentalphilosophie und Ontologie in der systematischen Theologie.* Ed. Hans-Richard Reuter. 1988, 2nd ed. 2002. Written 1929–1930.

Vol. 3: *Schöpfung und Fall.* Ed. Martin Rüter and Ilse Tödt. 1989, 2nd ed. 2002. Written 1932–1933.

Vol. 4: *Nachfolge.* Ed. Martin Kuske and Ilse Tödt. 1989, 2nd ed. 2002. Written 1935–1937.

Vol. 5: *Gemeinsames Leben: Das Gebetbuch der Bibel.* Ed. Gerhard L. Müller and Albrecht Schönherr. 1987, 2nd ed. 2002. Written 1938.

Vol. 6: *Ethik.* Ed. Ilse Tödt, Heinz Eduard Tödt (†), Ernst Reil, and Clifford Green. 1992, 2nd ed. 1998. Written 1940–1943.

Vol. 7: *Fragmente aus Tegel.* Ed. Renate Bethge and Ilse Tödt. 1994. Written 1943–1945.

Vol. 8: *Widerstand und Ergebung.* Ed. Christian Gremmels, Eberhard Bethge (†), and Renate Bethge, together with Ilse Tödt. 1998. Letters and papers from prison, written 1943–1945.

Vol. 9: *Jugend und Studium 1918–1927.* Ed. Hans Pfeifer, together with Clifford Green and Carl-Jürgen Kaltenborn. 1986.

Vol. 10: *Barcelona, Berlin, Amerika 1928–1931.* Ed. Hans Christoph von Hase and Reinhart Staats, together with Holger Roggelin and Matthias Wünsche. 1991.

Vol. 11: *Ökumene, Universität, Pfarramt 1931–1932.* Ed. Eberhard Amelung and Christoph Strohm. 1994.

Vol. 12: *Berlin 1932–1933.* Ed. Carsten Nicolaisen and Ernst Albert Scharffenorth. 1997.

Vol. 13: *London 1933–1935.* Ed. Hans Goedeking, Martin Heimbucher, and Hans-Walter Schleicher. 1994.

Vol. 14: *Illegale Theologenausbildung: Finkenwalde 1935–1940.* Ed. Otto Dudzus (†) and Jürgen Henkys, together with Sabine Bobert-Stützel, Dirk Schulz, and Ilse Tödt. 1996.

Vol. 15: *Illegale Theologenausbildung: Sammelvikariate 1937–1940.* Ed. Dirk Scholz. 1998.

Vol. 16: *Konspiration und Haft 1940–1945.* Ed. Jørgen Glenthøj (†), Ulrich Kabitz, and Wolf Krötke. 1996.

Vol. 17: *Register und Ergänzungen.* Ed. Herbert Anzinger, Hans Pfeifer, together with Waltraud Anzinger and Ilse Tödt. 1999.

SOURCES OF DAILY READINGS

27	6:230ff.	3	6:81	10	10:515ff.	
28	6:232–33	4	6:81–82	11	15:569	
29	6:275–76	5	6:80–81	12	6:408	
30	6:276	6	6:141–42	13	6:49–50	
31	8:535–36	7	12:440–41	14	6:83–84	
		8	8:38	15	6:84–85	
April	**8:49**	9	16:540	16	6:85–86	
1	11:403	10	6:288	17	6:86–87	
2	8:548–49	11	15:466, 469–70	18	12:468–69	
3	14:635–36	12	6:94–95	19	15:560–61	
4	15:471–72	13	10:469	20	15:563–64	
5	15:472–73	14	6:323ff.	21	11:423–24, 426	
6	15:474–75	15	10:319–20	22	16:488–89	
7	6:404–5	16	6:326–27	23	16:496	
8	14:973–74	17	10:320–21	24	16:528	
9	14:974–75	18	15:572	25	16:528–29	
10	14:975–76	19	4:47–48	26	11:356–57	
11	14:978	20	15:521	27	5:91–92	
12	10:460	21	13:361–62	28	6:350–51	
13	6:74–75	22	13:362–63	29	6:356, 358	
14	9:577	23	16:657–58	30	15:549–50	
15	16:473–74	24	6:52			
16	8:368–69	25	12:458	**July**	**10:504**	
17	10:463–64	26	12:455	1	5:15, 18	
18	10:461	27	15:569ff.	2	15:523–24	
19	10:462–63	28	11:456ff.	3	5:18–19	
20	10:465–66	29	11:458ff.	4	5:19–20	
21	16:471	30	11:461–62	5	5:24	
22	16:472–73	31	15:576	6	5:32–33	
23	16:472–73			7	5:79	
24	8:499ff.	**June**	**15:564**	8	5:80–81	
25	3:33–34	1	13:414–15	9	5:82–83	
26	6:69	2	13:380–81,	10	5:84	
27	6:70		383–84	11	3:124	
28	15:557–58	3	10:509	12	6:290ff.	
29	15:558	4	8:99	13	6:293–94	
30	5:35–36	5	16:651–52	14	6:171	
		6	16:653–54	15	11:415	
May	**6:77**	7	10:512–13	16	11:415–16	
1	6:78–79	8	10:514	17	3:62–63	
2	6:148ff.	9	15:514–15	18	6:335–36	

July (*continued*)

19 6:336
20 6:337
21 8:542–43
22 5:30
23 8:310–11
24 8:398
25 14:907–8
26 10:316
27 10:456ff.
28 10:458–59
29 6:403–4
30 6:45
31 10:504

August 6:219

1 8:205–6
2 16:553–54
3 6:219ff.
4 6:224
5 6:226–27
6 8:24–25
7 8:38–39
8 5:85–86
9 13:517
10 10:522
11 6:179, 181
12 6:188–89
13 8:28–29; 6:74
14 8:558ff.
15 6:268–69
16 11:464–65
17 14:868
18 8:567
19 6:173–74
20 6:65–66
21 6:276–77
22 6:279
23 6:283

24 6:37–38
25 6:352–53
26 8:26ff.
27 8:29–30
28 6:67–68
29 8:288–89
30 8:454–55
31 8:36

September 6:242

1 6:237–38
2 6:241ff.
3 6:361
4 11:430ff.
5 10:494–95
6 4:107–8
7 13:298–99
8 13:300–301
9 12:234–35
10 10:536–37
11 10:537–38
12 4:108
13 4:110
14 4:113–14
15 4:130–31
16 16:619, 621–22
17 16:622–23
18 16:624–25
19 16:626–27
20 16:627
21 16:627–28
22 6:64–65
23 10:328–29
24 4:67
25 15:534–35
26 15:504
27 15:505
28 15:526–27
29 10:330–31

30 10:332–33

October 12:426

1 11:379–80
2 14:144–45
3 14:146, 148
4 10:350–51
5 5:46
6 5:46–47
7 5:47
8 15:527ff.
9 3:58–59
10 11:387ff.
11 15:519–20
12 6:311–12
13 6:312–13
14 6:313–14
15 6:314–15
16 9:305–6
17 9:306–7
18 9:307–8;
    12:314ff.
19 13:324
20 16:325
21 13:353
22 15:518–19
23 13:387ff.
24 13:390–91
25 13:393–94
26 13:395–96
27 13:397
28 13:400
29 13:401–2
30 12:426–27
31 13:403–4

November 8:407–8

1 10:479–80
2 8:208

3	15:19	23	13:376–77	12	8:246
4	16:502	24	13:367	13	10:583–84, 586
5	13:375–76	25	10:501–2	14	15:537ff.
6	11:452–53	26	15:271–72	15	8:240
7	8:407–8	27	11:445–46	16	10:288–89, 292
8	13:348–49	28	11:448–49	17	16:633–34
9	15:529–30	29	11:451	18	16:634–35
10	15:507–8	30	13:355–56	19	16:635
11	8:429–30,			20	16:636
	432–33, 435	**December**	13:343	21	16:636–37
12	10:455–56	1	15:500	22	16:637
13	13:350	2	6:70–71	23	16:637–38
14	6:248–49	3	13:336	24	13:341–42
15	13:321–22	4	10:533	25	13:340–41
16	8:226	5	10:529	26	13:342–43
17	16:194	6	10:529–32	27	13:513
18	10:524	7	13:359–60	28	13:514–15
19	8:255–56	8	13:360–61	29	8:30–31
20	10:500–501	9	13:339–40	30	14:258–59
21	12:429	10	6:83	31	8:607–8
22	8:206	11	16:373		

INDEX OF SCRIPTURE
REFERENCES

392

John (*continued*)

11:16	Apr. 28
13:34	Mar. 18
14:5	Apr. 28
14:6	Nov. 14
14:23	May 27
14:26	June 11
14:27	Sept. 11
14:27–31	May 27
16:33	May 5
18:36	May 17
19:30	Apr. 14
20:17	Apr. 29
20:25	Apr. 28
20:26–28	Apr. 29

Acts

2:1–13	June 4
10:40–41	Apr. 22

Romans

4:25	Apr. 22
5:1–5	Apr. 4–6
5:10	Mar. 21
8:26	Feb. 23
10:17	June 23
11:6	Apr. 12, July 27, Nov. 12
12:11	June 7
12:18	Mar. 21
12:21	Sept. 6

1 Corinthians

2:7–10	May 21–22
13	June 2, July 18–19, Oct. 23–29, Oct. 31
15:17	Apr. 18, Apr. 22

15:20–23	Apr. 22
15:26	Apr. 16
15:35ff.	Apr. 23

2 Corinthians

1:20	Mar. 2
3:6	June 11, Sept. 30
3:17	Sept. 29
5:17	June 12
12:9	June 3

Galatians

3:28	July 12
4:6	June 5
4:9	May 5

Ephesians

1:10	Dec. 12
2:14–16	July 4, Sept. 6
4:29	July 7
5:14	Jan. 28

Philippians

1:21	May 4
4:7	Sept. 11

Colossians

1:16–17	Aug. 2
3:1–3	Nov. 27–29

1 Thessalonians

5:16–18	Feb. 19

1 Timothy

3:1–7	June 27

2 Timothy

1:7	June 4
4:8	Nov. 22

Hebrews

4:9	Jan. 24

James

1:8	Aug. 28
2:12	Sept. 29
4:4	May 24
4:14	Jan. 4

1 Peter

1:7–9	May 26
2:20	Mar. 13
3:9	May 23
3:14	Mar. 13
4:17	Sept. 27
5:4	June 19
5:5	Sept. 25

2 Peter

3:13	Aug. 10

1 John

2:15	May 24
2:17	July 31, Nov. 20, Nov. 25
2:22	Sept. 20
3:24	June 6
4:7–10	July 20
4:16	June 21, July 20
5:4	Oct. 31

Revelation

1:9–10	June 4
2:4	Oct. 30
2:5	Nov. 21
3:20	Dec. 4
21:5	Dec. 4